birdie & harlow

birdie & harlow

Life, Loss, and Loving My Dog So Much I Didn't Want Kids (. . . Until I Did)

taylor wolfe

HarperOne
An Imprint of HarperCollinsPublishers

HarperCollins books may be purchased for educational, business, or sales promotional use. For information, please email the Special Markets Department at SPsales@harpercollins.com.

FIRST HARPERCOLLINS PAPERBACK PUBLISHED IN 2024

Designed by Bonni Leon-Berman

Library of Congress Cataloging-in-Publication Data is available upon request.

ISBN 978-0-06-329382-3

24 25 26 27 28 LBC 6 5 4 3 2

For Chris.

Remember when you suggested I skip work in 2009 so we could go to Worlds of Fun instead? That's when I knew you were a keeper.

introduction

I Need Some Alone Time, but I Need Everyone to Come Along

I don't know how I got this way—how I turned into the person who struggles to be away from their child for more than a night. Now, a dog, I understand. Because dogs are the best. They just want to love you and be near you, and when you leave a dog, they don't seem to know if you're ever coming back. Which is why I chose to rarely leave my dog—it simply wasn't worth the risk.

But a kid? Well, I was sure that would be different. Because *I* would be different. If I ever decided to become a mom, which seemed rather unlikely for a large part of my life, I was going to be a chill mom.

I was never going to be that annoyingly sentimental woman I saw all over social media—the one sobbing on the first day of kindergarten, blubbering at every outgrown custom-embroidered cardigan that had to be packed away forever. I scoffed and shook my judgmental little head from afar as I heard stories about moms who hadn't spent a night away from their children until they were ten years old. That's an entire decade of attachment issues!

"That will never be me," I'd tell Harlow, my beloved vizsla pup.

"I'd hope not!" he'd respond from my lap. (Yes, Harlow talked.) "Now let's go try out that new life jacket you bought me. Boy am I glad you finally found a more dog-inclusive kayak rental." (*Harlow and I had indeed kayaked in the Chicago River together, and like most of our last-minute high jinks, it didn't really go that well.*)

I think about my and Har's kayaking adventure as my beloved human child, Birdie, tries on a new swimsuit for our upcoming vacation, and the 2T size barely fits her anymore, and suddenly I've become the blubbering fool, weeping over a swimsuit that no longer fits. It's two p.m. on a Tuesday, and I am crying over a swimsuit! It's ridiculous and *I know* it's ridiculous, but that doesn't stop me.

How did I miss the signs I was doomed to become this way?

Our entire Christmas tree was covered in ornaments with my dog's face on them, and yet I somehow assumed I wouldn't be a sentimental human mom. Was I that delusional? It's a definite possibility—it always is. The devil works hard, but my delusions work harder. Or was it the fact that I held so tightly to the belief that I wasn't a "baby person" for so long that I thought this might shield my vulnerability in some way? I honestly don't know which it is, and I suppose it doesn't matter. What matters is that in a very short amount of time, I became the woman I never understood. Even worse, perhaps.

My chest tightens if I look at a photo of Birdie taken six months ago and I can't remember every single thing we did that day. *What words was she saying? What foods was she eating? Was she crawling or walking? Why can't I remember? Why didn't I document it in one of the ten baby books I keep?* A heavy sense of regret settles deep in my soul because if I can't remember, surely that means I missed it.

But I didn't miss it! I lived it. I lived it like I live any other day, and then came another. I wasn't like this before I had a baby, where I'm suddenly nostalgic for any mundane moment that has come and gone simply because it happened. Every once in a while, a whisper of reason reaches the surface and reminds me that it's okay if I don't remember every single second of Birdie's life. But the fact I even have to remind myself of this? Well, it makes me feel insane. And it's just one of the many reasons why motherhood makes no sense.

I'm not sure who to blame for this behavior, but I'd like to blame someone (*anyone!!*) because it certainly can't be my fault. I was never going to be this way, remember? I said it only a few paragraphs ago, which is precisely how fast it sneaks up on you—the heartache of motherhood, I mean. I don't enjoy being caught off guard, especially when it comes to something that feels like it's taken everything you thought you knew about life and turned it on its head, shaken it up a bit, turned it over once more, and then smothered it with a layer of sentimental longing that leaves you more confused than you were the day before. That's kind of how motherhood feels to me. Like I am constantly missing who my child was yesterday (even if yesterday was an absolutely brutal no-nap kind of day) while still cherishing and loving who my child is today and wondering who they might be tomorrow.

I've heard some moms say they don't remember life before they had kids, but I do. I remember the car rides. And the vacations, flying to get to those vacations, ordering a drink on a plane—alone! What a thrill. And the leisurely grocery runs, trips to Target without begging Birdie to please just stay seated in the cart, for the love of God, stay in the cart for five more minutes. I remember sleeping, like *really sleeping*, and in bedsheets not covered in milk or marker or with a few random magnetic tiles hiding under the pillows. I remember it all. And as I allow my mind to do so, to make the list of all the things that were so much simpler before having a kid, I still choose the kid. Sappy (often completely unnecessary) heartache, constant worry, and all.

I tell Chris, my husband, that I desperately need some alone time, but I'll need everyone to come along. Him, the baby, the dog—everyone's gotta be there.

"Are you sure?" he asks.

"Yes," I say without hesitation.

"But why?"

"I have no idea."

I finish packing Birdie's bag and say, "You ready to go on an adventure?"

She claps her small hands together and says, "Yay, let's go!"

As we walk out of her nursery, we pass the framed photos on the wall, and she pauses to point at everyone and say their names. "Dadda, Mama, Birdie." And when we get to the final frame on the wall, Birdie will reach for the face she sees there and in her sweetest little baby voice say, "Hah-low."

It's Harlow's senior portrait, the one where he's photoshopped into a fancy black suit. Then Birdie will rest her head on my shoulder, and we'll stand there for a second longer, both saying hi to our boy. *Hi, Har. Hello, sweet boy.*

And it makes sense.

part one

a borderline unhealthy codependent relationship begins

GRIDLEY, KANSAS. 2010.

"You never want to break a dog's spirit. It's the worst thing you can do as an owner." Earl eyed me from his sprawling farmhouse porch, a pack of floppy-eared Hungarian vizsla puppies dancing at his feet.

I nodded and tried my best to smooth out my jeans, as if eliminating wrinkles might help make me look more responsible. Here I thought I'd driven over an hour to a farm in middle-of-nowhere Kansas to choose a puppy, but it was becoming clear Earl was the one choosing me. At only twenty-three years old, with my Jessica Simpson *Dukes of Hazzard*–era blond hair, high-top Converse sneakers, and Hollister ripped denim that barely graced my hip bones, I wasn't screaming "Miss Responsibility." I did not realize there would be an interview portion to buying a dog and regretted not bringing my cover letter so Earl would know I wasn't only captain of my high school basketball team, but I also created all the party T-shirts for my college sorority.

"I would never do that. I love animals," I stuttered, fearing my chances of bringing home one of the adorable red puppies for my boy-friend, Chris, was slipping away. I had set my mind on a puppy—not another Shutterfly photo calendar—for our two-year anniversary. A gift that I hoped he realized conveyed something of a permanence to my love for him.

"You gotta know, you can't punish these dogs," Earl said. "They're much too sensitive, and they can't take it."

Same, I thought. But luckily, for once in my life, I didn't add a quippy remark and simply nodded again.

For the sake of transparency, I should let you know that Earl's name wasn't actually Earl. But that's always how I've thought of him when I recalled the advice he gave me, so Earl it is. I'd found him and his vizslas online only that morning. I Googled "puppies for sale near Topeka," and Hungarian vizslas came up. Earl's bitch, Big Nose Kate, had a litter a couple of months ago, and there were a few puppies still available. For the sake of continuing transparency, yes, it felt weird to me too writing out, "Earl's bitch, Big Nose Kate," but I'm trying to keep it real and authentic here.

I didn't know anything about the vizsla breed, but I'd heard Chris, my boyfriend whom I was so eager to impress, talk about them a time or two. We spotted one in passing when we were walking around Kansas City's *très chic* Country Club Plaza, and he noted "what a cool-looking dog" it was. Our future was set right then and there as I imagined us walking around the plaza someday with our very own cool-looking dog, being the cool-looking couple that we were. The following Thursday I just happened to get off work early, so I called the number in the listing, asked if I could come see the available pup-pies, and off I went.

I didn't check any animal rescues or shelters first. Nor did I re-search the breed at all to see that, while vizslas are very affectionate and intelligent, they're also incredibly high-energy dogs that need a lot of consistent exercise and stimulation. I simply printed off the directions from MapQuest (my dang Garmin GPS had been so unreliable lately) and jumped in my Toyota Camry, ready to pick up a surprise puppy to celebrate a two-year dating anniversary with the man I intended to dog-parent alongside!

"What's your experience with training dogs?" Earl asked as he invited me inside the room right off the porch, a space with several large couches reserved just for his dogs.

I'd watched *Best in Show* at least a million times. Did that count?

"Well, I grew up with animals—cats and dogs. And they always loved me the most," I gloated, wondering if I should tell him about all the baby birds I'd attempted to save as a kid. However, recalling I never actually successfully kept one alive for more than a day, I figured I could keep that little anecdote to myself.

"But have you ever trained one?"

"Well, no. This will be my first," I admitted.

The pack of rust-colored puppies followed Earl's every move, except for one bulky-headed little guy who was always a step behind. I bent down to get a better look at the pup and gave the elephant-like ears that nearly covered his entire face a good rub. They were as soft as the crushed velvet Juicy Couture sweatsuits I ordered off eBay before my freshman year, determined to make a good first impression as a college student! And hidden beneath a forehead of the most delicious puppy wrinkles were a set of dark brown eyes that begged to be stared into. Some dogs turn away from a good stare down, but not this guy. He seemed as interested in what I was thinking as I was in what *he* was thinking.

"Hi, sweet boy," I whispered as we locked eyes. "Who are you?"

Earl told me I'd found the outsider of the group. Not because he was the runt of the litter, but because he was just a little more clumsy and less polished than the others. His snooty siblings seemed to recognize this and left him behind. As the youngest child of three, I could relate. It wasn't until I pulled the clumsy pup into my arms that I noticed a small white mark in the shape of two tall rabbit ears on his chest. I asked Earl if all vizslas had this mark or if it was special to the little outsider. He said several have markings of some sort, but it's not desirable if someone plans to show their dog. The dogs with the solid brown coats were the most sought after. As someone who also once had a less-than-desirable Playboy Bunny sticker mark on my chest from too much time spent in a tanning bed, I knew I wasn't leaving the farm without him. This was destiny.

Earl proceeded to show me around, pointing out the barn and the field behind it, where the puppies went to run out their zoomies.

"But these are not outdoor dogs," he said. "They need a couch, and they need their humans. However, they also need space to run because a walk or two won't cut it. A tired vizsla is a happy vizsla."

I wondered if he had that last line embroidered on a tea towel somewhere inside his big old farmhouse. I was going to bet he did.

"There's a dog park right by where we live. I can take him there every day," I said confidently.

"Puppies can't go to dog parks."

"Right. I meant when he's older." Damnit, this wasn't going well.

"You really gotta be all in with vizslas, because on the one hand you know you're getting an amazing companion, but also a lot of work. And you don't get to sign up only for the good parts—you sign up for all of it."

"Well, sign me up for all of it, sir," I mumbled because I wasn't sure what else to say, but I definitely regretted adding the "sir."

Earl leaned against his barn and looked from his dogs to me. "Do you know much about the breed at all?"

I frantically searched my brain. "I know they're a hunting dog, kind of like a red lab." I tried desperately to remember some other facts Chris had told me. Knowing Chris, he certainly rambled off at least ten, but I probably stopped paying attention around two or three. The only thing I could think to say was, "and that . . . a tired vizsla is a happy vizsla." I guess I could get Chris a tie or something for our anniversary.

Before Earl could respond, a pickup truck barreled down the dirt road, and two more fully grown vizslas jumped out from the passenger side and ran to greet him like they hadn't seen him in years. It was Doc Holliday and his brother. The dogs jumped in pure delight in Earl's presence, but also sat immediately upon his command.

"Vizslas are eager to learn and please, but you can't teach by punishing them." Earl had already told me this part, and I started to wonder if something about me looked like I was a punisher. Was it my gold nose ring?

"I won't. I promise." I looked toward the red dust cloud of puppies running toward the open field and saw the clumsy one struggling to keep up.

"They're a regal breed whose bloodline traces back to Hungarian royalty," Earl said proudly.

"Uh huh," I responded as I watched the little guy tumble straight through a pile of poop, a pile clearly left behind by one of the bigger dogs based on its size. "A psychic once told me I also have royal bloodline," I added, and Earl only stared at me.

The pup barked and yelped at his siblings to let him join the fun, but they paid him no attention. They'd already paired off, biting at each other's ears and mouths, and he was the odd one out. I wanted the clumsy little weirdo badly. He'd been through some shit but was still fighting for his place in the pack. But Earl had made his point, and I'll admit I was nervous about how to train him without some sort of punishment tactic. I'd grown up in a time of crating for bad behavior and rubbing a dog's nose in the carpet when they'd had an accident (no matter how long ago it happened). And this was for dogs without any royal lineage. I didn't even know where to start with a blue blood. And now that we're being honest, I wasn't *exactly* sure how the whole "hours and hours of exercise" thing was going to work either since I was more of a *Total Body Cardio Dance Workout with Paula Abdul* kind of gal, and that video lasted fifteen minutes at most. But then again, the choreography was rather simple, so maybe it was a workout the pup and I could do together someday. That's what companions did with each other, right? That idea of a "really great companion" sort of landed on my brain as rational words, but I wasn't entirely sure what that meant. I wondered if I, too, was a really great companion. The only thing I wasn't worried about, come to think of it, was Chris. I knew Chris would be in this dog-parenting game with me for the long haul. I knew two years was just the beginning for us.

Maybe that's why I turned to Earl and put it bluntly: "If you let me take that pup, I swear to you I will give him the best life ever."

Earl rubbed his palms together and glanced from his pack back to me.

"How?" he asked, a rather uneasy look on his face. "How exactly will you do that?"

Well.

Things to Pack: Hospital Bag for Me and the New Baby

- Pj's for me and baby.
- Toiletries.
- Going-home outfit for me and baby.

Things to Pack: Harlow's Weekend Bag While We're at the Hospital

- Sloth, Monkey, Pepe the Pig, Tom the Turkey, Taxicab, and Hot Dog.
- Favorite red blanket and pillow.
- Bully sticks and KONG.
- Food (kibble and fresh meat) and bowls.
- Jerky chews, peanut butter bites, dental sticks.
- Collar, leash, harness.
- Hiking pack—make sure the bear bell is attached. And a collapsible water bowl.
- Double-check hiking snacks are in the pack and identification card.
- Sweater and jacket. And booties!
- Anxiety meds, CBD oil, arthritis chews, ear drops.
- Musher's Wax.

HARLOW'S FEEDING INSTRUCTIONS: Two cups of kibble in the morning with fresh meat sprinkled on top (keep refrigerated). After breakfast, Harlow likes a dental stick: ask him to sit (and high-five) and then give him one. He'll try to trick you into giving him two, but don't fall for it. Repeat the same routine at dinnertime.

BEDTIME: I've included Har's favorite pillow and blanket; he'll ask that you cover him at night (and anytime he's lounging, actually). He'll start by nosing the blanket to get it over his head, then he'll need your assistance to cover him completely (he won't be content unless he's completely covered). And just an FYI, he snores—really loudly. But it's very cute and endearing.

ONE MORE THING TO NOTE: Anytime you leave the house, you have to say, "Bye, Har. We'll be right back." Then he knows you're leaving but coming back, so it's okay for him to relax. But if you don't say that, he'll anxiously pace until you get home. So just remember to tell him goodbye. :)

*And if you go on a long walk or hike, I've included his CBD oil (put a few drops on his food) and his arthritis chews and also some wax (it's in his hiking pack) for his paw pads so they don't get dry. And please make sure to give his hips and legs a little massage to ensure they don't get sore.

**If the pavement is too hot or cold, I've also included his booties.

hello, birdie

"Do we put Birdie in her car seat up here, or like *in* the car?" Chris asked, and I could see he was slipping into stressed-and-nervous Chris mode, my least favorite of his modes. Whatever my answer was, I had to give it confidently or risk a meltdown from all three of us. We'd been in the hospital for six days, and the newborn bliss was wearing off as it dawned on both Chris and me that the nurses couldn't come home with us. I'd asked.

"*In* the car," I said in a tone that alluded I knew this to be *fact* when I actually had no idea.

Chris glanced at Birdie, who was asleep in my arms like a perfect pink little angel, then to the cold demonic car seat next to our hospital bed. "I'm gonna go ask the nurse," he said.

Apparently, my tone wasn't that convincing after all.

"We put her in the car seat up here." Chris returned with a red face and a sigh of frustration.

"Okay, how was I supposed to know that?" I snapped back, knowing all too well the layers of his sigh.

We'd been so patient and gentle with each other the past few days, but like I said, our nerves were taking over. I understand that Chris and I probably appeared to be a mature couple in our thirties, well equipped to bring home a new baby, and sometimes we really were, but there were several more times when we actually felt like two very insecure teenagers with no idea what to do next. What were we thinking getting into this whole parenting nonsense?

I handed Birdie over and watched as Chris crouched on the ground and attempted to do the unthinkable: put a newborn into a car seat for the very first time. Birdie let out a high-pitched cry the second he put her down. It sounded more like a baby goat than a baby human, and she didn't stop the more he tried to buckle her in.

"Don't hurt her!" I said, certain it would help the situation.

"I'm doing it like we practiced, but it's not working!" he said back.

Chris had put together our stroller, locked the car seat stand in our car, and put together every piece of baby furniture and baby gadget we received. That's the kind of guy he is. Chris builds things, he solves problems, he mounts flat-screens on the wall (and hides the cords!). He does all the things I cannot (or will not) do, except he could not figure out how to strap our baby into her car seat. Two straps, three buckles, one baby. Two new parents near tears shouting at each other while also trying not to shout at each other.

"Just buckle her in!" I definitely did not shout.

"If it's so easy, you come do it!" Chris didn't shout back.

"I can't bend over—I just had a baby! And stop yelling at me! I don't want Birdie to hear us yelling at each other!" I yelled.

"I'm not yelling! Where's the nurse?"

In the midst of our fear and frustration, Birdie grew tired of her annoying new parents and fell asleep. Chris was able to buckle her in, we finally made our exit out of the hospital, and what ensued next was the longest, most stressful seven-mile drive of our life.

"I don't think I should take the interstate home," Chris said.

"Of course not!" A baby on the interstate? Not a chance.

Chris paused at stop signs for an extra five seconds, and we held our breath at every one of them.

"What a maniac!" I scoffed when a car zoomed by us going the speed limit.

"Seriously," Chris agreed.

We barely made it home in one piece, but when we did, I knew Har waited for us inside. My mom had picked him up from where he'd been staying for the week with a wonderful family who had two other vizslas, but I had promised Har we'd be gone for only a few days, not an entire week.

My throat swelled with emotion before our garage door even shut behind us. I couldn't wait to see my boy, but I was also heartbroken knowing how much his life . . . our life . . . was about to change. I knew that I wasn't going to be one of those people who just forgot about their dog once they had a baby. That was never the question. But with only three days of being a new mom under my belt, I'd drastically underestimated the amount of time recovery would take. And the amount of time feeding would take, and changing, rocking, feeding, napping, feeding, more rocking. Just baby time in general was an entirely new concept for me.

Before having Birdie, during one of the many pregnancy naps Har and I took together, I told him that I'd do everything in my power to make the change as easy on him as possible. To think of everything Har had been by my side for during the last ten years, how could I not? It was my time to show up for him.

I asked Chris to bring Birdie inside after I saw Har because I wanted a moment where he could see only me, no baby in my arms. Before I slid the back door open, I saw Har lying on the couch next to my mom, his sweet little face resting on her legs, and for the first time that I was willing to admit, he looked old to me. I finally saw what others had been seeing for years when they'd comment on his white face and his lumpy belly, and my throat got even tighter.

Harlow heard the click of the backdoor, and his ears perked up. The second he saw me sliding open the glass door, he bolted from the couch toward me.

"Hi, sweet boy," I said with a tired, raspy voice, as one tends to have after delivering a human.

But before Har got to me, he realized his mistake and quickly turned back around, heading straight for his toy basket. What kind of greeting was a greeting without his favorite stuffed Sloth? With Sloth dangling from his mouth and the biggest bounce in his step, he barreled toward me. Har was so excited he nearly tripped over himself ten times trying to get to me, his nails slipping on the hardwood floor like a cartoon dog running in place. I laughed and held back tears because I saw my clumsy little puppy again—of course it was still him.

"Hi, buddy. We're home!" I bent over to hug him as much as my postpartum body allowed, and Har wiggled uncontrollably.

Chris walked in next, and Har promptly ran over to him, giving him the same joyful greeting and paying no attention to the car seat dangling from Chris's arm.

"We have someone we want you to meet," I said as Chris placed the car seat on the floor and we both took two very large swallows of anxious air.

I'd been anticipating this introduction for nine months but secretly wondering if it would ever really happen for so much longer. Whenever someone used to ask if Chris and I wanted kids, I'd often respond that I wasn't sure if Harlow would approve. "He's not much of a baby guy," I'd say. But then again, I was never much of a baby gal.

"So what do you think, Har?" I pointed toward Birdie and prayed that she would pass the sniff test. My plan of sending Birdie to live on a farm for a while if it didn't work out no longer seemed as doable now that I'd, you know, met her. Much to my surprise, I'd grown a bit fond of my baby. "This is your little sister, Birdie."

Har looked from Birdie to us, from us to Birdie. Then in a move that surprised everyone, he hustled toward our pantry door, slid it open with his nose, and started digging around for something we didn't know was hidden.

"What's he getting?" I asked Chris.

"No idea," he said.

Harlow returned with the biggest, dirtiest rawhide bone hanging from his drooly mouth. It was a bone we hadn't seen in months, possibly even years. With a proud smile on his face and a prance in his step, he came barreling toward us and tried to drop the bone right on Birdie's face. An undeniable demonstration of Harlow affection.

I think he likes her, I thought, relieved.

no one's gonna buy the milk

TOPEKA, KANSAS. 2010.

"I know this is all new and kinda scary, but I swear you're going to like us," I said on the drive back to Topeka.

The clumsy puppy with the white Playboy Bunny mark on his chest watched me timidly from the passenger seat of my Camry. He wasn't nearly as energetic without his pack. Nerves had taken the place of his excitement, and I could see a slight tremble as he tried to curl into himself.

A cloud of dust and wispy tails lingered in my rearview as I turned off the dirt road and left the farmhouse and the puppy's family behind us. I suddenly felt like a monster for taking him away from his home. If I were in his position, I'd be looking for the exits so I could make a run for it.

"I promise you don't have to be nervous. You're going to a good home!" I said, perhaps a bit too confidently. *Am I a good home? Am I going to be a good mom?* I wondered, not for the first time in my adulthood.

Here's the thing: If I was given the choice to hold a puppy or baby, I'd choose the puppy every time. When my nieces and nephews were born, while I was always happy to meet them, that was kind of ... it. If I was forced into pretending that I wanted to hold them, I would ask to sit in a chair first, just like the children in the room. I would make the necessary oohs and ahhs and then try to get away as fast as possible before my lack of maternal instinct was revealed. It's okay for a child or a man not to know what to do when a baby fusses or squirms, but a (somewhat) grown woman? Well, certainly I should know *something* about taking care of a baby. But I never felt like I did, so I began to tell myself (and so did a few other people) that perhaps I should stick to dogs.

Thus, the puppy in the back seat.

The door locks clicked together, and the puppy's eyes darted from side to side at the unfamiliar and ominous sound. It was really poor timing on my part, as I had just been trying to explain to him that I wasn't a kidnapper. "We'll get you a nice bed and toys and everything you could ever want, okay?"

He rested his chin on the console and looked at me with his soft brown eyes as if he could understand what I was saying, so I kept talking.

"And we'll go on lots of walks and to the dog park—when you're older, I mean! Unless you don't like the dog park. I don't really like socializing, so if you don't either, it's totally fine with me. You can make the call on that one later if you want."

I made a list in my head of all the things I'd have to buy once we got back to Topeka. "We'll get you a crate, bowls, a leash, a collar, food." What else was I missing? Surely a lot. I had literally nothing ready for this dog, although I didn't dare say that out loud. I could already tell he was a keen listener. "Anything else you want?"

The pup tilted his head as I spoke, like he was really thinking about what else he may want.

"If you think of anything, just let me know," I said, and I could have sworn he nodded.

We pulled into PetSmart, and I worried the overstimulation of the bright lights and other shoppers might be too much for the little farm dog, so I held him close to my chest as the sliding doors welcomed us inside.

"You don't have to be scared," I whispered. "We'll be in and out."

But as soon as we stepped into the store, his ears perked, and he squirmed to look around. His curious eyes shot from the squeaker toys to the bones to the beautifully decorated treats up front. The sight of the pet store and all it had to offer didn't scare the pup—it excited him. Did I have a little shopper on my hands?

"Or we don't have to be in and out. Should I get a cart?"

We strolled up and down every aisle, filling the cart with more items than I could afford, but each new tennis ball, KONG, and squeaker toy placed inside only made the pup's wispy tail swing faster. His excitement was contagious.

"I don't typically like shopping with other people," I said as I bent over the handle of the cart to get closer to him, "but you might be the exception."

We got back to our apartment complex around four p.m. I thought about trying out the new leash I had just purchased but decided to carry him in my arms once more. Even though we'd only just met, and it usually took me weeks (sometimes years) to warm up to new-comers, I liked having this guy close to me. The way he eagerly leaned into my arms and looked up at me as I spoke made me think he liked it too. I gave a tour of the outside grounds, which included the dump-sters, the murky green pool we'd never go by, and the drainage ditch behind our building where I had a feeling we may play a lot (I was right!), and then we headed up the stairs to our three-bedroom unit. It was a bigger space than anything I'd rented in my short time as a renter post-college, but it was the last available and still cheaper than any of my previous apartments because that's what you get in To-peka, Kansas. Upon moving into the swanky penthouse, I promptly painted all the walls a dark brick red and bright mustard yellow be-cause it was 2010 and I had taste, okay? This was my first shared space with a boy, and I was going all in!

Much to our parents' dismay, Chris and I were living together unwed with no intentions to wed anytime soon.

"No one's gonna buy the milk when you give the cow away for free," my mom told me a week before move-in day, which still makes me shudder.

"I sure hope no one buys me at all, Mom. Ever." And how did she know I was the cow? Why couldn't Chris be the cow? Actually, why did either of us have to be a cow?

In my mom's defense, this statement was rather out of character for her, and I can't help but think she said it just because she felt she had to say something and chose to use the words her own mother inflicted upon her.

Despite my obvious "Yikes, Mom," a clear and deliberate retort in the moment, I would be lying if I told you those words didn't reverberate off my brain every now and again, shooting some unspoken ideology of energy down my spine. How could I be sure neither Chris nor I became a cow? There was no way I would ever marry a man without living with him first. I needed to know each and every creepy quirk—from toilet-seat etiquette to bathroom sink cleanup, fridge organization, the number of cups allowed on a nightstand, and other personal (often disgusting) human habits I won't mention—that you only truly know by living with someone. But at a time when all my Nebraska friends were getting married and I was content just living with my boyfriend, I sometimes wondered if I was sending the idea of an engagement off to pasture. I didn't necessarily care, but when you graduate college with a "serious relationship" and you're from the Midwest, people often tell you that you *should care*. And I hadn't quite learned to think for myself yet.

I brought the pup inside and showed him around our hand-me-down/T.J.Maxx-chic apartment. If dogs could read, he would have known this was a HOME SWEET HOME with a COFFEE BAR, BUT FIRST, TACOS, where we always remember to LIVE, LAUGH, LOVE and DANCE LIKE NOBODY IS WATCHING and DRINK THE WINE, preferably in front of the waxy artistic wine drawing.

"I have a passion for decorating," I bragged as he sniffed around. "This will be your bed." I set a brand-new dog bed down beside ours.

He gave it a glance, then promptly thrust his oversize paws onto ours instead.

"No, you sleep in your bed."

He darted from the room before we could discuss it any further. I chased the puppy from our bedroom into the bathroom and back into our bedroom. By the time I heard the click of Chris's work shoes on the stairs outside, a fancy pair of Allen Edmonds gifted by his parents for college graduation, I had chased the puppy all around his new dwelling, and he was warming up quite nicely. He had finally found another dog to play with him. That dog just happened to be a human who looked like me.

"Here comes Chris!" I said excitedly. "You're going to love him."

The pup's ears perked as Chris's keys jingled in the lock outside. We heard the door creak open, and Chris walked inside.

At this time in his life, Chris wore a suit and tie to work every single day. He also had a cleanly shaven face, not the beautiful dark beard he takes such precious care of now. Every morning he'd ask me to help tuck his tie under the backside of his crisp white collar, and I'd feel so grown-up and mature as I did it. We were twenty-three.

Chris sighed as he placed his shiny new briefcase next to the cherrywood entryway table, a hand-me-down from my mom, and he loosened his tie. If we were a 1950s sitcom couple, this is when he would have announced, "Honey, I'm home!" Instead, he said, "What should we have for dinner?" as he rounded the corner to the living room where I sat with the surprise pup, which was close enough. It's fun to think there was a time in our lives when I actually enjoyed this question. Look at me making tater-tot casserole for my boyfriend because we live together!

And then it happened. One of the single best moments I've ever had the pleasure of witnessing. The moment Chris saw the dog who was to be his, and the dog saw Chris.

"No way. Is that a dog?" His voice raised an octave higher, and the years fell off with each step he took toward us. "Did you get a dog?"

I nodded proudly as the puppy wiggled on my lap.

"For real? I can't believe this!" Chris crouched on the ground, and the two of them immediately started playing together. He was no longer a grown man tired after a long day of financial planning but a little boy rolling around on the carpet with his new best friend. "I can't believe you got a dog."

"What do you think?"

"I think it's great! What should we call him?" Chris asked as he held the puppy close to his chest.

"I was thinking of Harlow," I said. The name had been in my head since I picked him up, but I couldn't pinpoint why.

"Arlow?"

"Or that, but I actually said Harlow." The more I said it, the more I liked it.

"Are you a Harlow, little guy?" Chris held him in the air, and he let out a small puppy bark. "Should we take that as a yes?"

"Welcome to the family, Harlow," I said as he barked once more but this time a little louder. I wondered if he was going to be a bit chatty.

Harlow's Nicknames

Full name: Harlow Wentworth Jimmer Hillis Wolfe.

Also known as: Har, Harvey, Har Har, Harvard, Harbie, Carbies, Charbies, Carlos,

Harlow Santana, Harlizzo, Harlene, Mr. Wiggles, Chompers, Sweet Boy, Harlow Boy,

and most notably, Carl, for when Harlow was acting like a real Carl.

a humble beginning

I've always been a dreamer, to a fault. Growing up, my life aspirations were to play in the WNBA (I was a scrappy defender but struggled with making any baskets), run track in the Olympics (I peaked in sixth grade), and win an Oscar. I'm technically still holding out for that last one, but only because my speech is already written, and I'd just need to make a few minor tweaks regarding the "I can't believe I'm the youngest person ever to win an Oscar" section.

My parents were supportive of my dreams, perhaps because I was the youngest of three, and my wild ambitions kept me distracted and content to play on my own since no one really played games up to my standards except me. I had friends as a kid, but I didn't necessarily enjoy their company. I simply agreed to playdates with the ones I knew had the best toys, then I'd politely suggest we play in our own quarters. Unless they agreed to follow the scripts I'd already handed out to my leading Barbies, Alexis Macintosh and Savannah James, I really had no need for another child by my side to mess up my productions.

If I wasn't playing elaborate games of make-believe with my dolls, most storylines involving a tragic plane crash in the mountains or adultery (sometimes both!), I was working on my physical fitness. I loved nothing more than a casual backyard obstacle course to get my heart rate up in the morning. Twenty jumping jacks on the trampoline, ten pull-ups on the swing set, then five suicide sprints across the lawn while the crowd of adoring fans chanted, "Taylor! Taylor! Taylor!" *Is today the day she breaks the world record, folks? We think it might be!* The announcer in my head always pushed me to go a little harder, a little faster. For myself but also my fans.

After I'd won gold in all the events I was the solo participant in, I loved to relax and get away from the crowds by climbing the old tree that perched over the drainage gulch behind our house. Something about hanging out in a tree with my legs dangling over the edge made me feel wild and free. That is, until the concrete gulch actually flooded and overflow from the nearby lake surged beneath my dangling legs and flashes of the *Now and Then* scene when Sam almost drowns in the gutter scared me right back down from my tree. If I had a dollar for every time that movie affected a decision in my life . . . or better yet, *two dollars* for every time I paused the Devon Sawa scene as a child, well, I'd be a very rich woman right now.

Other than hanging out alone or trying to figure out if Devon Sawa was actually naked (*he wasn't! or was he?*), I occasionally hung out with my older siblings, Jade and Jordan. I suppose the three of us got along as well as any nineties siblings got along. We had no iPhone or iPad to fight over, so instead, we fought over old-fashioned things like who got to record the greeting on the answering machine, check the Caller ID box first, or move the tiny felt mouse in the Avon Advent calendar during the holidays. The real drama didn't start until we got one of those electronic handheld bass-fishing games. We proved rather quickly we couldn't handle the pressure of such advanced technology, and my dad had to take it away from us, but I always had a feeling he just wanted the magical digital fishing game all for himself.

My mom, whose name is Sandy, wasn't necessarily a stage mom, but I think she could have been if one of us had just an ounce more talent.

Or even just an ounce *of* talent. Looking back, she really didn't have much to work with, and I feel bad we may have hindered that life for her. I worry there's a Kate Gosselin haircut and rhinestone IT'S WINE O'CLOCK SOMEWHERE shirt out there still looking for the owner they never got to know. Every fall, Sandy would drive my siblings and me to Omaha so we could audition for the Omaha Playhouse production of *A Christmas Carol*. We'd practice "Consider Yourself" from *Oliver!* in our piano room until our voices were hoarse and our tap shoes had given us blisters. Jade and I both wanted to be actresses after our mom forced us to watch *Steel Magnolias* with her every Sunday afternoon, and we became mesmerized by the iconic acting skills of Sally Field and Julia Roberts. *Shelby, you need some juice. Drink your juice!* We perfected our own version of the juice scene, and I still tear up thinking about how moving I was as I screamed, "Stop it, Mama!" as Jade forced a cup of whatever we could find in our fridge down my throat. Landing a role within the prestigious Omaha Playhouse would put us on the map. And my brother, Jordan, went along because my mom promised him a new pocketknife for his knife collection if he at least gave it a try. My mom always thought Jordan had the best shot at actually getting a part, and I'm still not sure why, as he was the least theatrical or coordinated of any of us. He never once let my sister shove juice down his throat.

"Will you cut your hair to play Tiny Tim?" my mom asked me every year.

"Absolutely," I'd say, and I meant it. I wanted that role so badly I'd do anything. "I'll break my own foot if I have to."

After years of auditioning, none of us ever even got a callback. I'm not sure if it's because we weren't the right ages, didn't have the right look, or simply because we all lacked musical talent and talent in general, as mentioned above. You just never know with those things! But one thing was certain after all those Omaha trips, and that was the fact that I *had* to live in a big city when I grew up. We'd always stop by the Westroads Mall before heading home, and nothing made me feel more alive than stuffing a parmesan pretzel in my mouth while the energy of a food court buzzed around me. The neon lights, the greasy smells, the "number seventeen, your order is ready" announcements—it was all so exhilarating to me. I was a city girl through and through.

But first I had to get through a childhood in Norfolk. Ugh.

My parents dated in high school and got married shortly after. My mom often talks about how broke they were when my siblings and I were growing up. But other than the fact we were only allowed two Little Debbie Zebra Cakes a week, and the Schwan's man just stopped by around the holidays to deliver frozen spicy chicken tenders, I don't remember wanting for anything. I assumed our basement was carpeted with a mix of sample squares by choice; it was fun and eclectic! My fourth birthday party was a Hawaiian luau where we all danced in "hula skirts" made from torn-up garbage bags because it made cleanup easier.

My mom stayed home with us while my dad, Jay, worked long hours building up his insurance business. I had no idea what insurance was (still don't), but I knew it meant he was gone from morning until night, and if we were ornery, my mom would threaten, "I'm going to call your dad!" She made it sound so scary and ominous, but knowing what I know now, this call would have just entailed a weather update or tense chat about Nebraska football.

On the weekends, my dad refereed high school basketball games to make extra cash, and we would often go along to watch, probably because my mom needed to get out of the house with three small kids, and her options were limited. I loved being in the competitive atmosphere of a gym until one day, I realized the fans weren't always cheering for the players—sometimes they were yelling at my dad. And then I got pissed. I started to heckle the hecklers. If someone wanted to yell shit at my dad, they would have to go through me, his six-year-old daughter, first.

I think the final straw for my mom was a particularly high-pressure game where she was trying to keep me out of fights with drunk old men, when Jordan ran underneath the bleachers and nearly tore his ear completely off on a jagged piece of bleacher metal and had to be rushed to the emergency room. I remember watching him get carried out of the gym by a grown man I didn't know, a white towel soaked with blood held to his head, and all I could think was, *My mom really thought he'd make a better Tiny Tim than me? Ha!* Jordan couldn't even walk under a bleacher without ripping his ear off. How could he possibly execute a fake limp across a stage with theater lights in his face while proclaiming, "God bless us, everyone!" Made no sense.

Sometime after the bleacher incident (from which Jordan recovered quickly, and his ear only wobbles on really windy days now), I grew tired of not being financially independent and having to limit my Little Debbie intake. Jade and Jordan had money of their own—I'd found it stashed in their Fossil watch tins—so I wanted my own money as well. And thus I started my first business (of many). I began collecting Beanie Babies with the sole intent to resell them. Get in and get out, baby! My mom drove me around to small gift boutiques and floral shops all over northeastern Nebraska to scour their inventory after I'd get wind they got a new shipment in.

"Did you get the stuff in today?" I'd ask from our kitchen phone as my little foot dangled from the stool I'd propped myself up on. "I know you were expecting a delivery this morning." I knew because I had a full page of stores and their corresponding delivery schedules listed in my Lisa Frank notebook.

"Hello! What stuff are you referring to?" the old lady on the other end would reply as if I hadn't been making this same business call for several weeks.

"C'mon, Marilyn. Don't play games with me. You know what I'm looking for. I want the Beanies. I want the bears—Princess Di, Glory, Erin. If you have them, just tell me."

"Oh, those things. Yes, I think we got a few."

The Beanie sellers always tried to play aloof to the whole Beanie

Baby craze, as if it wasn't the biggest thing to hit their store since Precious Moments figurines.

Once I'd get confirmation the goods had arrived, I'd twirl my finger in the air to let my mom know we needed to get moving. Grab some chilled Frescas and start the Nissan minivan. It was go time!

"Take the yellow, Mom. TAKE IT!" I'd shout as we hit the last stoplight out of Norfolk. There was no time to waste. If we were only a minute or two late, the other collectors would beat us to the bears.

We did this for an entire summer until I had every Beanie Baby my heart could desire. And then I immediately sold them all and made a couple thousand dollars. I paid my mom what I assumed was enough to cover gas (my mom is into gas prices like my dad is into weather), and I even gave her an extra twenty dollars and told her to buy herself a new thong leotard for Jazzercise.

A few years ago, I asked my mom why she said yes to all those absurd Beanie Baby trips. Why did she give up her mornings to chase down my list of Beanie dealers when I know she had a long to-do list herself?

"To spend time with you," she said easily. "It was just a fun thing we could do together."

This comment unsettled something in me, and I instinctively called for Harlow, only to realize he was sitting right next to me. Why did I find myself suddenly longing to relive the bizarre Beanie Baby summer but not as the child this time? What if I was the mom driving the minivan with my daughter in tow, excited to see where her adventurous little spirit led us for the day as we chatted away about mall pretzels and one-handed cartwheels?

I hadn't even considered having kids, let alone the idea that people actually enjoyed outings with their kids. Could that really be me someday? It was a crazy thought I tossed around in my head as I wondered where it came from. That would never be me, right? I hated minivans.

hurricane harlow has entered the chat

TOPEKA, KANSAS. 2010.

As Chris and I got ready for our first night as dog owners, I put Harlow in the dog bed beside ours, and once again, he instantly tried to get into our bed.

"Should we put him in his crate? Or bring his crate in here?" Chris offered.

"Yeah, we could do that." I held Harlow in my arms, and he looked from me to Chris. "Or . . ." I trailed off.

"Or what?" Chris asked.

"Or we could let him sleep with us, but only for tonight. Think about how scary it must be as a little guy to be away from your mom and siblings the first night. I just feel so bad."

Harlow buried his face under my chin, making all the little puppy grunts he already knew I couldn't resist. His manipulation skills were rather impressive, even as a puppy.

"Okay, but I think we should really try to get him to sleep in his crate going forward."

"For sure! I totally agree."

Harlow fell asleep with his neck draped across my neck. I nudged Chris several times just to say, "Look at this adorable little thing asleep on me," and we'd just stare at him and all the cuteness. I slept with one eye open, assuming Harlow would need to get up and go to the bathroom, or worse, he'd simply pee on the bed. But he didn't do either. He slept as soundly as a puppy could sleep, only moving on occasion to further stretch his paws across me or to make a little suckling sound here and there. There was no way I could move this perfect little angel into a crate, at least not for the first few nights. But once he was comfortable in our home, maybe in a week or two, we'd definitely work on crate training.

··

"Wait a second. There was a time when you thought I'd actually sleep in a crate?" Har asked as he tried to stifle a giggle.

"Yeah, buddy, I did," I said as I shut off the lamp on my nightstand. "I was young, okay? I didn't know any better."

"Oh my God, that's adorable!" Har took one last drink of bedroom water, arguably his favorite water bowl in the house. "Bless your heart, your sweet heart."

"Good night, Har."

He jumped into bed, spun a few times just for the sake of pretending he still had some dog in him after all, I assume, and then promptly plopped down next to me—all seventy pounds of him in the perfect position to kick Chris and me all night long.

With Har's face just inches from mine, he scooted even closer. Like two little kids sharing a pillow at a sleepover, he turned to me and whispered, "Would you have slept in there with me?"

"Go to bed, Har."

"I bet you would have."

Of course I would have. And I should probably mention once more that Har talks. He didn't at first, but once he started, he didn't stop. We'll get to that shortly. He's always interrupting me.

..

After Harlow's first night with us, I had an early morning of recruiting teenagers to become culinary artists. Every day I'd stroll into high schools across Kansas and Missouri pulling a red cooler full of my ingredients, a suitcase with my projector and computer, and a knife kit slung across my chest. It was my job to inspire teenagers to pursue their dream careers while I prepared them jicama salsa to display my knife skills and pray they'd fill out the college application (and sign it) so I could make my quota for the month.

Before leaving, I put Harlow in the bathroom with food, water, and a toy filled with peanut butter and told him I'd be back as soon as possible.

"You don't have to worry because I'll be right back. Okay, buddy?"

Chris's job wasn't flexible, but mine was, and I knew I'd only be away for a couple of hours. I left a happy Harlow lying contentedly on the bathroom rug, playing with his peanut butter toy. *What a good boy,* I thought as I gently closed the bathroom door behind me.

After two hours of preaching to teens not to settle for a job they hated, while I myself was dressed like a chef from a reality show you just knew I was going to get eliminated from, I packed up my cooler and applications and tried to get the hell out of the classroom before the bell rang. I saw an ambitious-looking student waiting to ask me a question as I made my way toward the door, but I simply held up my hand and gave a strong "nope" as I ran out. Not today, kiddo. I had to get home to my own dream, my new pup.

I sprinted up the stairs to our apartment and flung open the door to the bathroom where Harlow was supposed to be sleeping. Inside our small bathroom, a hurricane had hit: Hurricane Harlow. Kibble and water covered the linoleum floor—apparently Harlow preferred his bowls tipped over and empty rather than full and upright. Every towel that was hung and toilet paper square was strewn across the small space. The shower curtain was barely hanging on to its cheap silver hooks; I'd gotten home just before it was completely pulled down. And the rug was no more. Only threads of it remained, most of them stuck to the wet toilet paper pieces on the floor. And in the midst of it sat Harlow, tail wagging, peanut butter toy in his mouth, and so happy that I was back.

"What'd you do, little guy?" I asked as he jumped on my legs, zero remorse shown.

There was a brief moment as I scanned his destruction when I wondered what I had gotten myself into. Would I ever be able to leave the house again?

"No," I heard him say with a smirk and a wiggle, and I wondered if he really knew what I was thinking. *Did I know what he was thinking?*

"I don't think so either." I laughed because what did it matter? I had no friends in Topeka or hobbies to speak of, besides yelling profanities at the cult we lived nearby. I wasted far too much time circling their commune, imagining all the cutting and *very witty* things I'd say to them if they ever happened to be outside mowing their lawn or having an evil crafting hour in their garage as they added more puff paint to their horrible protest posters. *Someday . . . someday I'll give that hate-filled group a piece of my mind.* Until the day it actually happened, and the second I saw movement appear at the front door, I completely panicked and ran home as fast as my swishy Nike running shorts would allow.

"Anyway, let's go play." I scooped Har into my arms and took him outside to run some laps in the parking lot and play with the neighborhood kids near the apartment dumpsters.

With Chris rarely home during the day and me not knowing how to socialize with new people, I had a lot of time on my hands, and I spent it all with Harlow. The first thing on my list was to teach him how to walk on a leash. Harlow eagerly took it in his mouth and pulled, and I realized teaching me to walk on a leash was on his list as well.

For the first few weeks, there was a bit of a power struggle as to who got to walk whom, but in the end, we both decided it was best if Har walked me, especially as he grew bigger and stronger. And after we'd had enough walks for the day, we'd stop by the dog park so Harlow could hang around other humans, and I could hang around other dogs.

"We really got to get this potty-training thing down," I said to Harlow one night after we'd stood outside for ten minutes, he finally pooped, then told me he was ready to go back inside only to immediately pee once he hit the carpet.

Harlow tried to rip the rag from my hands that I was using to clean up his pee spot, a favorite new game of his, and I knew he wasn't listening.

"I mean this, Har. You can't pee inside."

With his face low to the ground and butt high in the air ready to pounce, he looked at me like he had no idea what I was complaining about. Sometimes I felt like he understood me, and other times I wondered if we were getting anywhere at all.

"I appreciate that you poop outside. Trust me—I do. But you have to pee outside too, okay?"

Harlow saw a moment of weakness—I had many during those first weeks of potty training—and he grabbed the rag from me and took off with it in his mouth, a victorious bounce in his step. Earl's words rang in my head: *You can't punish these dogs . . . you'll break their spirit.* And so I let Har run. And then I praised the hell out of him when he behaved well and tried my best to ignore when he peed all over the apartment.

A few weeks later, during one of the many times I rushed Harlow to the vet, certain he was about to die from something I'd made up in my head, I learned that he had a urinary tract infection. Harlow was peeing all over our apartment because he literally couldn't control it. I didn't even know puppies could get UTIs, but apparently, it's pretty common. I felt awful thinking he might have been in pain. What if I had punished him? How many other puppies had been scolded for an infection they truly couldn't control?

"I'm sorry, Har. I had no idea," I said as we waited for the vet to return with his antibiotic prescription.

But Harlow wasn't listening. He'd been given a milk bone and couldn't be happier pushing it around the linoleum floor as if it were a grasshopper he couldn't contain.

His infection cleared up within a week, and it made potty training so much easier. But the idea of Harlow being in pain really bothered me because it wasn't just about him—it was about all the other dogs as well. And I'm not just talking about puppies with UTIs, but in regard to how dogs in general are treated by their humans. I started noticing things I hadn't before, like the neighbor dog always chained up outside or the friends who just got a puppy but never missed a happy hour. Something about bringing Harlow into my life opened up a part of me that made me so much more sensitive to everything. For once, I wasn't just in my own world.

Reasons I Took Harlow to the Vet His First Year

When he ate an entire box of Cheerios, and the dry cereal coated the roof of his mouth in a layer so thick that every time he swallowed, he made a hacking sound like an old smoker, so I was sure he had kennel cough.

When I worried he had eaten three blocks of cheese and two loaves of bread. He had not. He simply hid them in our couch cushions for a rainy day.

When I thought he had a skin disease because his nose was raw and bloody. He was fine. This was simply the price he paid for burying and hiding things around our apartment. Like cheese and bread.

When I did not know it was my responsibility to help ease things free from his backside. Like long strings of grass, long strings of plastic bags, or long strings of anything else he found to eat. Most likely stuck, thanks to cheese and bread.

When his gums turned black and I thought he had gum disease. It was actually just the skin of blueberries, caught in his teeth, and I still have no idea where he got into blueberries.

When he did in fact get kennel cough.

dear google, why do people have kids?

CHICAGO, ILLINOIS. 2018.

It wasn't until my final "I'm-not-sure-if-I-want-kids" friend casually mentioned that she and her husband had started trying for a baby that the panic started to set in. The panic didn't creep in because Chris and I weren't trying or even because the phrase "trying for a baby" has always made me rather uncomfortable because I'm a graphic thinker, but it was because I still didn't know if I ever wanted to try. What did everyone else know that I didn't? And how did they know it? What was I missing?

I turned to the one person I could trust with all of life's hardest questions: Google.

Dear Google, why do people have kids? Or why do people like *kids? And how do you know if you're ready to be a mom? And what happens if you don't like your kids? Or you realize you hate being a mom? Or that wiping their boogers makes you gag even though everyone says it won't once it's your own kid? It's still their boogers! And can I still go to Pilates and then Nordstrom Rack right after if I have a kid? Or sleep in? What about edibles? Can I still take a few of those when I*

feel like it? Or live out my career dreams? This is a very big choice to
make, Google, so PLEASE HELP ME. I don't get it! Where is my
baby fever?

Night after night, with Harlow in my lap and Chris next to me
browsing memes about the corporate world, I scoured mommy blogs,
stalked cool moms on Instagram, and read one parent post after the
other, hoping something might click.

"What are ya looking at there?" Chris would sometimes ask.

"Porn!" I'd respond quickly. "Lots of it!" And then I'd fling my
phone across the room hoping he wouldn't ask more.

I don't know why I was ashamed to admit what I was actually
searching. Chris never pressured me to get pregnant, and for all I
knew, he had his own secret search going on. But if I had to guess,
I suppose it's because society often tells us it's perfectly okay for men
not to know if they're ready to be a dad. Humorous, even. We make
jokes about men getting cold feet, but if a woman isn't ready to be a
mother, well, she's just cold.

So there I was, a cold, childless woman, with a uterus growing
crustier by the day. Or was it my eggs getting crusty? I'd have to ask
Google again, but it was safe to assume it was everything! Everything
on my decrepit body was getting crusty as I settled into my thirties.

"You know if you wait much longer, you'll have a geriatric pregnancy," a friend once noted.

"That's fine. I've always loved old people," I responded. "I'd be
thrilled to give birth to one."

The female body is incredible, and I'm very thankful for mine.
However . . . HOWEVER, the fact that our prime reproductive years
often begin in our teens when we're barely capable of taking care of a
new ear piercing, let alone another human, and then start to decline
at the age of thirty?! Thirty, when things are just getting good and
stable, when you're finally feeling okay in your own skin and body, so
the idea of growing another body in the one you've just settled into
might seem a little more doable than it once did. How in the hell does

that make any sense? I don't know who came up with that timeline, but we need to change it.

As I was saying . . .

At family get-togethers, Chris and I were the only couple without children. Relatives either jabbed us with, "When are you guys gonna have one of these already? Don't they look like fun?" as they dangled their screaming kids in our face, often held upside down by their ankles like a tiny toddler piñata, some sort of dark sticky substance all over their faces and hands.

"It does look fun," I'd mumble as I'd slowly back away in my white denim.

Or they went the opposite route and kept their little ones away from us altogether, assuming that since we had no children of our own, that certainly meant we would try to eat theirs.

Neither way bothered me because, at the end of the day, Chris and I would return to our quiet and oh-so-clean home and admit to each other that being around children all day did not sell us on having one.

"Thank God. Me neither," Har would chime in. "Those things are *a lot.*"

Har was right. Kids were a lot. And maybe they weren't meant for the three of us, and that was okay.

..

And then one day both Chris and I caught a glimpse into the secret, more tender side of parenthood that outsiders don't often get to see. Or maybe I just never looked for it before. It was a moment or, more specifically, a feeling that all my researching and Googling simply couldn't provide for me. There was nothing particularly special about what we saw, and I'm still not sure why it captivated us in the way that it did—why it made both Chris and me think, *That* could *be us.*

Our little peek behind the curtain happened at Mama's Fish

House in Maui, Hawaii. So there's a good chance mai tais played a part in all of this, or just the fact the entire restaurant was basically a culmination of what every tourist dreams Hawaii might be like. Nearly everything I knew about Hawaii was based on two *Full House* episodes from 1989, and with the colorful leis adorning every neck, soft Hawaiian ukulele music, and fruity drinks served in tiki mugs, Mama's Fish House was not letting me down.

A couple who appeared to be around the same age as Chris and me had the coveted table near the window overlooking the beach, a spot where your eyes were instantly drawn. They also had an adorable toddler in her own miniature lei who sat in a high chair between them and happily clapped her hands together and babbled among them. The three of them together looked so . . . content. Dare I even say . . . relaxed? Okay, that may be one emotion too far, but still, everything I'd read or witnessed about bringing a toddler into a restaurant, presumably while also on vacation, shouted "Don't do it!" But not these three. Certainly something must be wrong with them.

I continued to observe the mystery family from the corner of my eye (in a very non-creepy way, I promise), or at least that's what the mai tais told me, marveling at the way the parents gazed at their daughter and she back at them. It was as if they were the only three people in the restaurant, in the world even—just mom, dad, and baby. *And the creepy lady staring from what she thinks is "afar" as she makes up a fictional story in her head about who these people are but is actually only one table away.*

"You want to join them?" Chris joked.

I was caught. Of course I was. "I just think they're a cute family is all."

And then we both watched as the perfect little toddler grew agitated with her high chair, rocking from side to side, arms outstretched, probably tired of the boring dinner, and we held our breath as we waited for the tantrum. But a tantrum never occurred—at least not in front of us. In one swift motion, the dad swooped the small child into his arms, smothered her with kisses, and then walked her out of the restaurant and onto the beach.

A tiny hand enclosed in one much bigger, the father and daughter took slow steps in the sand and then even slower ones as the little one toddled along unevenly. They stopped to pick up seashells and look up at seagulls, and when the dad pointed out that mom wasn't far, just watching from inside the restaurant, the toddler's eyes lit up with recognition and love as she waved to her. And from behind the window, her mother did the same.

I told myself to stop intruding on a moment that wasn't mine, but before I did, I wanted to know. I wanted to know what that mother felt—not just in that idyllic little vacation moment, but in all the moments. When her hand was held, her shoulder laid on, her lap rested upon, and her eyes peered into by the tiny little being whose love was so pure and unconditional, because it was quite literally made by her own.

When I finally turned away, I saw Chris was still engrossed.

"They don't make it look so awful," I said quietly. "Having a kid, I mean."

"I know." He took a slow sip of his drink. "I bet we might even enjoy it."

Like I said, it could have been the mai tais.

How to Interact with the Only Child-Free Couple at Family Get-Togethers: Option 1

If an adult couple has made the choice not to have children, it is safe to assume they HATE all children, and thus you must keep your own children as far away as possible. If you do not, you will risk the following: your children being stepped on, dropped, mowed over, or given alcohol and drugs (people without children do not know that kids can't have alcohol or drugs), or exposure to curse words, conspiracies, big cities, Lizzo, nose piercings, sleeve tattoos, or the horror that some adults do not have children, which is far too confusing and, frankly, dangerous for a child to comprehend.

If caught in an interaction with a child-free couple and also your child, try to cause a distraction that will allow your child to get away. Possible distracting conversation starters: brunch, European vacations, their "fur children," designer shoes and handbags, Phish concerts. Child-free couples love to talk about themselves and the things they must do to fill their empty lives, so an engaging question is key.

carl, are you serious?

CHICAGO, ILLINOIS. 2019.

Harlow was the first person I told when I found out I was pregnant.

"I can't believe it," I said, the three positive tests still in my hand.

"Me neither," Harlow responded.

Har and I talked to each other. Like, a lot. So much so, I often forgot that not everyone had lengthy conversations with their dogs on a regular basis. I'd find myself in public saying something like, "Carl, are you serious? We've talked about this. You don't get two treats from the Club Lucky treat jar!" And then I'd catch someone giving me an odd look, so I'd quickly try to act like I was on my phone to cover it up. *In case we've forgotten, Carl was Har's naughty alter ego.*

"What's that guy's deal?" Har would ask when he'd notice the person staring as well.

"I don't know. Some people are just weird," I'd mutter, and we'd carry on our way.

Or there were the times we'd pass the bus stand full of dirty barbecue dishes from outdoor diners at Smoke Daddy, and Har would act all casual, like he had to tie his shoe or something, just so he could bend over and get a lick of a leftover. I'd immediately catch him and say, "Nice try, buddy, but I told you I'm onto this little charade," and then he'd bark back, "There's no charade. I actually need to stop right here and send a text message. Is that okay?" He didn't even have a phone! So I'd pull one way while Har pulled the other, both of us insisting we were right, and suddenly everyone eating at Smoke Daddy on Division Street was staring at us.

"You are causing a scene," he'd say under his breath, his belly flat to the ground refusing to move. "Just let me assist in cleaning one dish, and we'll be on our way. Is that so much to ask?"

I never let him—not on purpose, anyway. But I did take Har to Smoke Daddy for his birthday lunch one year, and we both agreed it was one of our favorite lunches together. Second only to the time he jumped through the window at Vinny D's trying to get his birthday hot dog. A real Carl move, if I've ever seen one.

I'm not sure when exactly our conversations began, because it didn't happen right away. But I know that once I started listening, Har never stopped talking. A certain look in his eyes or perk in his ears, even just a tilt of his head—it all said so much. Chris recognized the secret language Har and I spoke, but he wasn't nearly as fluent as we were. But how could he be? Har and I spent literally every day together, just the two of us. Of course, we had to learn to talk to each other. The days would have been so lonely otherwise.

"Should I get another test?" I asked him.

"I'm one step ahead of you," Har said as he pulled his leash from the wall. "We better get to Target ASAP."

Other than dirty dishes from Smoke Daddy, there were few things Harlow enjoyed more in life than stopping by the Target in Wicker Park, where dogs are not only allowed but celebrated. He'd find any excuse to lead me there knowing precisely where he had to stand (or throw a tantrum on the cement) to make the magic glass doors glide open.

"Hi, Harlow," the manager would greet us as we walked in.

"Hi, Carol. The store looks even better than it did yesterday, as do you!" He'd beam back, ever so delighted to be in his happy place. She'd give him a little back scratch, and then Harlow would prance up and down the aisles, inspecting every item on the shelves as if he were the manager. Sometimes I think he really thought he was.

But today we had no time for lollygagging.

"Okay, Har. We have to get in and out. No time to chat with all your friends."

"Absolutely. Got it! Oh look. There's Carol!"

I gave his leash a hard pull the other way to let him know I was serious. He rolled his eyes and huffed but knew not to push me. I was anxious, and he could feel it. Har often picked up on my anxiety before I did.

Everything about the pregnancy test aisle made me uncomfortable. Thanks to birth control and the Lifetime movie starring Kirsten Dunst called *Fifteen and Pregnant*, I didn't have a lot of pregnancy scares. Okay, I didn't have any pregnancy scares. This was my first one, at age thirty-two, when I was in a serious relationship *with my husband*, and I still looked over my shoulder as I tossed the test in my basket to make sure that no high school teachers saw me.

I splurged and bought the expensive tests this time, mostly so I didn't have to come back and do this again. The kind that actually spelled out the word "PREGNANT." As in, "Yes, moron, you are." Apparently, it took three cheap tests and two expensive ones for me to actually believe it.

Well, kind of. I was still skeptical. I needed a doctor's confirmation.

"Hello. Yes, I'd like to schedule an appointment, please." I paced our bedroom while Har snored loudly on the bed, legs and arms stuck straight in the air, his afternoon napping position of choice. He was positive that whatever this was could wait until post-nap.

"What will we be seeing you for?" the receptionist asked.

"I'd like to confirm a pregnancy." I tried to be casual.

"You want to confirm a pregnancy?" she repeated in a tone I didn't love.

Now I was feeling defensive. "Yes, that's correct." Certainly I wasn't the first to call an OB-GYN's office with such a request.

"We don't do that," she said.

"You don't?"

"No. We don't."

"Okay . . . well, you should."

Of all the things an OB-GYN should confirm, why not start with whether or not a woman is starting to grow another human in their body? I've had my earaches confirmed. Sore throats. Sinus pressure. Hell, even an ingrown eyelash (twice!). And yet here I was, unable to find out if I had an ingrown baby or not.

"Did you take a test?" the receptionist asked.

"Yes," I said, our annoyance levels matching each other's.

"Congrats. That's your confirmation. We'll see you when you're ten to twelve weeks along."

When exactly is that? I wondered. My sister had tried to explain pregnancy time to me on more than one occasion, and I never understood it. Allegedly, you start counting the weeks from the start date of your last period, but a baby is usually conceived ten to fourteen days *after* your period starts, so how does that make any sense unless someone is time traveling here? It was lost on me, but apparently until that magical ten-to-twelve-week window arrived, all I had to rely on was a ten-dollar piece of plastic I bought at Target. And every other pregnant woman who had come before me, fictional movie characters aside, just accepted this?

I decided to do some deep breathing. Paced around the room for a bit. Looked down at my phone. Told myself *no*. Looked at Har, and his face said, *Do it*. Okay, I had to call back.

"'Ello. Can I schedule a checkup please?" This time I spoke with an accent. "Just a general checkup is all, love."

"Ma'am, we have Caller ID."

I promptly hung up. Well, shit.

I sat down next to Harlow, and he instinctively stretched his head back into my lap and looked up at me. "Sorry," he said, now fully moved on and ready for a post-nap neck rub.

The wrinkles he had on his forehead as a puppy traveled down his body, landing on his neck, leaving folds and folds of goodness that begged to be pet. His face was white now, like it had been dipped in a bucket of sugar while the rest of his body stayed cinnamon. But when I looked into Harlow's dark brown eyes, all I could see was the puppy I picked up on that small Kansas farm nearly ten years ago.

That twenty-three-year-old version of me who drove to the vizsla farm simply because she got off work early and wanted to impress her new boyfriend with a cool anniversary gift had no idea what she was setting in motion that day. Then again, we never do at twenty-three. Nine years later, that impromptu little choice I made on a random Thursday was the closest thing to offspring I had ever known, and maybe all I had ever wanted to know.

How could Harlow and I still be as close with a baby in the picture? We literally shared a pillow at night. Wherever I went, Harlow went. Where I sat, Harlow sat. Could my lap hold a seventy pound dog *and* a baby? (Yes, Har was a very big vizsla, or as some fellow dog walkers even noted, "the biggest vizsla." But he wasn't overweight, just big chested!) Anyway, what if Har didn't like the baby? Then what? Would Chris and I have to separate because we had no other choice? He and baby would go live in Napa, and Har and I in London, and then one summer Harlow and baby would find each other at camp and realize they're sisters! *Sisters—we're more like twins!* And I know you just read that line in an accent, so please make no mistake that in my head Har has perfected the English accent. *You want to know the difference between you and me?*

I'm kidding, by the way. I know that idea doesn't make any sense because Har and baby wouldn't be twins, obviously! And *The Parent Trap* storyline is very flawed. Who sends their kid to summer camp in a limo?

Tangent aside, I just wanted Har to be happy, and I worried

throwing a baby into the mix would be hard on him. People thought I was crazy when I admitted this. "You can't let a dog keep you from starting a family," I'd often hear. First of all, Har is not "just a dog," and second of all, he *is* our family. Our family had already started. A family consists of a lot more things than only a baby. Come on, people. This isn't 1995! Hawaii aside, Har did nearly everything with us. We planned road trips we knew he'd love, went to restaurants where he could join us on the patio, and camped in places where he could roam. Har's joy brought us joy.

We'd heard people love their kids as much as their dogs (sometimes even more), but could it really be true? Chris and I got so much secondhand joy watching Harlow be happy that we began to imagine adding even more joy but with a baby. So we weren't necessarily *trying* when I found out I was pregnant, but we also weren't *not* trying. We were just warming ourselves up to the idea, assuming it would take a lot longer than it did.

After Harlow napped and I spent an hour or two overthinking how to get a "pregnancy confirmation," we set out on our fifth walk of the day, this time to meet Chris in the West Loop after he got off work, as we did every day. But today, we had news to share. Life-altering news.

We crossed the busy intersection at Ashland and Division, and Harlow glanced up at me as the Chicago traffic crawled by, the city sounds of horns, sirens, and truck exhaust surrounding us.

"Not here, Har," I begged, knowing all too well what his glance meant.

"Yeah, I gotta go now," he responded as he started to zigzag in the crosswalk, sniffing for a spot.

"Of all places, buddy. Please. We've talked about this."

"I know we have, and I keep telling you you're asking too much." He was already mid squat. "Now watch my back for me."

There was no stopping him. In the middle of one of the busiest intersections in Chicago during five o'clock traffic, Harlow decided now was the time to relieve himself. And I'm not talking about number one—we're talking about the kind that requires cleanup.

You're probably thinking, *Get him to grass, you terrible dog owner. Don't you remember the promise you made Earl?*

Of course I remembered the promise! I reorganized my entire life to live up to that promise, but the terrible truth is that Harlow preferred the pavement. He preferred sidewalks, curbs, empty pots, large rocks, anything with a hard and preferably elevated surface. I took him to the dog park (a big grassy area with plenty of great smells) at least three times a day, every single day, no matter what the Chicago weather brought us. We also went on multiple walks with patches of grass on every block, but he still sought out the pavement. Once, Har actually landed a turd on a tall exposed pipe. I couldn't believe it.

"How'd you do that?" I asked in disbelief. "And better yet, why'd you do that?"

"Because it's my pipe," he said smugly, "and now everyone knows it."

Apparently, it's a vizsla trait. Something in their elitist bloodline makes them think their shit needs to be higher than everyone else's. Or when a pipe isn't available, in the middle of a goddamn intersection.

As Harlow squatted, I willed the stoplight to stay red just a little longer. He was taking his sweet time—no modesty shown whatsoever as the cars inched closer and closer and his back arched higher. Sweat gathered at my hairline as I watched the adjacent light fade from green to yellow. The only one wearing a look of shame at this moment was me.

With a bag covering my hand, I picked up his mess as fast as my humility allowed, and we shuffled out of the intersection. Harlow trotted beside me looking just a little too content about the scene he'd just caused. I shook my head and tossed the black bag into the closest trash bin and wondered for a moment if this was a sign. If Harlow taking a big dump in the middle of an intersection was his way of telling me what he thought about the new road Chris and I were about to go down.

What if this happened again, but next time I had a baby? How would I pick up after Har, make sure the baby was okay in the stroller, and get out of the way of traffic? Then again, I suppose my first battle would just be getting out on a walk. We lived four floors up, and it wasn't the easiest setup to get a dog out, let alone a baby, stroller, and a dog!

My stomach turned with anxiety as my mind began to spiral. Everything I felt didn't line up with what I expected to feel. Where was the joy and excitement I'd seen all my friends have with their pregnancies? The only thing I felt was fear and uncertainty, which then opened the door for guilt to come rushing in, because how dare I feel anything but elated about casually getting pregnant in my thirties when I knew so many others struggled?

By the time we reached the block of Chris's office, I was so anxious I thought I might faint. There was so much change on the horizon. So much change I couldn't control and wasn't ready for.

It was Harlow who saw Chris approaching first. He pulled at his leash and ran to greet him as Chris crouched to the ground and opened his arms wide as he always did, an after-work reunion scene that had been making me smile for nearly a decade. Chris is a tall guy, standing well over six feet, but he'd always get to Harlow's level to say hello.

Chris was meant to be a dad. I'd known it since the first day I met him. Well, maybe not the first day—we met in a musty basement of a frat party while he manned the keg—but over time, I could just tell. Knowing this didn't make my uncertainty any easier. What was wrong with me? Why was I so scared and unsure of this mom thing? Where was my "baby fever"? I'd been waiting for that damn fever for years, and it still hadn't arrived.

I took several deep breaths and tried to act casual. "Hi! How was your day?"

"Kinda stressful, actually." The three of us stopped and waited at the crosswalk. "Why are you making that weird face?"

"No weird face. This is just my face," I said, and Har looked at me and furrowed his brows, and I furrowed mine right back. He'd better not say a word. "Why was it stressful?"

"Just lots thrown on my plate I wasn't expecting," Chris responded. The light turned green.

"Well, ready for another thing thrown on your plate?" I said as we stepped out into the intersection.

"What's that?"

Don't do it like this, I begged myself. Just because I was anxious didn't mean I had to make Chris anxious. I should make it special. I could bake him a cake or hide the test under his pillow. Wait, a urine stick under a pillow? That sounded like a weird tooth fairy fetish. I could buy him a dad mug, or dad socks! *Don't just blurt it. Don't just blurt it. Don't just—*

"I'm fucking pregnant."

I blurted it.

How to Interact with the Only Child-Free Couple at Family Get-Togethers: Option 2

If an adult couple has made the choice not to have children, it is safe to assume they are actually looking for someone to change their mind, because they don't realize the grave mistake they are about to make. This can be you! You can save them! There are a few ways to go about this, but start by reminding them that everyone has children. It's. Just. What. People. Do. Bring up things like: lonely holidays, growing old, not being selfish, grandchildren, dying alone, the fact that dogs are not children, and dogs will eat you if you die alone and they get hungry enough. That last one is a little morbid, but so is not having children!

If caught in an interaction with a child-free couple and also your child, this is your chance to show them how great it is to be a parent! You can do this by: insisting they hold your child or having your child dance for them, sing a song, retell a funny story that literally never ends, say a (silly) swear word, or force a hug. Child-free couples love to talk about themselves and the things they do to fill their empty lives, so providing examples of parenthood being so much more fulfilling than their current superficial "hobbies" is key. Perhaps say something like, "I never knew what love was until I had my children. I thought I did, but I was wrong"—thereby insisting the child-free idiots standing before you are also loveless. That one hits hard (but in a good way!).

there's a baby in there

"You're really pregnant?" Chris asked for the fifth time as we continued our walk from River North toward our condo in Noble Square. "Was not expecting that."

"Makes two of us."

"Three of us," Har added as he pulled to walk toward his favorite pet store on Milwaukee Street and I pulled him the other way.

"Why'd you take a test? Is your period late?"

"Yeah, but it always is. But today I remembered it was really late."

"How late?"

"Um . . . a week? Or two?"

For the next ten minutes or so, Chris processed the news by continually saying, "Whoa" and "Are you sure?" While I responded, "Yes" and "I know."

As we crossed the street toward Noble, I noticed a look in Chris's eyes I was lacking in my own. He was excited. Maybe if he could feel that way, so could I.

"So we're going to have a baby." I tried the words out to see how they felt.

A smile crept across his face. "It's crazy. But it's good though. We said we'd start trying eventually. I just can't believe it happened so . . . quickly."

Quickly is right. I won't get into too many details here—if you are reading this, I have to believe you know how babies are made—but I do want to pause for a moment. Chris and I had been conditioned to think we were going to have a "helluva time" getting pregnant in our thirties. I didn't know a lot about infertility, but I did know my mom had a "magic" small wooden turtle figurine known as the "fertile turtle" that I was told was blessed by some witch doctor hundreds of years ago that was in high demand among my sister's friends. (I was later told the turtle was purchased at a gift shop near the Grand Canyon in Arizona.) But the point is, the turtle made its rounds through my sister's friends, and then it trickled down to my brother's friends, and suddenly *my* friends were asking about the magic turtle. *Did it really work? Could they borrow it and find out? They were ovulating next week, so like, seriously, how could they get their hands on the magic turtle by then?* I was skeptical of its powers, but I also refused to touch the tiny turtle or assist with the handoff.

Seeing the lengths so many of my friends went through to get pregnant, I assumed that when Chris and I started "kinda trying" we were just testing the waters. Our feet were still dangling on the edge of the pool. The water hadn't even touched our waists yet, which everyone knows is the hardest part of getting into a cold pool. Certainly I couldn't get pregnant from just sitting on the edge, could I? Was that damn turtle around me and I didn't know it? Perhaps that's why I craved the confirmation so badly. Were we the couple who managed to take the plunge without the initial discomfort and gasp that always follows the first jump in? If so, should I feel smug about this? I always hated pools that weren't heated. But right now, all I could feel was stunned and incredibly unprepared.

The following day, we found ourselves in a cramped MRI-center waiting room on Halsted Street. It took a lot of phone calls and a little bit of begging, but I finally found a way to have someone in a doctor's coat confirm my pregnancy. I aggressively bounced my purse in my lap in an attempt not to wet myself. My instructions were to come in with a full bladder for the ultrasound, and I took that as my first future-mom assignment. I came in with the fullest bladder.

Twenty minutes passed, and we still hadn't been seen. My legs couldn't cross any tighter nor could I bounce my purse any faster.

"I am going to piss myself!" I whispered to Chris through gritted teeth as I wobbled toward the bathroom. Thank God the door opened easily, or my bladder would have taken matters into its own hands.

The moment I walked back out, relief written all over my face, the receptionist called my name.

Back in the exam room, with my legs in stirrups and a paper gown doing a half-ass job to cover me, the tech handed me what looked like a turkey baster and said I could "insert it when ready."

"Myself? I put this in myself?" I'd never heard of such a thing. Then again, this was my first ultrasound.

"Yes. Is that okay?"

I nodded. First, self-checkouts at grocery stores, now this. I looked toward Chris, and he blushed and turned away.

Once the baster was inside, the tech took over. Her eyes were fixated on her computer screen as she jerked the tool around like it was a stick shift. Left, right, up, down, oops there's a pothole, don't hit the deer! About ten minutes and five thousand gear changes later, the process was over, and we were both sweating.

As the tech removed her plastic gloves and studied the screen in front of her, I wondered if she beat her top score. Did that round get her on the leaderboard? It should have.

"Uh huh," she muttered to only herself as she zoomed in on something neither Chris nor I could see.

"Is everything okay?" Chris asked.

"Oh yes," she finally said in a thick Russian accent. "There's a baby in there."

There it was—the confirmation we'd been seeking. Chris and I looked at each other with wide eyes and anxious smiles.

Based on the ultrasound, I was probably only five or six weeks along. It was too soon to hear the heartbeat, but I was given a tentative due date of February 3. And that made things feel very real. I had a due date!

Oh my God, I had a due date.

The list of things I needed to get done before this date started to stack on me before we even stepped out of the clinic.

I needed to finish my manuscript. How could I write with a baby around? And what about stand-up? I wasn't doing a lot of comedy, but I did have a few shows lined up for the summer. Was that dream over now? Most comedians got famous first, then had the babies. I stood no chance doing it the other way around.

And then there was Har! What about my boy? How would I break it to him that this was really happening? Of course he knew about the pregnancy tests, but now it was real. His life was about to be flipped on its head, and how could I do that to him? The fear about going on walks while hauling a stroller up and down four flights of stairs came crashing back. I was lost in a swirl of hows and whats when Chris stopped and grabbed my hand, a rare form of public affection neither of us was known to display, and told me how excited he was that we were going to be parents.

"Me too," I said.

And I *was* excited. I was just also really overwhelmed. I knew both of our lives were about to change. I was just going to be the one to feel it happen first.

And you know what? I was right. It started with migraines, and then the nausea hit. It hit me in the morning, the afternoon, and at night. It hit me all damn day. I'd use the few moments I had of feeling okay to take Harlow on our walks. I was not going to give those up even if it killed me, and sometimes it felt like it actually might. Okay, that may be slightly dramatic, but no one prepared me for how truly awful morning sickness can be. It was as if I had a case of the flu that never went away.

One Friday morning, Harlow and I attempted to walk to our favorite bagel shop about a mile away. Halfway there, I had to stop and sit on the curb because I thought I was going to faint.

"I can't do it, Har." I put my clammy hands on the back of his head as he dutifully sat down beside me.

"You don't look so good," he said as his ears shrugged toward me with concern. And then he turned back in the direction of the shop. "But I also really want a bagel."

"I feel like I could pass out." My once-sweaty forehead now felt icy, and my teeth chattered uncontrollably. This wave was a rough one.

A woman pushing a double-wide stroller approached, and I did my best to sit as close to the street as possible so I wouldn't get run over by her toddler mobile.

"Are you okay?" she asked, taking pity on the mess I certainly appeared to be.

"I'm ten weeks pregnant," I said in between heavy breaths. I'm not sure why I told this stranger the truth when I hadn't even told most of my friends yet.

"Oh God, no. I'm sorry. I had it bad too," she said, and I realized that's why I told her—I wanted sympathy. I'd been miserable for almost five weeks and had hardly muttered a word to anyone about it because of some unwritten rule I felt I had to follow about not announcing "too early."

Would men do the same? I often wondered.

Ted in marketing couldn't make it in today because his throat hurts, and he's worried it might grow worse throughout the day. Meanwhile, Lynette in accounting is quietly dry heaving at her desk hoping no one notices as she secretly grows a tiny human in her body.

For the record, I don't think anyone should have to work when they don't feel well, including Ted. I also think women should announce their pregnancy whenever the hell they want to announce, whether that's week four or week twenty-four. Perhaps we could normalize both timelines.

"It gets better. I swear." The woman gave me one last empathetic glance before continuing on her way, presumably to get the bagels I knew I wouldn't be eating that morning.

How did women willingly do this more than once? I wondered as I watched her walk away, two sets of tiny feet dangling from the stroller. *Just get to twelve weeks,* the little voice inside reminded me. That had become my mantra after I left my ten-week appointment with my OB-GYN. She told me that most women feel much better at twelve weeks, and I clung to that hope. Our twelve-week genetic test was less than two weeks away. Everything would be better after that appointment.

"Come on," Har said as he stood up, pulling on his leash for me to do the same. "Let's go."

"I don't want to," I whined.

"But it's time to keep going. C'mon," he said once more, and I knew I had no choice in the matter.

I begrudgingly stood up from the curb and tried to pull Har back toward home, but he held his ground. Pointing to the bagel shop, he wanted his normal route. "We're going home, Har."

"No," he resisted. "This way."

"Goddamnit, Carl," I mumbled as I let him win, dragging my defeated feet behind his triumphant ones. "We'll get your stupid bagels."

harlow and the city

"I can't live in Topeka anymore, Chris. I am miserable here," I said after eight months of living in Topeka.

About ten months previous, I had agreed to move anywhere Chris's job took him (us). I think I actually said, "I could be happy anywhere as long as I'm with you." Lol.

And then we learned his assigned territory was Topeka, and as it turned out, I actually couldn't be happy anywhere. Chris wasn't happy either; he just needed confirmation from me. We left in May 2011 and literally did not look back. A few weeks before our departure, a Christian radio host named Harold Camping predicted that May 21, 2011, was going to be the end of times. I didn't believe it because I'm not crazy, but I also kind of believed it because I'm a little crazy. I was so happy that we were leaving Topeka and moving to Chicago, a city I had dreamed of living in as a little girl from a small town in Nebraska, that it made sense to me it was probably too good to be true. Of course the world would end right before we got out of Topeka. Of course!

On May 22, when the world didn't burst into flames, I'd never been so grateful to be alive. It was almost as exhilarating as the day I got released from the medical study I participated in during college to make some money to go on spring break.

"It's a good thing we're getting out of here," Chris said that morning as Harlow and I danced around the kitchen. "I think living too close to a cult was starting to get to you."

Who, me? Never.

There wasn't one thing about Topeka that sent us packing but rather the toll of eight months living in a place we didn't love, with zero friends, all the while wondering if this really was where we wanted to set up our lives. The longer Chris stayed with his investing office and built up his book of business, the less likely we were to leave. We knew things could eventually get better in Topeka, and staying there would grant us "a very comfortable life down the road," as so many of our family members reminded us when we told them Chris was considering quitting his job. However, "comfort" in this context seemed to only refer to financial means, which is obviously important, but what about every other aspect of life?

Chris and I hadn't even hit our mid-twenties at this point, and we wanted to see the world. We had both grown up in Nebraska, attended college there, and only landed one state away in Kansas because of Chris's internship that turned into a job. The idea of moving to a city like Chicago, a place I'd only been on family vacations to see a Cubs game and eat deep-dish pizza at a chain restaurant, felt wild and exciting.

I also harbored a little secret that only Chris and Harlow knew. I wanted to try stand-up comedy and improv. Chicago was a comedy hub. The dream gnawed at me throughout college. I thought I could tuck it away when I graduated, but the more I imagined staying in Kansas forever and never giving comedy a try, the more it ate at me. Could Chicago be a place where we actually chased our dreams? Where we could surround ourselves with people and experiences that were different from the bubble we'd both grown up in? Was it finally time to get uncomfortable?

With an overpacked U-Haul and an energetic young Harlow, it took us two days to get to Chi-Town. And it took me approximately three days to learn to never call it Chi-Town again. I had high hopes for the move and what it must be like to be a cool big-city gal. I envisioned myself prancing around downtown in high heels and pencil skirts, going to happy hours with my new work friends at trendy little bars that were on or near Michigan Avenue, and saying things like, "That restaurant is okay if you're a tourist, but it's not where real Chicago people eat." I obviously wasn't a real Chicago person, nor did I have a job or even friends, but I figured all those things would come soon enough. Certainly an advertising agency or fashion magazine would hire me in no time. Never mind that I had zero experience in either field. Movies like *13 Going on 30* and *How to Lose a Guy in 10 Days* reminded me that such pesky details didn't really matter.

What I didn't envision was sitting in standstill traffic on I-94 for over an hour in a U-Haul that stank of beef jerky and body odor with no air-conditioning. This was never a part of my dream, and yet it's exactly how we were first greeted in the city.

Roughly two hours later than anticipated, we pulled onto Wrightwood Avenue in Lincoln Park to get our first look at our new Chicago home. We passed one gorgeous brownstone and limestone after the other, each tucked behind a black wrought-iron fence, some with actual gaslight lanterns next to their massive front doors. It was like a block straight out of a movie based on a book—and we got to live here!

And then we pulled up to our house—or the house with the garden-level apartment we'd rented.

It was an old yellow Victorian house, but not just any yellow. It was a pale, sickly yellow with missing paint chips and smudged windows. It was easily the ugliest house on the block. We found the apartment on Craigslist and knew it didn't look amazing, but we liked the location, and it was all we could afford. Rentals in Lincoln Park that allowed large dogs weren't easy to come by, so we signed the lease sight unseen and both hoped it might be better in person. Unfortunately, it was not. It was worse.

The rocks that surrounded the steps down to our front door absolutely reeked of urine. It smelled like a dog run in an apartment complex, and Harlow was ecstatic. He couldn't lift his leg fast enough.

"Welcome to Chicago, Har," I said as I held my breath.

"I already love it here!" he responded with his nose pressed to the urine-stained rocks. "Love, love, love!"

The yellow Victorian garden-level apartment had exposed brick on the inside, which was very cool to a small-town Nebraska girl. It also had a lot of centipedes, spiders, and mold from flooding every time it rained, which was a little less cool. I'm not sure if you've ever been stalked by a centipede the size of a lizard while you were in the middle of a daytime anxiety-shower, but it's rather unsettling. Thank God for that exposed brick though, right? We shared one washer and dryer with eight other people. The machines only took quarters, and they had to be quarters in their prime. Anything too dull or old, like a quarter that had clearly seen some shit in its life, would be eaten on the spot. No second chances given. Quarters were never as precious to me as they were the first year we moved to the city. I used to get into arguments with my nieces and nephews back in Nebraska about who got to raid my dad's coin jar (me, obviously!). Damn kids.

Chris started his new job immediately; it was at an exciting new startup called Groupon. Coupons on your phone for places you actually wanted coupons! How innovative! Cheap manis, pedis, and cheese fondue for all!

Every morning, Harlow and I would set up shop at the tall bistro table in our kitchen (he figured out how to crawl his way up onto the stool, and admittedly, I never tried to stop him because I enjoyed the company), and we'd job search for a bit before bailing on what seemed like one boring desk job after another and then head out to explore. I was nervous to venture out past the familiar blocks in the beginning. I'd never lived so far from my family or in such a big city, and everything felt very intimidating.

There were moments that first summer when I found myself daydreaming about moving back to Nebraska. The idea of it felt so comforting and easy compared to Chicago. All my grand visions about city living were falling short—no one had prepared me for how hard it can be. Our car was constantly getting tickets because that's what happens when you street park and don't follow the signs. *Why must parking signs be written like a riddle?* I'd have to carry our groceries for blocks when I couldn't find a spot close by, and my arms would nearly snap off by the time I got inside. Or sometimes I'd ride my bike to get groceries, but I swore the Trader Joe's employees would purposely fill one bag much heavier than the other to punish me for forgetting my reusable one so they could watch me tip over on my Schwinn when I tried to ride home.

There were also rolling blackouts our first summer—another thing I'd never experienced but had only heard about on the news. One blackout lasted four days, and all the groceries I'd purchased (and nearly broke my arms and bank account for) went sour. I cried in our tiny bedroom that night as a thunderstorm rattled our windows because I was frustrated, running through my savings, and most of all, I was scared. It was pitch-black in our basement apartment, and Chris was out partying with his new Groupon work friends. I felt like Tom Hanks in *Big*, minus the whole having-sex-with-your-adult-boss thing. Sure, I may have looked like a grown woman on the outside, but I'd never felt so much like a kid just scared to be alone in the dark in a city I didn't know.

But I wasn't completely alone. I never was, thanks to Harlow. I'd pat my chest, and he'd army crawl his way to the top of the bed and rest his head on me.

"We shouldn't have moved here," I confided in him that night. "We should just get back to Nebraska already. We can tell everyone we gave it a try, but it didn't work out."

"But we haven't tried yet." Harlow yawned and stretched his paws toward me. "Let's just try first, okay?"

"You can have a yard in Nebraska," I reminded him. "Wouldn't that be nice? A backyard just to yourself."

He closed his eyes and nestled back up. "Yards are nice, but we get to see more on our walks. Tomorrow will be better."

"How do you know?"

"Because we'll go on another walk."

And so that's what we did, every day, several times a day. Harlow pulled me one block farther to another street we'd never seen before, and then another, until we found ourselves walking all over our gorgeous new neighborhood. There were parks everywhere! Of course, we had to get to the slides early before the children arrived or we'd get some glares, but that wasn't a problem. I'd never seen a dog love jungle gyms as much as Harlow did. He'd run up the stairs, across the wobbly bridge, and then soar down the slide. Over and over and over. I'd stand in the wood chips at the bottom of the slide and watch as his floppy ears blew in the wind each time. Sometimes I'd run and hide when I knew I was out of sight, and then he'd fly down the slide even faster to come find me.

"I found you!" he'd shriek as he threw his wiggling body into mine as I crouched in a hidden jungle gym spot meant for a five-year-old.

"You did, buddy. You sure did," I'd say and put my face in his.

Was it normal to have this much fun with a dog? I'd sometimes wonder this when I'd catch onlookers viewing our antics. I must have looked like an insane woman, running up and down a jungle gym, laughing gleefully as my dog chased behind. But it never stopped me because it tired Harlow out, and we had fun together. And perhaps I was (am) a little bit insane; I just hadn't fully leaned into it yet.

On the way home from our park adventures, we passed grocery stores where I could actually bring Harlow inside, and I learned to shop like a city dweller: grab what you need for the day, and plan to go back the next. It started to feel as if Harlow and I were figuring this city stuff out.

And then I got a job offer. Which was good! My bank account barely had enough for two more months of rent, and that was it. I had a few freelance writing payments coming in, along with ad revenue from my blog, but both of those barely paid for Harlow's food. My blog, which for a *very short time* was named *The Pantyhose Diaries* after I landed a summer internship working at a large publishing company where all female employees were strongly encouraged to wear pantyhose, eventually became *The Daily Tay* once I left that job at lunch and never returned. I quit for several reasons, one being I was tired of all my male employees flaunting their bare-skinned upper ankles in front of me. Sure, they wore suit pants and loafer socks, but there was always that little window of skin that got to feel the breeze when they crossed their legs and dangled their foot in the air. And it was too much for me! I tossed my itchy Target pantyhose (which may have also been tights, because I've never actually understood the difference) into the bathroom trash at lunch and walked my bare legs on out of there.

I didn't start *The Daily Tay* to make money or with the hopes it would be my job someday. To be honest, I didn't think real people actually had that option—only Perez Hilton and a handful of very stylish Mormon moms. I started my blog because I enjoyed writing, and my favorite college English professor told me I should keep at it. Plus, a blog was easier to keep track of than my Limited Too diary, so it made sense.

As you may have guessed, in the beginning, I wrote mostly about how much I hated wearing pantyhose and hated being told I had yet another snag in said pantyhose. When I took the job recruiting for a culinary school, I wrote about my time spent putting on cooking demos for Family and Consumer Science classes in high schools across Kansas and Missouri. I wrote about my micromanaging boss in a very mature style with post titles like, "The Devil Wears Pur-

ple Blazers from T.J.Maxx," or about the time I got written up by a
teacher for fainting in her classroom because she thought I was faking
it to leave early. I wasn't (this specific time). I actually had swine flu
and didn't know it. I think I fainted before I passed the food samples
out, but I don't really remember because I had swine flu, Mrs. Lindy
from Olathe West, OKAY?

Once Harlow came into my life, my blog shifted once again. My
posts became a little less snarky and a little less focused on talking
shit about my jobs because Harlow made me a little less snarky, and
he became my most important job. After posting consistently for a
couple of years and sharing my site with friends, who then shared
with their friends, my audience started to grow, and soon small ad-
vertisers and other bloggers were asking to put clickable links on my
site. Would I allow some ads for twenty dollars a spot? Oh hells yes,
I would.

The twenty-dollar ad payouts were exciting, but they weren't paying the Chicago rent. When I got the offer for a recruiter position
at a staffing agency that specialized in placing HVAC profession-
als, I felt like I had to say yes. Did I know what HVAC stood for
when I got the offer? No, I did not. (It's heating, ventilation, and air-
conditioning, not "heavy vacuums" as I previously thought.) I took
the job because it had "recruiter" in the title like my previous job, and
that's what you do when you're fresh out of college—you follow the
familiar keywords in a job posting like breadcrumbs. Doesn't matter
if you want the position or not; you're just excited to get a response
to the hundreds of cover letters and résumés you pushed out into the
black hole of online job ads.

Tell us why you want this job. I actually don't!

What motivates you about this position? Money.

Tell us something interesting about yourself. I graduated with a degree
in English and a minor in history, and everyone told me those degrees
wouldn't pay the bills, but I am here to prove them wrong! Studying
the work of Jonathan Swift and Franz Kafka greatly prepared me for a

career in HVAC recruiting, as both writers often focused their stories on the inconveniences of everyday life. Had they been around when AC units were invented, the frustration of one suddenly not working would have undoubtedly played a central theme at some point.

Why should we choose you over the other candidates? Unless the other candidates have theater degrees, you probably shouldn't.

Like every other job I accepted out of college, I didn't want the HVAC position. I wanted to work for myself (or for a fictional fashion magazine where I wrote approximately one article per quarter, as I was far too busy sipping appletinis in stilettos at swanky work events), but I hadn't figured out how to do either just yet. So in the meantime, I had to say yes to the steady HVAC paycheck.

i guess i don't want
a steady paycheck

CHICAGO, ILLINOIS. 2013.

"I just went to a college reunion with some of my sorority sisters. They're all married with, like, five kids living in mega-mansions, and most of them are doctors or lawyers, and I was like, 'Well, I just got a new bike! And I'm really good at playing Zip Zap Zop.' Both are pretty big deals in Chicago, you know? But Nebraska? Not so much. One of their five-year-olds actually scoffed at me. He was like, 'A bike? I got that when I was three.'"

This was how I began my first stand-up set—in a classroom with lighting much too bright for an open mic, even a makeshift one.

"'Well, good for you, asshole,'" I continued, no idea if anyone was listening. "'At least I don't have crusty snot all over my nose. Like, take some pride in your appearance . . .' So anyway, it went well. And me and crusty-nose got along a lot better later when I had to babysit him, you know, because he was 'my boss' or whatever. I'm a little unemployed at the moment, so I have to take any job I can get."

I rambled for four minutes about not wanting to go to baby showers, having no idea what I wanted to do in life, and the homeless man in our alley with two shopping carts full of treasures who had more drive than I did. My pulse was pumping so loudly behind my ears I could barely hear myself talk, let alone if anyone laughed. My hands were clammy, my limbs were numb, and I blacked out the majority of my first attempt at stand-up at Chicago's infamous Second City.

The Second City is a comedy club and improv training center. It's also where all my comedic heroes started: Gilda Radner, Tina Fey, Chris Farley, Tim Meadows, Shelley Long, Steve Carell, Amy Poehler. I could fill a book (it just won't be this one) with all the greats who sat in the same brightly lit classrooms. I enrolled the moment my credit card balance allowed it.

While my friends in Nebraska got their master's and doctorate degrees, I got a certificate in improv stating I could make a killer sandcastle without even one grain of sand! When I found out the Second City hosted an open mic for stand-up comedy, I figured I'd give that a try as well.

Everyone in the room at the open mic was a comic, their face in their joke notebooks just waiting for their own four minutes. Everyone except for Chris, who came to support me. When I got done and sat back down beside him, my face stung with heat, and my tongue was thick with anxiety.

"I don't know what just happened," I whispered. "I hardly remember any of it."

"You did good. People laughed!" he said.

For the next year, I rode my (new) bike to open mics all over Chicago. I'd belly up alone at whatever dive bar hosted for the evening, buy my one PBR beer, and then wait for the list to go out so I could add my name to it. In the winter, I'd splurge and get an Uber because it's hard to bike in snow and I'm not that hard, although I know a lot of Chicagoans who are.

The general rule every new comic is told is that it's going to take them at least ten years of grinding to feel like they're getting anywhere. Ten years of open mics night after night where no one is listening because everyone else is just waiting for their own turn. Ten years of hoping you get booked for a show where you get paid absolutely nothing, and then you take that absolutely nothing and go buy a drink at an open mic after your show because the open mics never stop. But if you love it, it doesn't matter. You can't get enough.

I loved it for a few years. When I did my first show at the Laugh Factory, I remember peeking out from the green room to see a line of people waiting to get in—actual paying customers waiting to see me tell jokes on stage. Well, maybe not me specifically; I was just a guest spot on the lineup, but they were still going to see me whether they knew it or not. I felt like I'd made the big time.

The host introduced me, and I hoped the audience couldn't see my knees shake as I walked on stage. But once I grabbed the mic and moved the stand to the side, faking all the confidence I didn't have, I started into my material, and it all just flowed to me. I didn't miss one beat or punch line. The stage lighting was so intense I couldn't make out a single face in the audience, but I could hear them. And they were laughing. People were laughing at jokes I had written. What a thrill!

"It was so cool, Har," I'd tell him later that night as we sat on the couch together, his sleepy face in my lap.

"Can I come with next time?" he'd ask with eyes barely open.

"I'll find an open mic where you can come in. How about that?" I'd hear Har snoring and realize he'd already fallen back asleep on me.

No matter what time I came home or how tired he was, the moment Har heard me open the front door, he'd jump from bed and come out to the living room to say hello and ask me how the jokes went. Did the punch lines I practiced in front of him hit? Did the new material about Gardetto's go over well? (It didn't, but sometimes I'd lie and tell him it did anyway.) It took me a while to come down from the buzz of a show or even just hosting an open mic, so this was our little late-night ritual, and I loved it so much. We'd sit on the couch next to each other, usually sharing a string cheese or two, and catch up on the few hours we'd missed together.

At this time, we'd left the yellow garden level and now lived on the first floor of a slightly less decrepit house on Seminary Avenue in Lincoln Park. We were moving up! The top half of the house had white siding that needed replacing, and the bottom half consisted of light-colored brick that was trying so desperately to keep up with the prettier brownstones surrounding it. Other than the occasional rat that found its way in through vents, drawn from the restaurant dumpsters located in the alley, the inside wasn't terrible. We had a large window in the front sitting area, perfect for Har to gripe at anyone he didn't approve of walking on his sidewalk. And on one particular evening after I'd returned from hosting an open mic at the iO Theater, with Har snoozing in my lap, it served as the perfect window to watch a light snow drop from the Chicago night sky. It was one of those snowfalls where you could tell the entire sky had stayed up late waiting for it. Every brownstone on our street, even the ugly ones, God bless them, illuminated in the winter glow.

"Har, it's snowing," I whispered.

With the blanket still draped across his head, a look we often referred to as "Grandma Harlow," he turned toward the window, then back to me. "I'm glad you're back home."

I pulled him closer, and he nestled his face right into the crook of my neck, just like he did when he was a puppy back in Kansas. "Me too, Har."

I don't know why, but I could just tell this was one of those nights future-me would ache to relive. There was nothing particularly significant about it. I'd certainly seen snow before, and we'd go on to live in much nicer homes where we didn't watch the rats fight for stray pizza slices from our back porch. Chris and I would both get better jobs and make more money and get to do all the things we dreamed about doing in our twenties but couldn't afford (i.e., eat at Chicago's best restaurants), and yet, for some reason, coming home to Har in our crappy apartment on Seminary Avenue after a night of doing comedy and watching the snow fall from our one big window felt so perfect in that moment it nearly stung. I stayed up later than usual, clutching Har just a little tighter as I watched the snow hit the pavement, having no idea why I felt the need to hold on to such a mundane moment but also not questioning it. Perhaps it was one of those rare glimpses when life lets you know "a good old day" is happening while you're still living it. Or perhaps it was the two Old Styles and fiery shot of Malört I had while hosting the open mic. I guess I'll never know.

My pursuit of being a stand-up comedian wouldn't last too much longer. I loved being on stage and feeling the energy of laughter from jokes that I had written, but the late nights went from exhilarating to exhausting. I started to look forward to coming home so much more than I did leaving. I missed Chris, Har, and our couch. I told myself a career in comedy just wasn't in my future after all.

Unless.

Unless there was a way I could do it from our couch?

strengths: quitting jobs; weaknesses: leaving my dog

CHICAGO, ILLINOIS. 2011.

The HVAC staffing job didn't work out. Neither did the next staffing job or passing out flyers on Michigan Avenue about restaurant coupon books or dressing up as a giant cookie to inspire elementary students to sell cookie dough for their school fundraiser. It's too bad the fundraising company went bankrupt, because I was actually pretty good at blasting *Jock Jams* in school gymnasiums and pumping up kids to be tiny door-to-door salespeople, but apparently not as good as I thought since I got laid off one week before Christmas in 2012.

I really tried to have a steady job.

Well, I kind of tried.

Leaving Har every morning for nine hours killed me. The first time I had to do it, I literally ran to the train at five p.m. the second I was allowed to shut off my computer. I was like Melanie Griffith in *Working Girl*, sprinting down a busy street in a pencil skirt and sneakers with her heels dangling from her computer bag, not because I was late for anything but because I had to get home to my boy.

Harlow must have heard my keys in the door because the moment

I opened it, he was waiting on the other side in full wiggle mode, his entire body waving from side to side in pure glee to see my return. His body was very much awake, but his eyes still looked sleepy to me. I took a small amount of comfort in the thought he might have slept the day away.

"Hi, bud," I said as I knelt to the ground, and he put his paws on my shoulders. It should come as a shock to no one at this point that we embraced hugging—sometimes referred to as jumping—in our house. "How are you? I missed you. I missed you so much."

"You're back! You're back!" Harlow said as he tap-danced his back paws. "You're finally home!"

"I know. I hate leaving you." I put my bag on the table. "So what'd you do all day?"

"Oh, not much," he said casually.

I turned to hang up my coat, and that's when I saw what he did all day . . . and it was not napping sweetly on the couch. Harlow chewed. He chewed everything he could find. Books and magazines were pulled from the coffee table, and the ripped-up pages were scattered around our living room. One of Chris's fancy Allen Edmond shoes was hidden in a couch cushion. One of my nude high heels reserved only for bachelorette party weekends was in the other cushion. I saw toilet paper, tea towels, a half-eaten wicker basket, and traces of trash all over. And that was just in our living room.

I turned to look at Harlow, and he was no longer wiggling. He knew I knew. Harlow cowered low to the ground and wouldn't look at me.

"What did you do, buddy?" I said calmly, knowing this was my fault.

"I don't wanna talk about it." Harlow turned away from me and scurried into the bathroom. I followed after him with his leash in hand, knowing he'd need a walk, but I found him trembling in the bathtub, refusing to leave.

"It's okay, Har. We all make mistakes." I crouched next to the tub and put my face in his. Other than the first few weeks when we brought him home as a tiny puppy, Harlow had never done destruction like this. He was a pleaser, not a destroyer, and my heart ached to know how anxious he must have been alone all day.

When Chris came home a short time later, he found both Harlow and me sitting in the tub. I'd been petting him and telling him it's okay over and over until he'd finally calmed down.

"What the heck happened out there?" Chris asked, and Har immediately began to tremble again. I shot Chris a look that said, *Don't bring it up*, and he immediately shut up. Ten minutes later, we were all in the bathroom, Chris crouching next to the tub, Harlow and me still in it, both of us telling Har it was okay and that we forgave him.

Later that night when we were on a walk—Harlow happy as ever to be out of the house and the chewing situation long forgotten—Chris and I replayed the events that had just occurred.

"So basically, he destroyed some of our best shoes, our favorite books, dragged the trash all over the house, and then we were the ones apologizing to him? Telling him how much we loved him and would he just come on a walk with us and leave the bathroom already?"

"Pretty much," Chris said as he bent over to give Har a little butt pat.

We shook our heads and wondered if we had the most sensitive dog in the world or the most manipulative. We'd learn later it was both.

Har hadn't been crated since he was a puppy, but after his chewing rampage, we had to start crating him again in fear he might eat something that could cause himself harm.

"Don't worry. I'll be right back, Har," I said on repeat as I locked him inside the small enclosure. "I'll be right back, right back I swear!"

"Are you sure? Can you just stay with me? I don't want to be in here. Please don't go, I'll be good," he begged, and I'd have to walk away with my eyes shut because it killed me to see him in there.

"Right back, Har. I'll be right back," I said over and over until I also believed it.

I'd remind myself that he was safe and okay in his crate. He had toys, bones, and a KONG filled with peanut butter, and I even paid money I did not have so that a dog walker would come by twice a day to let him out. But it didn't get any easier leaving Har, and I couldn't figure out what was wrong with me as I'd obsessively worry about him all day long. Why was I so miserable away from my dog? Was it because I couldn't see an end in sight in what I was currently doing? Or because I hated every job so much and when I felt something was off, my entire psyche would flip out until I set it right again? (One of my many special talents.) Being an idealist is both soul sucking and incredibly motivating; it usually depends on the amount of coffee consumed. People left their dogs all the time to go to work. It's just what people did. Had they all just accepted their fate and misery, or was I simply being dramatic and childish?

The days I spent in a cubicle making sales calls knowing Har was at home locked in a crate made me feel like I too was locked in a crate. It's not how a dog should live. It's not how any of us should live. I was only twenty-four and started to crumble at the idea of being stuck in terrible sales jobs for the next forty-plus years. The highlight of my day was walking across the street to Whole Foods to buy a salad I couldn't afford and then sitting behind the building to eat it just to be alone and feel the sunshine on my face. But then my thirty minutes of freedom would end, and I'd have to scurry back to my crate.

I tried to remind myself that plenty of people hated their jobs. This was just my first dose of reality, right? I needed to grow up and stop acting so entitled. But every once in a while, when I'd look in the mirror as I begrudgingly got ready in the morning, I'd catch a glimpse of the little girl who would have broken her own foot to play Tiny Tim or who sold Beanie Babies for thousands of dollars to grown-ass adults, and a small voice inside would whisper, *Find a different fucking way.*

A Quick Rundown of My Job History 2009–2012

- High school recruiter for a culinary school. Highs: I set my own schedule and learned killer knife skills. Lows: I walked through high school hallways dressed like the Iron Chef and encouraged students to "live their dreams" by enrolling in a for-profit college that was insanely expensive.
- HVAC recruiter. Highs: the Whole Foods across the street. Lows: literally everything else.
- Elementary school fundraiser lady. Highs: I got to see a lot of nice gymnasiums in small towns across Wisconsin. Lows: I had to put on sales presentations in said gymnasiums to an audience generally under the age of twelve, enticing them to sell cookie dough and frozen pretzels with prizes like glow-in-the-dark yo-yos, sticky hand toys, and furry key chains.
- The job I found on Craigslist selling restaurant coupons. Highs: I set my own schedule. Lows: I sold actual physical coupons (door to door) during a time when the internet was around.
- The job I found on Craigslist handing out flyers on Michigan Avenue. Highs: I got to work outside on Michigan Avenue. Lows: I had to work outside on Michigan Avenue.

I also started several of my own businesses during this time and invented a few things. *Have you ever heard of the Blankron? As in the blanket apron? Because who wants to be cold when they're cooking?*

a different fucking way

You never forget the first time you get laid off. More importantly though, you don't forget the moment you decide it will be the last time you get laid off.

My manager from the school fundraising job called me unexpectedly one morning, and as soon as she told me that someone from human resources was also on the line, I held on to Har a little tighter. Oh no, *had I accidentally played a* Jock Jams *song with swear words at my last elementary school kickoff*? The Waukesha moms had been giving me the evil eye throughout the entire BMX bike show.

"Is this about Waukesha?" I asked, still bitter a territory in Wisconsin had been thrown on me when I was supposed to only have Chicago metro.

My manager didn't hear me, or at least she pretended not to, and continued right on with her script. The call had nothing to do with the BMX bike show or the Waukesha moms. I was just being laid off, is all. The fundraising company was facing some challenges, had to make some cuts, and I was one of them. I just sat there nodding and saying "okay" until eventually I realized I was the only one still on the line.

"What happened?" Har asked when I put my phone down.

"I lost another job—that's what happened."

"Good. I didn't like that one," he said.

"No, Har, it's not good. What if I have to go back to an eight-to-five office job?" The fundraising job wasn't perfect, especially with the northbound commute on I-94 that made my traffic anxiety so intense I'd often leave for an eight a.m. appointment three hours early just to beat rush hour. Some of the best naps I ever took were in my car in a Dress Barn parking lot somewhere in Wisconsin waiting for my next cookie dough appointment. "I can't go back to a cubicle. I just can't."

"So don't," Har said flippantly as he looked toward the window to bark at someone passing by and then casually turned back to me. "You make your own choices, don't you?"

"It's not that easy," I grumbled.

"Sure it is," he said as he stretched his way off the couch and meandered toward the front door. "We meet plenty of people at the park who have jobs they don't hate. Why are you always thinking about the people who do?"

"Who in the hell have you been talking to at the dog park?" I asked.

"Everyone you haven't been," he responded. "You should try socializing sometime. It might be good for you."

"What? Have you, like, been networking this entire time?" Har always stood near the humans while I gathered near the dogs, so it made sense.

"Let's just go," he said at the door.

"I'm not going on a walk right now. I just got laid off!"

"Perfect. That means we've got plenty of time for a long one then." He nosed at his leash hanging on its hook. "C'mon now."

"I'm not kidding, Har. Can't you just let me sulk here for a second? I'm depressed. I'm not going on a walk, okay?"

"Okay, but I think we are."

"No, we are not."

We went on a walk.

One block turned into five, then ten, and soon enough, we found ourselves on the beach at Lake Michigan with the downtown skyline hovering behind us. The cold December air whipped across the white caps and stung my face in a way that normally made me look away. But today I faced it head-on. I wanted to feel the burn in my eyes and tingle in my throat as I watched the angry waves crash onto the frozen beach over and over. Har sat by my side not saying a word until eventually I stood up, so he stood up.

"You ready?" I asked.

"Are *you*?" he said with a full body shake.

We left the icy, frustrated waves behind us and started our walk back home.

I'm not going to claim that staring at a lake changed my life or anything. The frozen dead rat Har attempted to put in his mouth later probably had more of an impact on me, if I'm being honest, but that's beside the point. The point is, I found more clarity on our walk than I would have sulking on the couch. Sulking can be great and necessary, but in this moment, I needed to get out of our house, out of my head, and next to a big angry lake that didn't give a shit about me to remind me how insignificant I am. (It also helped to find a dead rat, to remind me how short life is, especially for a well-fed Chicago rat, sadly.)

As I was saying . . .

I forced myself to believe that getting laid off might actually be a good thing. It was a bit demoralizing pumping up children to sell pretzels and cookie dough, but I continued to sleep in the Wisconsin Dress Barn parking lot week after week because I knew it was better than working in a cubicle. And was I about to settle for "better than a cubicle"? Absolutely not. But I might have if I hadn't received the shove I needed that morning.

When we returned to our small garden apartment on Belden Avenue, I got out a notebook and every self-help book I owned (I would have also listened to the Tony Robbins cassette tapes I stole from my dad as a child, but they were back in Nebraska), and I made a plan. I needed to make money, but I wanted to do it on my own terms. And my own terms were as follows: spend all day with Harlow, go on as many walks as he demanded, write consistently and grow my blog, and use my resources.

I added that last part only because a self-help book told me to, but I wasn't sure what resources I had. This was a time in my life when I was walking around in holey sneakers with no soles because Harlow had eaten them. When my sister sent me a new pair of Nikes for my birthday, I nearly cried, so resources weren't exactly in abundance for me at the moment.

But there had to be a way. There was always a way.

I had a small internet following thanks to that trusty old blog of mine, *The Daily Tay*, one of the only consistent things in my life other than Chris and Har. As someone who was guilty of frequently losing interest in one project so I could move on to the next, I'd stuck with my blog because it never felt like a chore to me but more like an extension of me. I'd started to see other bloggers make their blogs their full-time jobs and wondered if I could do the same. I didn't have a niche, and every professional blogger said you *had to have a niche*, but what I did have was an abundance of time and, perhaps most important of all, I had the drive to keep moving toward what I really wanted—and that was to be my own boss and the freedom that came along with it. *Within Harlow's terms, of course.*

It was never the fear of taking a risk that kept me up at night; it was always the fear of *not* taking one. What if I could actually create a job I wanted, but I never got the chance to realize it because I was too busy searching for jobs I didn't want? Such a chilling thought forced me to start writing even more blog posts and wonder what else I could do to pay the rent until my blog hit Perez Hilton/Mormon Mommy status . . . What could I invent?

"You mean other than the Blankron?" Har asked with a smirk as he watched the wheels turning in my brain.

"That was a good idea! Chicago winters are cold, and the blanket went around your waist and had pockets!" I said defensively.

"Oh, I know. I went with you to buy the fleece and the Velcro," Har said with a giggle as he pretended to lick his paws. "And I'm just as surprised as you are that it didn't take off. I personally love crusted food on my blankets."

I guess there was a reason why people didn't often wear aprons on the couch, even fleece ones.

"Well, if you have any better ideas, I'm all ears," I said, wondering if there was another fabric I could use that was better than fleece for flicking off food.

"Don't overthink it. Just make something easy. Like the bin store we always go to where you buy the same stuff. Make something like that."

"The bin store? What are you talking . . . Oh, you mean Urban?" There was an Urban Outfitters surplus store on Clark Street where nearly all the clothes they sold were piled into bins, and all were less than ten dollars. It was me and Har's favorite place to dig for cheap T-shirts in Chicago. "You think I should make T-shirts? So many of those already exist."

"So make a new one!" Once again, Har strolled his way toward where his leash hung on the wall and thrust his nose underneath it. "Let's talk more about it on a walk."

As we wandered around the park, I paid extra attention to the street style worn by the people around us and saw that graphic T-shirts were everywhere. This either meant the market was already completely oversaturated, or that there was always room for another. Thanks to Harlow's confidence in me (and also his judgment), I decided it meant the latter.

"Using my resources," as the self-help book instructed, I decided to create my first T-shirt with my biggest audience in mind. Nebraska! It's where I was born and raised, it's where I attended college, and in the beginning, it's where the majority of my blog readers lived. And most important of all, football season was right around the corner, and if this idea was going to work, my bank account was wanting to know as soon as possible.

If you're not familiar with Nebraska football fans (lovingly known as "Cornhuskers") and college football, it's religion to them. Second only to actual religion (preferably Catholic or Lutheran or Methodist if you're the rebellious sibling). Whether the team wins or loses, Nebraska fans fill Memorial Stadium to capacity every single game, every single year. And they do it in brand-new tailgating T-shirts.

With the help of a mom-and-pop screen-printing business located in my hometown, I designed and ordered twelve tailgating T-shirts (the minimum order I could place) and paid the invoice with my credit card. But before I clicked *Submit*, I asked my parents if they'd be willing to loan me some money if I couldn't sell all twelve T-shirts and found myself in a spot where my credit card bill *and also* my rent were due. They said yes, as they always did when I really needed it. It's a lot easier to take that leap of faith when you know you have a safety net underneath you, known as your parents, ready to help you back up again. Not everyone has that net of support (and privilege), and I'm forever grateful that I did.

The alley behind our apartment became our photo studio because there was a brick wall with a little bit of graffiti, and brick walls with graffiti were very much in style. I insisted Chris snap several hundred photos of me in front of the brick wall wearing my new T-shirt, with my hands tucked deep in my jean pockets and my eyes locked on my feet. (Staring at your feet for blog photos was also very much in style.) I posted the photo to my blog and Facebook and was ready to keep track of orders with a pen and paper (if I got any), but I also cleared a spot under our bed just in case I had to hold on to extra merchandise for a while.

I took a deep breath and clicked *Post*, then forced myself to walk away for one minute. When I came back, the likes and comments had already flooded my post. In less than five minutes, I sold every shirt

I had ordered. Within an hour, I already had orders for at least fifty more. When I got to a hundred by the end of the day, I realized this little T-shirt gig might actually tide me over for a few weeks, maybe even months?

"We're doing it, Har! I think I just stalled having to find a real job for at least another month or two!"

"Let's head to Oz Park to celebrate," he suggested, already at the door ready to go. "Dipped cones from Dairy Queen on me! And by on me, I mean you, obviously."

To this day, I've sold many thousands of graphic T-shirts and sweatshirts. I have a few incredible employees who help me run the business, so it's no longer just Har and me, but for the first few years, I packed every single order in our living room, sometimes until three or four in the morning, hoping to meet customer deadlines. Every single morning, Har and I would tie garbage bags full of packages on our backs and walk the five blocks to the closest post office. (I was scared to move our car and lose our close parking spot, so walking several blocks carrying heavy garbage bags made more sense to me.) I got to know the employees at the Lincoln Park post office so well that I'd bring them boxes of donuts when I had a big drop-off day.

"What exactly are you shipping in all these packages?" one of the postal workers finally asked.

"T-shirts," I responded, and they looked surprised.

"T-shirts? Really?"

"Yup," I said with a shrug and a laugh.

"Well, good for you. It must be a shirt everyone wants."

It wasn't just one shirt; I quickly expanded into a few different options. But I'll admit—even ten years later, I never thought selling simple graphic tees, a market I was sure was already at its max, would allow me to finally work from home and be my own boss, answering to no one except for my dog.

Things I Want to Remember About Our Chicago Homes

Alternative Title: Things I Don't Want to Remember About Our Chicago Homes

- UGLY YELLOW HOUSE ON WRIGHTWOOD: Playing hide-and-seek with a young Har to tire him out during the long Chicago winters. Learning (and following) the politics of shared laundry spaces—you must give someone at least one hour before you remove their clothes from a unit to lap them, but then you must do it as fast as possible because you NEVER want to be caught performing the lap! I shudder just thinking about it. And also digging our car out of snow for forty-five minutes and placing two lawn chairs in its spot on the street because DIBS! (This is a lie—I never participated in dibs because Chris is Mr. Never-Piss-a-Neighbor-Off, but I dreamed about participating.)
- THE TINY BROWNSTONE ON BELDEN: The luxury of reaching the dryer from inside our shower so I always had warm towels, and vacuuming the entire apartment from the same outlet. Getting laid off ten days before Christmas and deciding I'd never work for anyone but myself again. Walking Har to the Lincoln Park Zoo to see the coyotes, then Oz Park to get a dipped cone at Dairy Queen, and listening to "Madness" by Muse on my walk to the Second City, and again when I jumped on the Clark bus immediately after for even more classes at the iO Theater.
- UGLY HOUSE ON SEMINARY: Falling asleep to the hum of the train at night, the bathroom sink that would often rip from the wall if you looked at it wrong, and the chauvinistic landlord I had to call to fix it who claimed he was cousins with the Belushis. (Every old landlord in Chicago claims this.) Packing customer orders until the

(cont.)

wee hours of the morning while Har watched from his bench in the front window and then walking five blocks to the post office with several garbage bags full of MARRIED AF T-shirts.

- OUR FIRST CONDO ON NOBLE: Also our first parking space, first fridge with an ice maker, first home with more than one bathroom (*were we royalty now?!*), and our first bedroom where nightstands fit on BOTH sides of our bed and I no longer had to crawl over to "my side." WE WERE LIVING! Playing hide-and-seek with an old Har to tire him out during the long Chicago winters.

here we are

CHICAGO, ILLINOIS. 2019.

Our genetic appointment was in an office downtown, right off of Lake Shore Drive, about a fifteen-minute drive from our condo on Noble Street. Chicago driving isn't usually that enjoyable, unless you're on Lake Shore during the tiny window of time when the traffic actually flows. Lake Michigan is showing off on one side and the Chicago skyline on the other, and you're just one small human, stuck in the middle, admiring the beauty.

It was going to be a perfect July summer day in the city—the kind where Pulaski Park pool would have a line to get in as long as the ice cream carts surrounding it. The beach wasn't packed yet, but it would be soon. As I let myself get lost in the vastness of Lake Michigan for a moment, I wondered if we'd get a lake view from our hospital room when I delivered in February. Of course, the scenery wouldn't be nearly as sparkly or inviting in February, but I still held out hope.

Over the past few weeks, my anxiety about motherhood was (finally) turning into excitement. We had names picked out, nursery color schemes, future family vacations . . . the baby pretty much had a full-blown personality at this point based on how much I talked to (projected on) her every night. We didn't know the sex yet, but I was certain she was a girl. I could just feel it.

On the way to our appointment, Chris and I rambled about MamaRoos, DockATots, Dunkaroos, Boppys, Bumbos, and Dumbos (who in the hell thought of those ridiculous names?). If anything could turn my excitement right back into fear, it was browsing the baby aisles in Target. There was so much shit. Did one really need all that shit? How did one decide which shit to buy?

Day by day, a little voice reminded me, *Every mom was a new mom at some point.*

"You'll hear the heartbeat today," I told Chris, as if he'd forgotten. "It's like a *womp, womp, womp* sound." I did my best to imitate the underwater-like noise from my ten-week appointment.

I heard the heartbeat for the first time on my own a few weeks ago; Chris had a last-minute work thing and wasn't able to attend our appointment. My first trimester had been so full of migraines and nausea that I was hoping hearing the heartbeat might make all of that magically go away. I wanted to have that special moment so many moms describe—the movie-scene moment with goose bumps and tears when they just know everything is going to be okay. But that didn't happen for me. By the time the ultrasound began, I had waited for more than an hour in a hot and stuffy waiting room and was starving and feeling faint, again. I enjoyed hearing the heartbeat, don't get me wrong, but I won't deny I enjoyed getting out of that appointment with a prescription for anti-nausea pills even more. Anyway, I was grateful to have Chris there so we might finally have the movie moment I had been hoping for all along.

We pulled into the parking garage and saw it was twenty-four dollars for two hours—typical downtown parking.

"This baby is already costing us," I joked.

Unlike our first ultrasound appointment at the MRI clinic, we were barely in the waiting room for five minutes before a woman showed us back into an exam room. She handed me a gown and told me I could keep my pants on, just unbuttoned, and left the room to let me change. I raised my eyebrows toward Chris as if to say this was already going so much better than the first time. No vaginal stick-shifting!

The tech returned, dabbed a little jelly on my stomach, and started to move her wand around my abdomen. I looked back toward Chris, anxious to see his reaction to the heartbeat. He smiled at me and then looked intently toward the screen. The tech continued to move her wand until it seemed she found what she was looking for. We all stared at the screen at what appeared to be a tiny dark sac. I waited and waited. The sound I heard at my ten-week appointment never came.

"I'm so sorry," the tech said quietly. "I can't find a heartbeat."

Well, look again, I wanted to say. *It was there a few weeks ago.* But I didn't say anything. I just sat there with my pants unbuttoned and jelly on my stomach, not fully understanding the situation. I looked at Chris. Certainly he would make sense of it. But instead, his head fell, and he let out a long, slow breath. It was as if that one breath held all the excitement we'd shared, the late-night conversations about becoming parents, and the early giddiness of knowing something big was on the horizon. It held the tiny striped golf onesie he brought back from his golf trip last weekend, the *How to Be a Dad* guidebook he ordered, and the old-school car map we bought for all the family road trips we were going to take. It all disappeared in that one breath. Just like the heartbeat had disappeared from inside of me.

The tech handed me a box of tissues and quickly excused herself from the room.

"I'm sorry," Chris said as he hugged me.

"I don't get it. It was there. I heard it."

I remember this moment so vividly and how strangely fake it felt to me. It was as if I was watching another version of Chris and me—the version where we were two people who had just lost a child and had no idea what to do next. *How sad for them!* For us, I had to remind myself. In my head, we were still lingering between the version of two very excited parents-to-be and the version of Chris and Taylor from a few months ago who frivolously wondered if they were even ready to have kids.

How did we end up playing out the version of us I never once imagined?

Shame and guilt hadn't joined me just yet, but they would soon. They'd remind me that I'd heard the heartbeat, but I hadn't fully appreciated it. *You took it for granted,* they'd whisper. *You, silly little fool, just assumed the heartbeat would always be there.*

We heard a knock at the door, and Chris looked at me to see if I was ready to face whoever was on the other side. I changed from the gown back into my shirt—a shirt I would later donate to a secondhand store because I couldn't stand to look at it in our closet. I signaled to Chris to open the door.

An older man entered the room in a manner that told me this wasn't his first time facing a couple who'd just learned their baby no longer had a heartbeat. He was kind and gentle and did his best to explain the situation to two people still very much in shock.

The dark sac we'd seen in the ultrasound was much too small for a fetus twelve weeks along. I had what's called a "missed miscarriage," which basically meant the fetus died in my womb, but my body didn't realize it. Based on the size, it had probably stopped growing a couple of weeks ago. There was no bleeding, no cramping, no sign at all that the little girl I'd been calling Gigi was no longer with me.

I thought back to the beginning of the month, when we'd traveled to Nebraska to see our family and tell them the big news. We hadn't told a lot of people, but there was no way I could keep it a secret while we were visiting, so we decided to share. "We're having a baby!" we had squealed to both of our parents. There were tears of excitement and shock—they were certain we'd never have kids. I flounced around in my loose-fitting dresses, basking in the attention while also openly complaining about how hard it was to be pregnant and how did so many women do it? Everyone toasted champagne as I held my soda in the air with a smirk and a playful eye roll. And now I wondered, *Was I even still pregnant then? How could I be so foolish?*

I had some real trust issues with my body after this, especially considering I still had pregnancy symptoms showing up even after there was no longer a heartbeat. I felt as if my body knew it screwed up and then tried to push everything under the rug, like it had a team meeting with everyone but me.

Okay boobs, we need you to keep being tender and big. And head, keep those migraines pounding. We'll keep nausea coming, and maybe, just maybe, if we all carry on like nothing has changed, she'll never notice something has gone terribly wrong.

And I didn't notice. How in the hell could I not notice?

We were given phone numbers to call and instructions on what to do next, and I sat there thinking, *There's a next? This isn't the end of it?*

We left the same way we came in, but it all looked and felt like a completely different office. Chris and I kept our heads down, not wanting to make eye contact with the other couples in the waiting room. We were the people you didn't want to be, and with only a glance, you could tell we'd just faced the situation everyone in the waiting room was trying to avoid. It was best we get on our way before our bad fortune rubbed off on anyone.

On our drive home, the stoplight turned red as we neared the crosswalk off Michigan Avenue, right by the Water Tower, a popular shopping center always flooded with people. I watched as tourists and locals pushed their way around our car, and I wondered which secret is harder to keep—the one when no one knows you're pregnant or when no one knows you've just miscarried. At least I only had a few people to "un-tell."

When we got home, Harlow greeted us with Sloth toy in his mouth like he always did, but as soon as we sat down on the couch, he dropped it at our feet rather than shoving it in our face like usual. He didn't have to ask if something was wrong because he knew. Harlow always knew. He crawled on the couch and laid his head on my lap, and we all sat there in silence until the silence got too loud.

"I can't just sit here with this," Chris said. "We gotta go somewhere."

"Okay, where?"

"I don't know. Are you hungry?" he asked.

"No."

"Me neither."

So we decided to walk to lunch. Harlow led the way like a sled dog, pulling us along, knowing it was up to him to keep us moving. We walked down Milwaukee Avenue until we came to an intersection and had to make a choice. I think we might have stood there all day, not sure which way to turn, if not for Harlow who made the decision for us.

We found ourselves sitting on the patio at Big Star on a hot Monday afternoon. Big Star is a popular taco joint in Wicker Park where you go to feel the sunshine on your face, enjoy a cheap tasty taco, and drink a pitcher of margaritas until your arms and legs feel tingly and warm. It's not exactly a spot to grieve a miscarriage, but that's where we ended up because it's where Har knew we needed to be.

Harlow and I passed Big Star nearly every day on our normal walking route. We'd peek in and watch groups of people snacking on queso and sipping salty-rimmed margaritas, and we'd wonder, *Who gets to hit up a patio to day-drink on a Monday afternoon? They must have fun lives*, we'd agree as we continued on our lunch-break walk, sticking to our usual weekday routine.

Today, we were the ones on the patio, although the taco baskets in front of us sat untouched. I watched the people going to and from the L Train, the daycare kids walking like a line of ducklings heading toward the park, and the dog walkers passing by. I'd never longed to get lost in the mundane happenings of a normal day quite so badly.

If you're pregnant and this chapter just scared the shit out of you, please turn the page and take a breather with me.

A Breather

When you're pregnant and anxious, everything feels like a sign. Please allow me to say that the previous chapter was NOT your sign. Simply because you read about someone having a missed miscarriage does not mean you will have one. If you're anything like me, you're probably shaking your head right now, perhaps even calling your OB and thinking about moving up your next appointment so you can hear that heartbeat for reassurance, and wondering, *How do you know?* I don't know. But here's the thing that's hard to grasp about pregnancy (and life): none of us know. And yet we have to keep showing up anyway.

If my dad were writing this, he'd add, "Don't let the fear of striking out keep you from playing the game." But I don't speak in clichéd sports references, so I won't be adding it. But damnit, it's fitting for so much, isn't it?

I do know that looking for signs (particularly the bad ones) isn't helpful in any way. Rather than thinking about everything that could go wrong, you have to make yourself think about all the things that could go right. It's not easy, but I can assure you it's well worth your time to give it a try.

here we are (still)

CHICAGO, ILLINOIS. 2019.

The hospital called me while we sat at Big Star pretending not to be miserable to schedule my dilation and curettage to remove "what was left."

Before agreeing to have the "D&C" procedure, I'd already had a few other calls with my doctor to discuss my options. I found it so frustrating that I couldn't just sleep and mope around for the next few days, but instead I had to make some tough decisions and make them quick. I didn't have much time to debate this.

One option was a traditional D&C surgery, as mentioned above. The other option was a pill that I could take at home but had to be taken vaginally (let me pause there and let you think about that for a moment), and I could try to pass everything on my own. This would involve a lot of cramping and a lot of blood. So much blood that I was advised I stay near a bathtub "just in case." My very own *Carrie*-themed prom night right at home. How fun! I'd later write a stand-up set about this conversation and the horrors so many women go through and rarely talk about. I'd note the reason I didn't choose this second option was because my vagina couldn't take pills. Well, unless they were wrapped in turkey. Or smothered with peanut butter in a way that the pill was so hidden my vagina wouldn't notice it. Now, crushing the pills might seem like a good option, but I feel like once you start crushing pills for your vagina, you're going down a dark road. We all know it's just a matter of time before your vagina is snorting them—a tale as old as time!

I don't think anything about a miscarriage is funny, but we all work through things in our own way. What I didn't know then was that only two days after that comedy show, I'd find myself back at the hospital for yet another D&C. But we'll get to that soon enough.

On our third wedding anniversary, Chris anchored his arm under mine as I slowly shuffled out to our car after my surgery. The diaper I had on bulged from my backside, and I was certain everyone could see it through my pants, even though they were "loose and dark," just like the nurses advised. Chris reclined the seat for me and placed a brown paper bag in my lap in case I threw up again.

"You good?" he asked before he started to reverse.

"Uh huh," I said through a drugged lens.

As we made our way out of the hospital's parking garage, we had to pause as a man hurriedly dashed from his car back toward the elevator. He had a car seat under one arm and a new diaper bag slung across the other. Neither Chris nor I said anything. We just watched.

When we got home, I went straight to bed. I heard the pitter-patter of Harlow's paws on our winding staircase and waited for him to join me. Rather than high-jumping into our bed like he usually did, he sauntered over to my side and rested his chin on the bed next to my face.

"I'm sorry," he said quietly.

"I know."

"What can I do?" Har asked as he nosed my arm slightly.

"Just be with me." I patted the space next to me, and he slowly climbed up.

Harlow stayed with me all day. I remember waking up between painkiller-induced naps to find his head right next to mine on the pillow. Most of the time he was wide awake, simply by my side.

The morning after the surgery, as I got ready for my first shower, I looked at myself in the mirror. The body I'd examined with such amazement only a few days ago now looked and felt so foreign, like it had betrayed me. As I peeled off the enormous underwear and enormous pads, I thought about all the photos I'd seen of women wearing the same big underwear, but theirs always came with a caption about, "True life postpartum. What it's like after you have a baby!" What about the caption where you only go home with the pads and big underwear, no baby?

In the days that followed, Harlow and I spent a lot of time sitting alone on a bench at the dog park. A gnawing feeling of loneliness followed me everywhere, and I couldn't escape it. It wrapped itself around me like a shell, and if I wasn't careful, I'd fall back into it and would find myself watching things unfold around me, rather than actually living them. I started texting Chris every day around three or four p.m. asking if he'd get to come home early from work. As someone who had thrived while working from home alone and with only a handful of friends who lived nearby, this feeling of isolation was new for me. I had always been so content, even happy, on my own. I didn't understand it.

But then again, when I really forced myself to admit it, maybe I *did* understand it. For the past couple of months, I'd thought about one thing every single day, several thousand times a day. Whether it was regarding what I could or couldn't eat, what activity I shouldn't do, how my clothes fit, how my face looked, what was happening inside of me at that moment, or next week, or in nine months—and then one day, it was all gone. And what was my mind supposed to do? Just shut all of that off and move along? I suppose some people are able to do that, but I couldn't. I still seemed to have all those emotions and thoughts for the life I was supposed to be living just floating around, but now they had nowhere to go, nothing to fill, and it left me feeling empty.

When I was pregnant, I'd long for my old habits and routines, and now I had the chance to get them back. Bring on the wine and poke bowls! *This is what you wanted, remember?* That little voice, the one packed full of shame and guilt, that immediately reminded me that I didn't appreciate the heartbeat, taunted me all day long. *You didn't even know if you wanted to be pregnant, so why are you so sad?*

Yes I did! Maybe not at first, but I did. I'd fight back with myself, with whatever fueled the voice that told me I had no right to be sad.

In the midst of my loneliness, anger and guilt surrounded me as well, because it was true. I had been so unsure about this pregnancy and if I was ready to be a mom, and then the moment it was taken away from me, I was completely shattered. Did I really have a right to grieve like the women who knew from day one they wanted to be a mom? Or what about the women who had tried for years to get pregnant and then miscarried? Certainly their grief was more warranted than mine. Who was I to be so upset?

These were the arguments I had in my head as Harlow and I sat on the bench at the dog park, tears rolling down my face under my dark sunglasses. Eventually another dog and their owner would show up, and we both knew it was our time to go.

Since I had my D&C surgery on our actual wedding anniversary, Chris and I decided to "celebrate" our anniversary a week later. As I blow-dried my hair and put on makeup, I said to Chris a hundred times, "Should we just cancel dinner? We could stay in."

"We can stay in if you want, but we haven't been to dinner in months," Chris said patiently. "I really think we should just try to go."

He was right; I should at least try. For the past couple of months, I'd been so nauseous and exhausted, we'd rarely left the house past seven p.m.

So, I filled in my eyebrows and brushed on my bronzer and tried to pretend I was excited to go eat sushi at one of our favorite restaurants in the West Loop. As we strolled Lake Street, I was surprised at all the people out and about. Everyone seemed so happy and tipsy, soaking up the warm evening as Chicagoans do once summer finally arrives. It was as if I'd thought that just because my summer nights had been put on hold, so had everyone else's.

Right as we crossed the street toward Momotaro, the sushi spot where we were headed, we passed by a couple doting on their precious newborn. Chris and I exchanged a look and then hurried by, but not before it felt as if every last ounce of air left my body, and my shoulders instinctively hunched downward, and I put my face toward the ground.

Chris put his arm around me and whispered, "Do you want me to go punch that baby?"

"What?" I whispered as I glanced at him and laughed.

And I continued to laugh, far too hard, considering how dumb it was, but Chris doesn't punch people, and he certainly doesn't make jokes about punching babies. But in that moment, it was what I needed to hear, because it wasn't just the baby that made my shoulders hunch, although that was a big part—it was more the look of knowing between Chris and me. Because only a week ago, the look we exchanged when we passed a baby had meant something entirely different.

I continued to see pregnant women and newborns everywhere after I miscarried, and I hated it, and I hated even more that I cared. Was this my baby fever? Had it finally arrived wrapped in heartache and resentment? I'd sometimes look at photos of myself from before everything happened, before I took the first pregnancy test, before I heard the heartbeat and then didn't hear it. And I wondered if I got the chance, would I go back to being her? Would I go back to being the woman who didn't know if she wanted a baby, who didn't secretly track other pregnancies that were able to keep growing at the same time she lost her own? Who could scroll social media without the fear of another pregnancy announcement popping up like a tiny bomb, exploding in a way that made her angry at strangers for being happy and angrier at herself for caring? Would I do it? Would I go back to not knowing? No. It was always no. Because at least now, I knew.

..

"You're super fertile after a miscarriage, so you'll be pregnant again in no time," I was told by people trying to comfort me.

But what these people didn't know is that I'd had a partial molar miscarriage, which meant I didn't have the option of getting pregnant again "in no time." I had a lot of time, in fact—at least six months before my doctor would clear us to try again. I was sitting on the floor in our living room staring at absolutely nothing, my favorite pastime as of late, when my cell phone rang, and it was my OB-GYN's office. I picked it up easily because I hadn't known to be scared of that number yet. My doctor told me they'd gotten results back from my D&C, and I fought the urge to respond, *Did the baby make it?* I was feeling dark and cynical and wondering why she was calling to give "results" for a procedure I didn't want to have, to remove a baby I *did* want to have. I was here; the baby was not. Couldn't they just let me move on already?

I wish I could recall exactly what my doctor said next, but I was stuck in such a thick fog just waiting for the appropriate time to say, "Thank you and goodbye" so I could hang up, that when I heard words like "cancerous tissue" and "we'll need to continue to monitor you," I wondered if they'd called the right person.

"Wait, wait, *what?*" I said as I shook my head, feeling as if I were crawling on all fours to get out from the back of my head where I'd safely been hiding. "Did you say cancer? I could have cancer from all of this?"

Har woke up from his nap and tilted his head my direction. "What's going on?"

I pointed toward the phone and ran my hands over my eyes. This nightmare was never ending. What was a partial molar miscarriage? Couldn't I just normal-miscarry like everyone else?

My doctor told me partial molars were very rare, occurring only in 0.005 to 0.01% of all pregnancies, and I recall feeling like I sensed excitement in her voice. She had a meeting with her colleagues later and was going to share my results. I was her first!

Well, it wasn't a total loss then! Glad I could give you something cool for show-and-tell.

Looking back, there's certainly a chance I imagined my doctor's excitement. I wasn't her biggest fan. But you also don't forget sensing excitement in someone's voice when you're having your first cancer scare. Other than it being rare, I learned that a fetus has no chance of surviving a partial molar pregnancy. I'm not blaming Chris's sperm, but they basically got too aggressive, and rather than following the rules of reproduction and sending in only one sperm to fertilize my egg, two wrestled for it. Typical toxic masculinity, am I right? I could just imagine two Affliction-wearing sperm, slamming Monster energy drinks, fighting about whose turn it was to fert' the egg. And rather than being mature sperms about it, knowing one should stand back, they both went in and made an extra copy of Chris's genetic material in the process. An embryo should have only forty-six chromosomes, but in a partial molar, there's sixty-nine. *Thanks, guys.*

After the partial molar pregnancy is removed, any molar tissue left behind has the potential to grow, and that's where the cancer stuff comes into play, also known as persistent gestational trophoblastic neoplasia (GTN). Still with me here? Yeah, me neither, so I'll make it quick. One sign of persistent GTN is a high level of HCG (a pregnancy hormone), and that, ladies and gentlemen, is why I wouldn't "be pregnant again in no time." After my miscarriage, I had to get my HCG back down to zero and for at least six months before we could start trying again. If I didn't, it would be too hard to know if HCG was present because I was growing a baby in my uterus, or growing cancer. Gender reveal parties were bad enough; I was sure no one wanted to attend a cancer reveal party.

For the next four months, I received weekly blood draws to monitor my levels, a painful weekly reminder that I was stuck, unable to move forward until I found out if cancer was inside of me or not. After each blood draw, I'd obsessively stare at my computer, refreshing my patient portal to see if my results had come in. I'd work myself into such an anxiety hole I'd nearly throw up waiting to see if my HCG had dropped each week. In the beginning, my numbers dropped by the thousands. I'd be at zero in no time! And then one week, it only dropped by a hundred, then fifty. The next week it was twenty and soon only ten. My doctor assured me everything was okay; I just needed to give it more time. *More time.* She said it so flippantly, as if it were something that was just in abundance. But when you're hoping to get pregnant after a miscarriage, the last thing you have is time.

When a rare moment of clarity would find its way to me during these dark months of waiting and blood draws, I'd remember that cancer could be looming inside any one of us; I was simply the one monitoring it. How's that for a positive pep talk? I actually took relief in the thought that a ton of stuff could be going wrong in my body at any time, and this was just one I was choosing to focus on.

In an attempt to distract myself from the worrying and waiting, I decided I should do something more useful with all my anxiety (and anger), but what might that be? Well, back to stand-up, of course! Isn't that why comedy was invented? And thus, new material was born. Thirty minutes of miscarriage jokes—what more could the world want? Apparently a little more lighthearted humor, as one drunk heckler noted about ten minutes in. Luckily, I didn't hear what was said during my set, although I was told to my face after. But I didn't care because the set wasn't written for her; it was written for me and every other woman who's been through a miscarriage and has had to listen to the unending list of stupid shit people say to you after.

This was unknowingly my last stand-up show in Chicago, and I performed it on a Thursday night in October. The next day, Chris, Harlow, and I were supposed to depart on a cross-country road trip to show Har the ocean—something we'd wanted to do since he was a pup. Before leaving, I scheduled an ultrasound with my OB for Friday morning. My HCG numbers had plateaued for weeks, and something just felt off inside of me. I'd been persistent about this at my latest checkups, but my doctor insisted we wait a few more weeks and do a few more blood draws. I waited until I couldn't wait any more. Something wasn't right, and I knew it, so I demanded to be seen.

I listened to Lizzo on repeat as I rode the elevator to the ninth floor. *I just took an HCG test; turns out I'm one hundred percent not fixed.* I hummed the remix I'd created over the past two months of blood draw visits. I kept my eyes fixated on my phone in the waiting room as I always did, fearful of making contact with the pregnant women. The time was 11:11, and I made the same two wishes I'd been making since I'd started the blood draw appointments—for a healthy pregnancy someday and to be in a better place than I was now. I intentionally left the second half of my wish vague so the Universe could have some creative control.

My name was called, and I followed the nurse where I was told to go. It didn't dawn on me that I hadn't been in an ultrasound room since the "there's no heartbeat" appointment until my feet were in the stirrups and it was much too late. I tried to count the speckled tiles on the ceiling to keep my anxiety from suffocating me, but they swirled and bounced together. Before the tech even began, I had tears streaming down my face—the kind that come from somewhere so deep inside you didn't even know they were still hiding there.

"I'm so sorry," I mumbled. "I don't know why I'm doing this." I'd just talked for thirty minutes about my miscarriage the night before to a room full of strangers, and now I couldn't keep it together for one minute for an ultrasound?

"Do you want me to stop?" the tech asked.

"I'm fine," I said between hiccups. "You can continue."

The ultrasound revealed that I was right. My uterus lining was thicker than it should be, and I'd have to undergo another D&C surgery immediately. In another time, I might have made a thick uterus joke about how "guys liked them that way" or "more cushion for the childbirth pushin'," but I had no jokes today. I just lay there in a daze thinking, *Again?* There would be no road trip the next day but instead another awful hospital visit. Another month of wearing bulky pads, scrubbing blood out of sheets, and worst of all, signing a goddamn waiver agreeing to an "emergency hysterectomy" should it come to that during surgery. I was still processing all of this when the tech told me I could go back to the waiting room and my doctor would see me shortly. *Go back?* Go back into that room full of pregnant women with their hands resting on their bellies and their sonogram images dangling from their purses? My hands shook, and my face was red and streaked with tears, and I wanted to go anywhere except back to that waiting room.

"Is there . . . is there anywhere else I could wait?" I asked meekly. I'd never felt so small in my life.

She nodded sympathetically and then led me to a small dark room where I sat alone with my knees tucked to my chest, for once not caring how long I had to wait.

Things Not to Say to Someone After a Miscarriage

At least you know you can get pregnant!
> Do you tell someone with uncontrollable diarrhea, "Well, at least you know you have a butthole"? No, no you don't. Because it's not helpful in any way, shape, or form.

Better that it happened now rather than later.
> Really? Would you say this to someone about any other terrible personal situation?

It just wasn't meant to be.
> Nor was this comment. Ever.

You'll get pregnant again in no time.
> Stop.

This is why you should wait a while before you announce your pregnancy.
> Someone actually said this to me, to which I kindly responded, "You are so right! I forgot that not talking about pregnancy prevents miscarriage."

Things to Say

I am here for you.

an hcg number reveal

I woke up from my second D&C surgery thinking about peonies because those were the kind of flowers we brought my mom when she had her hysterectomy. My brother and I picked them on our walk to the hospital, which was approximately two blocks from our big purple house, and even though the silky petals had tiny ants crawling all over them and I was worried they'd bite me, I held the peonies as tightly as I could in my small hands because I knew my mom would like them. She always commented when they bloomed at the start of every summer in Nebraska.

But it wasn't summer. It was late October in Chicago, and I was wincing in pain from my uterus contracting so intensely.

The nurse who pushed my hospital bed back to the recovery room stroked my arm and whispered, "I'm so sorry you had to go through this."

I tried to smile and nod between tears, but all I could think of were the peonies. I remembered thrusting them toward my mom as she lay in her hospital bed, excited for her to see what I'd brought, but instead, she flinched and turned away from me because I'd accidentally pushed on her newly stapled stomach. My sister and brother yelled at me for being careless, and I remember feeling so embarrassed and scared.

Why did my uterus hurt so badly? It wasn't like this last time. I didn't remember feeling any contractions. I wiped my eyes and groggily asked the nurse, "Did I have to get a hysterectomy?"

I thought about signing that form a few hours earlier. Was it only hours? And I thought about signing it a few months earlier too. Both times that I had to give permission to remove my uterus if an emergency should arise during surgery, I looked at Chris and sighed with frustration and fear.

"I hate this," I'd muttered.

"It's just something they have to put on there. It will be okay," he responded.

They have to put it on there because it's happened to someone, I thought but didn't say out loud, because I knew Chris was thinking it too. Everyone who signed it thought it. And for all the time I spent not knowing if I wanted to have a baby, nothing made me more certain that I did than signing a form agreeing that if something went wrong, I might not ever be able to.

The nurse looked at me and gently grabbed my hand. "Oh, honey, no. You had a D&C."

Even in my drugged-up state, even as my insides felt like they were being wrung like a dish towel, I felt relief. "Okay, good." At least I could still have one of those.

My doctor came by a short time later to tell me that surgery had "gone well," and as I curled over in pain and scrunched my face together with each contraction, I wondered what exactly that meant. She felt that they'd gotten all the leftover tissue this time, and as the extra cherry on top, she gave me an additional medication to soften my cervix, which was probably causing the contractions. I wish I would have asked why I wasn't given the softening medicine during the first D&C if it helped with the process, but I just nodded and said okay. I was nauseous and sore and just happy to be leaving with my uterus still intact. But as my doctor walked away, I hoped that I'd never have to see her again. I knew it wasn't her fault that I was lying in a hospital bed again, dry heaving from the anesthesia of the same surgery I'd just had a few months ago. Doctors are only human like the rest of us, not superheroes like I often build them up to be in my head. But then again, when someone is working away on your insides, making choices and scrapes that could change life as you know it, you kind of pray there's a cape under those scrubs.

A few days later, Chris, Har, and I were on a walk near Division Street, careful not to get too far from home, because the first days (and sometimes weeks and even months) following a D&C, it's not uncommon to pass clots that you'd rather not be waddling around with, and I'll just leave it at that. My phone rang, and it was the number that instantly made my head feel heavy and my knees weak, the number that had brought instant dread for the past three months—my OB-GYN's office.

"It's them," I said to Chris.

"Answer it," he said.

"Yes, answer it!" Har reiterated.

But I couldn't do it. I just stared at my phone while Chris and Har stared at me. Fear paralyzed me from simply accepting the call and saying hello because once I said "hello," I couldn't go back. I let it go to voicemail. It felt like it was the one small strand of control I could have over this, and Chris and Har didn't say a word.

As we crossed the street toward our house, a gust of wind hurled down Division Street, taking the hats from anyone who didn't see it coming and grabbing leaves from trees that didn't have many to give. The mums that sat on stoops, once cheerfully welcoming the start of autumn, now looked tired and defeated. The Pulaski Park swimming pool had long since drained the water and kicked out the children in exchange for litter and anything the neighborhood trees couldn't bear. You could feel in the air that the season was getting restless; it was time for a new one.

Before we walked inside, I took a deep breath and lifted my phone to my ear to listen to the voicemail. Chris hoped my HCG had dropped from four hundred sixty to forty-five. I was being more realistic and hoped for ninety. But we were both wrong. It was nine.

"Chris! I think she said nine! I swear she did."

"No way. Let me listen!"

I passed the phone to Chris and played the voicemail once more so he could confirm it. He heard the same thing I did. My HCG had actually dropped below ten. After my first D&C in July, my numbers were around eighteen thousand; today they were nine! I felt like I could finally open the door and begin to leave the room I'd been trapped in.

Before I was able to see a new specialist in Chicago, I returned to my OB's office one last time to get a blood draw. I sat in the waiting room surrounded by pregnant women holding their bellies and checking their Bump apps and reminded myself that they might have had their own struggles to get to where they are. Or maybe they didn't. It honestly didn't matter because I thought less about the women sitting next to me this time and more about the women in the other waiting room—the ones we don't see.

About a week later, we were able to take Har on the road trip we'd promised. We didn't make it all the way to the ocean since our timeline had changed. Instead, we took Har sightseeing through Yellowstone with stops in Wyoming, Montana, Utah, and Colorado. Chris had always wanted to explore Moab and Jackson Hole, and Har and I wanted to wear our new fall jackets in a different setting.

"Just one pic. That's all I want!" Har begged as he discreetly growled at the herd of buffalo standing right outside of our car in Yellowstone National Park. "Just to show my friends back home."

"Absolutely not, Har." I double-checked to make sure the car doors and windows were locked since he knew how to work both. "You're not going to be one of those tourists who ends up on the news getting charged by a buffalo after you tried to get a selfie."

"Fine." His eyes darted from window to window. "I just can't believe these things. They're the biggest dogs I've ever seen. But I could take them on," he added under his breath with that mild growl again.

"Really, Har? Because this morning you were hiding in the shower when Chris turned the stove on. But now you want to fight a herd of buffalo?"

I finally received a zero on my HCG test in a small hospital in Moab, Utah. Before leaving Chicago, we were cleared to go on our road trip, but only if I continued my blood draws along the way. Chris and Har explored a dog-friendly hike nearby while I sat in a waiting room anticipating my results, while also wondering how in the hell life had led me to a small hospital in Moab, Utah, waiting to see my HCG levels. Six months ago, I didn't even know what HCG meant, and now my life revolved around it. How had that happened? How had so much changed in such little time, especially during a year when I found myself constantly feeling like I was at a standstill, unable to move forward no matter how hard I tried?

I was handed my results in a sealed white envelope, and I waited to open it until I got back in the car with Chris and Har by my side. As Chris slid the envelope open, both of us on the edge of our seats waiting to see if I'd finally hit zero, something about the scene felt familiar, but I wasn't sure why. And then I realized it was a scene I'd once imagined for us, but in my version, we weren't opening an envelope to find an HCG number, but to find out the sex of our baby. So many others got that version. Why couldn't we? I felt sorry for myself for just a second, and then I accepted that that wasn't our scenario today. But maybe it could be someday.

Chris unfolded the paper inside the envelope and smiled as he read it. "It says zero, Tay! You did it!" He handed me the paper, and we hugged, and for the millionth time, I cried. The tears were so layered with different thoughts and feelings I didn't even know what caused them anymore. Relief, longing, sadness, joy, gratitude—the whole gang was here at this point.

Later that afternoon, as the three of us sat under one of Utah's famed arches (the one that allows dogs to sit underneath it), Har sighed with content and rested his head across my legs. Today alone, he'd tackled his first slot canyon as if he'd been a mountain dog his entire life, he'd bounced in and out of the shallow river that flowed through the red canyon, and he'd run zoomies through the sand until he was coated in Utah's landscape.

"There's so much to see out there," Har said softly as he stared off into the rust horizon, a horizon that seemed to match his own coloring just perfectly.

"You like it here, don't you, buddy?" Chris leaned into Har to give him a good ear scratch, and Har relished in it. "Because I do too."

A lot of times Chris needed me to interpret for Har—*What did he need? What did he want?*—but not out here. They seemed to know exactly what each other was thinking.

"There is a lot to see. You're right, Har," I said. "I'm glad we're here."

I thought about the HCG results tucked into my hiking backpack. I brought the paper along rather than leaving it in our car, like I thought someone might take it away from me if I left it behind. And I thought about how every other time in my life when I felt like I was at a standstill, I never actually was. Life was still moving right along and taking me with it, and when I finally crawled out of my head long enough to notice, I'd always ended up somewhere I never expected to be.

part two

rita wilson's husband
has covid

CHICAGO, ILLINOIS. 2020.

It was a snowy Tuesday night when Har and I sat together in a cozy neighborhood bar called Bucktown Pub trying not to think about the stranger in our house opening every door and turning on every light, doing her final walk-through before *our* home became *her* home. Of all the things I miss about Chicago, it might be the neighborhood bars I miss the most. Especially the ones that allowed Harlow to sit on a stool next to me. How can one ever be lonely when there are bars that allow dogs to *sit on stools*?

We'd sold our condo and were leaving the Windy City, something I never thought we'd actually do. But 2019 had been an eye-opening year for Chris and me, so we were ready for a change. We were ready to make 2020 our best year yet. *Ha ha!* I loved Chicago so much and everything it had taught me, but when we came back from our road trip West, we couldn't shake the urge that there was more out there we needed to explore. Or at least that's what Chris said, and I went along with it because the idea of change is always very exciting to me. The act of it, not so much, but I'm always on board in the beginning for the fun, dreamy part. It also didn't hurt that we planned our move during one of Chicago's longest stretches without sunlight. I think we went eight full days without seeing any sliver of light in January 2020 (a foreshadowing of things to come). I considered myself a pretty tough Midwesterner when it came to Chicago weather, but even that was a bit much for me. It was almost as grueling as the winter of 2019 when the temperature reached such extreme lows our walls started popping. Chris said the foundation of our condo contracted or something. I'm not sure; I'm not a scientist. I just know it was too damn cold. The only way I could get Har outside to go to the bathroom was to drive him to the park, but even our car refused to be in those temps. It just stopped working in the middle of the street, one block into the three-block journey. Instead of an orange check-engine light, there was just a message on the dash that said, "Fuck this. I'm out."

Chicago weather aside, which I could obviously talk about for hours but won't because this isn't a phone call with my dad, Chris and I knew the move would be good for Har. We'd noticed that his hips had started to stiffen, and getting up from naps or going on longer walks wasn't as easy for him as it used to be.

"You okay, bud?" I asked when I saw him limping a bit after coming home from the dog park.

"I'd be better with a denty stick," Har responded quickly as he glanced from his treat jar back to me.

"Well, obviously." I handed him a green dental chew and rubbed his back legs. "But do your hips feel okay?"

"Completely fine. Didn't you see how fast I was today? I got all the garbage before anyone else."

"You did, Har. You sure did."

I also knew he probably wouldn't tell us if he was in any pain, unless of course we accidentally stepped on the back of his heels—Har absolutely hated that. But who doesn't?! I took him to the vet almost immediately and did my best to settle both of our nerves while we waited for the doctor to return with his X-rays.

"I don't like it here," Har panted. "Can we go?"

"Soon," I responded, hoping the X-rays didn't show what I'd always feared they'd someday show.

"How about now? Or now? What about now? Maybe now?"

The door creaked open, and Har tried to bury his face under my sweatshirt as if it were a blanket. No matter how often I switched clinics or made sure we only saw the kindest veterinarians we could find, Har's anxiety about visiting the dreaded doctor only got worse with age. When I saw the X-rays tucked under the vet's arms, I wished Har had been wearing a sweatshirt I could hide beneath as well.

"Did you see anything?" I hoped I sounded casual, but as I gripped Har's fur, I wondered who was panting louder.

"Other than what appears to be a little early arthritis, he's a healthy big boy," she said, and I wanted to hug her, and I don't ever want to hug anyone without four legs.

Har's vet went on to tell us there was a lot we could do to help loosen up his joints, and I feverishly took notes, ready to do them all. There were special treats, pills, CBD, water therapy, acupuncture. As I wrote everything down, my mind began generating new T-shirt ideas I could create to cover any of Har's additional costs. I'd do whatever it took to make sure I got my boy for at least another decade.

"One more thing that would help," the vet noted as Har pulled me toward the door, ready to get the hell out. "Try taking him on walks with hills or different levels of elevation. Let him jump up on park benches and things like that."

I thought about our daily visits to Pulaski Park where I'd run in circles begging Har to chase me and not eat park garbage, and as fun as those were, apparently they weren't doing much for his aging hips.

"What about mountains?" I asked. "Would those help his joints?"

"Well, sure, but there aren't a lot of mountains in Chicago."

But I'd heard there were mountains in Colorado. For the past few months, Chris had been asking if I'd ever consider moving to Denver. He'd found a few jobs he was interested in there, one in particular that he was pretty serious about, and wouldn't it be nice to get a little change of scenery? I was hesitant to leave a city I felt so lucky I was able to live in—until Har's vet appointment. And then I thought a move West might just be what we all needed.

Chris accepted a new job, and we quickly began house hunting for cute bungalows *in Denver!* (This was the "fun, dreamy part," until it wasn't.) Unlike me, who started new jobs every other week in my twenties, Chris worked at the same company for nearly ten years, so this was a pretty big leap for him (for us). We'd also been given the green light by my new doctor to start trying for a baby again. Like I said, it was 2020, and anything was possible! *Until approximately two weeks into March, at which point most things were not in fact possible in 2020.*

The night I took a pregnancy test and saw two lines indicating it was positive, Chris was on a flight to San Francisco. My period wasn't late, and I wasn't showing any symptoms. I'd actually just poured a glass of wine, but before I took a sip, something stopped me. It was just a feeling that told me I was pregnant, and a test confirmed it.

"Holy shit," I gasped as I held the little plastic test in my hand.

"Oh what, you believe those things now?" Har asked.

"Yes, Har, I do. It's called growth." But just to be safe, I took two more.

I didn't even consider telling Chris in a cute way this time. That simply wasn't me, and I'd accepted it. Instead, I texted him a blurry photo of the results and said, "You better call me when you land." That was kind of cute though, right?

"Are you serious?" Chris asked when he called me, still on the plane.

"I am. I took a couple of tests."

"Wow. Okay. Wow." His uncertainty was louder than his words, and it caught me off guard.

This wasn't like the first time around; we actually knew we were ready to be parents this time. Right?

"Why are you sounding so weird?" I looked at Har and gave him our "Chris is being annoying" look that we occasionally exchanged when we were being catty.

"What now?" Har slapped his paw on my arm, and I rolled my eyes and pointed toward the phone.

"I'm not. I'm excited," Chris said, but I knew the expression on his face without even seeing it. He was distracted, eyebrows and lips scrunched together, much too deep in his head for his own good. "Things just feel a little strange here, and we haven't even gotten off the plane yet. I don't know. I might end up coming home early. We'll see how this all plays out."

By "this all," Chris meant Covid. He landed in San Francisco Tuesday, March 10—as in, the last normal Tuesday for life as we previously knew it. We were only a few days away from the NCAA basketball tournament being canceled, and we had no idea. *Not the basketball tournament!* A few people in Chicago had started wearing masks, but I didn't think much of it. It was just a bad flu, right? Or a bad cold? What was it exactly? I wasn't sure, but I do recall coughing in Target was very frowned upon, so if you felt so much as a speck of dust in your throat, you might as well get the hell out.

But I didn't have my true "oh shit" moment until a few days later when it was announced that Tom Hanks tested positive. *Not Tom Hanks!* If America's dad could get it, then no one was off-limits. *Also, this is my second time mentioning Tom Hanks. That guy has really made an impact on me!* Har and I immediately drove to the closest Mariano's grocery store at nine p.m. so I could stock up on "the essentials." But once inside, I realized I didn't know what "the essentials" were, so I just bought a lot of chips and pasta. I picked up my pace as I wandered up and down the aisles, and each shelf grew emptier than the previous. The toilet paper aisle was completely bare, just like the cleaning supplies and medicine. I'd never seen our beloved Mariano's like this, and it gave me such an eerie feeling of vulnerability. I was here only a few days ago, and the shelves were stocked. How had things changed so quickly? *What other changes are looming in the darkness?* I wondered.

"You should come home," I texted Chris. "I'm getting a little worried."

He took the next flight back to Chicago, and I made him change clothes in our hallway before he stepped inside. And once Chris got home, things started to spiral—in Denver and Chicago. We put in a panic bid on a house in Denver we'd never seen in person and knew we couldn't afford.

"We just need a house!" I sobbed, my first trimester hormones already raging with fear and anger on top of everything else unfolding around us.

"This isn't a good time. We shouldn't have put that bid in." Chris paced our bedroom, regretting the bid the second he agreed to it. "We're in a pandemic. We have no idea what's going to happen!"

"We have a baby coming!" I screamed in case he'd forgotten.

"Guys, stop yelling, please." Har wiggled between us, begging Chris and me to lower our voices. Har couldn't stand it when we talked (or argued) too loudly, which we didn't do often, mostly because we knew it made him so uncomfortable.

"I'm sorry, Har," we said at the same time.

Our Realtor called to tell us the house had nineteen other bids and was already one hundred thousand dollars over the asking price. We'd heard the Denver market was crazy, but one hundred thousand dollars over asking price? In a pandemic? We immediately backed out, and I could literally see the relief wash over Chris's face.

"It wasn't meant to be," he said, and I knew he was right.

But did I still cry and somehow want to make it Chris's fault because I was feeling emotional and irrational? Yes. Yes I did.

The closing date for our own condo was March 30. That was supposed to give us three more weeks to pack up, say our goodbyes, and find a unicorn of a house in Denver. But in March 2020, plans changed by the hour. We'd heard rumors a shelter-in-place was coming but had no idea what that meant. Would it mean we couldn't leave our house? Or city? Or even the state? I'd just watched the movie *Contagion* (which Tom Hanks *isn't in* but he *should have* been), and my mind was having a heyday envisioning armed guards in hazmat suits not allowing us to walk out our front door, let alone load a moving truck.

"What if we can't move out, so our buyer can't move in? And then neither can her buyer, or her buyer, and we start an entire waterfall effect of throwing off the moving chain?" I asked Chris as we sat in our living room, glued to the news and the Covid death count it displayed. "And then all these people have nowhere to live during a pandemic because of us?!"

"I'm not sure," Chris responded, "but I think this is going to get a lot worse before it gets better."

The news showed clips of people fighting over toilet paper and hand sanitizer, eggs and milk. If we continued like this, how bad would it be in three weeks? What would people be fighting over then? I think Chris and I both secretly imagined leaving Chicago in a moving truck as apocalyptic scenes played out around us—people looting our vehicle (looking for toilet paper and eggs, probably), forcing us off the road with masks and weapons so we had no other choice but to walk hundreds of miles until we found an underground community that was initially skeptical of us but finally took us in after I explained I was pregnant (and also once had a large Instagram following in the old world). I understand how dramatic this seems, but it was our first pandemic, and everything felt so insanely dramatic.

After a lot of phone calls and a lot of back-and-forth arguing between Chris and me—*What if we stay? What if we don't? What if we . . . ?*—we decided in a matter of hours to move up our closing date and get out of Chicago in the next forty-eight hours.

We slept on an air mattress in our living room our last night on Noble Street. Everything else in our condo had already been sent away with the moving truck.

"I'm going to bed," Har said as he started up the spiral staircase toward our bedroom, as he did every night.

"Har, no. We're sleeping down here tonight," I said with a heavy sigh.

He paused halfway up and peeked his little head through the railing. "But our bed is up here."

"Not anymore, Har."

As the three of us tried to sleep on the uneven air mattress, either sinking low to the ground or suddenly bursting upward each time the other moved, I stared at the lights from Division Street sneaking in through the curtains and tried not to think about what lay ahead. Furloughs were happening in every industry. Would Chris be next? Would we find a new house? Would we even still move to Denver? I listened extra hard to the familiar sounds of our home that night—the heat coming on, the mysterious fridge hum, the occasional siren outside—and hoped they would drown out the chaos in my head. The world felt like it was crumbling around us as we prepared to leave the place we called home, and I finally understood the uncertainty in Chris's voice when I had told him I was pregnant. *What were we doing?*

Eventually the night noise of our sweet condo lulled me to sleep, as I knew it would because it had so many instances before, and when I woke up, it was time to say goodbye.

We left Chicago on the grayest of gray days. Chris drove the U-Haul full of our houseplants in front, and Har and I followed behind in our car. Moving companies won't take live plants across state lines and even though we were just starting our first pandemic and had no actual idea what the road might look like ahead of us, we knew it would involve our houseplants. One must never leave behind the fiddle-leaf or bird-of-paradise! All our friends and favorite places in the city were on lockdown, so the only thing we were able to say goodbye to on our farewell bucket list was Har's park, Pulaski Park to be specific.

"Get one last run in, buddy," I said as I opened our car door for him, and he sprinted toward his favorite corner.

There was a light mist in the air, like the sky was too tired to commit to rain or snow, so it decided to just make everything a little damp and dirty-looking instead. I pulled my hood over my head and watched Har sniff around for park garbage and thought about all of the time we had spent here, and at every park in Chicago, for nearly the past ten years. How could we leave the city that had taught us so much? Sure, the weather was kind of terrible, and the parks sometimes had a lot of garbage, especially in the summer, but it was our home. I couldn't take Har from his home.

"Okay, let's go," Har said, suddenly appearing at my side.

"Are you sure? We can stay longer." He was being strong for me, bless him.

"No. No, it's time," Har said, already walking toward the car without me. "Let's get out of here. It's too wet."

"But, Har, it's the last—"

"Oh my God, let's just get going! I said I'm getting wet, okay?!" He shook his ears and shouted at me at the same time. "And you know I hate getting wet! Must I spell it out for you?"

It was true. Har hated the rain; he acted as if it was actual acid on his back should a raindrop ever strike him.

"Such a goddamn diva," I muttered to myself as I left our beloved Pulaski Park for the final time and took off my coat so I could properly dry off Princess Harlow.

As we drove out of the city, I could barely look at the skyline as it disappeared behind me. I hated to leave it in such a hasty way.

Har rested his head on the console and looked at me. "You know it will be okay, don't you?" He was in a much better mood now that he was dry and lovingly covered with his car blanket.

"I don't know, Har. Everything just feels extra bleak, like the world is ending or something," I said.

He yawned. "You said the same thing last time we moved."

"What? No I didn't."

"We even danced in the kitchen when the world *didn't* end. Don't you remember?"

The Harold Camping apocalypse. He was right. "How do you remember that? You were just a puppy." That felt like a lifetime ago.

"Because I remember everything we've done together, but especially the adventures."

"Well, it's different now. It's real this time." I'd never seen I-94 so empty. Not one single person had honked or flipped me off, and it was unsettling.

"It's just another adventure. We'll figure it out like we always do." And then Har closed his eyes and didn't even look back as we left the city we loved so much.

remaining a united front

"I'm not sure you guys are gonna figure this one out," Har said as he watched Chris and me scramble to calm down a screaming Birdie at three in the morning. "I honestly don't know what you two were thinking bringing her here."

It was our first night home with Birdie, and we'd gone through every swaddle blanket, burp cloth, pajama set (for both Birdie and me), and crib sheet by 3:30 a.m. and didn't know what to do. Har's judging eyes as he glared at us from the comfort of our bed, angry that we were interrupting his sleep, didn't help the situation. Chris and I were starting to turn on each other.

I found him hiding in the hallway after he'd put in another load of laundry and I exploded, "What in the hell are you doing out here?"

"I just need a second, okay?"

I patted Birdie's back, who sounded like a screaming baby goat against my damp chest. "Oh *you* need a second?" I was in a permanent state of damp lately. Damp from breast milk, night sweats, spit-up, and God knows what else, but Chris needed a second? Oh, screw that. "It's your turn. You take her!"

I thrust Birdie into his arms, and we started to argue with each other simply for the sake of arguing. Unable to form actual sentences or logical thoughts (I assume due to our sleep deprivation), we resorted to griping at one another like two children who had just discovered sarcasm.

"*Okay, Tay, you know everything, don't you?*"

"*Yup, Chris, I guess I do!*"

"*Okay, Tay!*"

"*Okay, Chris!*"

We went back and forth like this for longer than I'd like to admit, neither willing to drop an argument that made literally no sense. I'm truly embarrassed Birdie had to witness her mom and dad like that on her first night home. It wasn't what I envisioned when I dreamily hung her fancy white nursery curtains and delicately washed all of her precious newborn onesies so many weeks ago. But things can get kind of ugly those first weeks when you're exhausted, unsure of yourself as new parents, and your baby won't just go the fuck to sleep. We had changed her, fed her, burped her, and still she cried. Those were the three things the nurses told us to do, so why weren't they working? What were we doing wrong? The fear was heavy in our eyes, and perhaps even heavier in our souls, as Chris and I started to wonder if we'd ever sleep again.

"We have to remain a united front. We can't let her sense our weakness," I finally said after neither of us had spoken in a while. Had it been five minutes or two hours that we'd been sitting in our hallway covered in a mix of dirty and clean laundry? Time stopped making sense long ago.

"I know," Chris agreed. "I'm sorry."

"Me too."

"But you have to stop snapping at me when I say I'm tired. It's not just you feeling it," Chris said.

"Okay, I'm sorry." It wasn't a competition for who was more tired. Chris was right.

But if it was, I would win. Hands down.

"I'm just going to put her back in her magic crib and hope it works," Chris said as he walked back toward our room. "It should be dry now."

Her "magic crib" was a bassinet that plugged in and was supposed to respond to a baby's cry with noise and motion and lull them back to sleep. But it hadn't quite worked for us like that, unfortunately. The reason it wasn't dry and why we were in the laundry debacle at 3:30 in the morning was because Chris hadn't secured Birdie's diaper tightly. When she pooped, she started to cry, and when she cried, she set off the magic crib, which set off the motion sensor rocking her side to side, making the diaper looser and looser. Do you see where I'm going here? It was kind of like that urban legend that circulated the internet about the robotic vacuum that rolled over a piece of dog poop and shot it all over the house. It was like that, but on a smaller scale. Once the robotic bassinet loosened up the diaper completely and caught wind of the poop, it shook it everywhere. It leaked out of the diaper and out of the straitjacket Birdie slept in and splattered the walls and pad by her feet. For all the warning stickers on the bassinet, not one of them mentioned "shaking shit" as something to look out for, which I think is a huge miss on their part.

The bassinet was an arm's length away from where I slept (and by "slept" I mean transitioned between chills and night sweats), so I caught it right away. Thus we spent the next hour soothing Birdie, cleaning the bassinet, and doing more laundry. We also left a little time to "discuss" with one another about the proper way to put on a diaper. The side that says BACK goes on the back. You'd think this would be enough in regard to diaper instruction for a grown adult, but I'll be the first to tell you it's not. Why not put FRONT on the front as well? And maybe add a "pull side tab until here" mark, "but don't pull too hard because the side tab will rip and everyone will end up in tears." And then add a sweet little message like you find on tea bags. Something like, *"Hey, I know this is really hard and you're suddenly looking around at every other human on Earth wondering how the hell they did it, or how their parents did it, because there are literally humans everywhere, so that means they made it through the newborn stage, so you can too. But seriously, what the fuck? How did they do it? Idk, but they did, so you can too! And remember to double-check the folds if you have a baby girl. You got this!"* Just a thought for diaper companies.

Chris set Birdie back in the bassinet, pacifier in mouth, and I waited for her to cry, but she didn't. She suckled her paci and actually fell asleep, or so it seemed. I held my breath until I felt it was safe to release it. When I finally did, the sigh I let out was as heavy as the exhaustion I felt throughout my entire body.

And then she woke back up.

I didn't even bother to look at Chris because I knew he was already fast asleep, and seeing him in such a state would just piss me off again. Instead, I did my best to barrel-roll myself out of bed, as one does when they've just had a C-section and it's difficult to sit up with abdominal muscles that have literally been cut apart, and I put the pacifier back in Birdie's mouth. She was content again. As long as the paci stayed in Birdie's mouth, she was quiet and happy to suckle away like a real-life Maggie Simpson.

I rested my head on the hard thin ledge of her bassinet and wondered if I could attempt to sleep standing up. With my arm throbbing as I hovered it above Birdie's little head, sure to keep her paci in place, I closed my eyes and thought, *This isn't so bad!* But a few seconds later, the rest of my body screamed, *Yes it is, you moron!* I stood like that for a while, my body curled over her bassinet, doing everything in my power to make sure Birdie fell deeper and deeper into her sleep, while I did my best to keep from collapsing.

"I can't do this," I whispered to absolutely no one. "I just need to lie down." I'd never felt the pain of exhaustion like this before. When I had my wisdom teeth removed, I lay on the couch for five days. I'd just had a baby removed and hadn't lain down once.

I expected to lose sleep. I expected to be tired. But what I didn't expect (which is almost comical to me now looking back) is that my body would hurt so much in the process. For my entire pregnancy, I feared the pain of giving birth but hardly put any thought into the pain that came after. Sure, I'd been told to take home the spray bottle the hospital provided for "postpartum washing," and I assumed I'd be wearing big pads in my underwear, but that was it. I wasn't prepared for the overall trauma your body (and mind) goes through after creating and then delivering a new human into this world. So many people suggested I make a "birth plan," but not one suggested I make a post-birth plan.

It felt like I was trying to learn how to be a new mother while my own body was shouting, "Hey! Mother *me*—I need help too!" But we're not supposed to admit this as women, right? It makes us look weak or selfish to acknowledge we still have to take care of ourselves as we learn to take care of another. After all, women have been giving birth since literally forever and in much worse conditions. How did they manage? I still don't know the answer to this, but if I had to guess, it's because women have been warriors forever.

I lost my focus for a second, and Birdie's pacifier fell from her mouth. She started to squawk even before it completely departed her lips.

"Please, God, just let her sleep," I prayed as I replaced it. I'd never prayed as much as I did that first week home as a new parent. "Just let her fucking sleep, God. Please." I'd also never said "fuck" so much to God before, and I'm sorry about that, but I think He understands.

Eventually my prayers of profanity were answered, and Birdie drifted off to sleep. I hunched my way back to our bed, and Har was in my spot, so I politely nudged him to scoot over.

"I was asleep," he said with a groan and glare.

"Just scoot a little, Har," I begged.

He promptly stood up and huffed his way to the bottom of the bed. "That thing is loud," Har muttered as he glanced toward Birdie.

"I know, buddy, but it will get better." I lay down and patted my chest, my symbol for Har to come back up and lie with me. I hadn't snuggled him in over a week since we'd left for the hospital, and I missed him so much.

"I'm fine down here," he replied as he curled into himself.

"Har, please?" I asked once more, but he resisted. He'd been giving me the cold shoulder since we got home, and it killed me. "You're still my best boy," I whispered, but he wouldn't look at me.

Knowing I couldn't help the situation at four in the morning, I fell asleep and hoped tomorrow would be better. Just kidding! That's what a sane person would do. Instead, I lay there in a coma of weariness and postpartum hormones and wondered if anything would ever be the same.

Things I Often Wonder About Cavewomen and Motherhood

- How did they do it—birth and recovery? Like, I know how, but also, HOW?
- What was their first post-birth meal?
- When they spilled breast milk or let it spoil on accident, did they also cry?
- Did they worry they didn't get enough bump pics (or bump cave drawings) immediately after their bump was gone?
- Same for newborn pics (drawings).
- Did they stay up late at night to look at the cave drawings they did get?
- Did going to Target (or their version of) and seeing a newborn make them want another even though they were still overwhelmed with the one they just had?
- How did they maintain a 67–72-degree temperature in the cave nursery?
- What did their partner's nightstand look like compared to theirs?
- Did they have a wipe warmer?
- Which sippy cup was their favorite?
- Did they worry their pet wolf was mad at them for having a baby?

the storm

After leaving Chicago, we stopped in Nebraska to see family and wait just a bit for "things to get back to normal." We assumed the pandemic would be over by mid-April, or May at the latest, at which point we could all remove our masks and our worry and rejoice in the fact that Covid was a thing of the past! *Thank God that terrible time is over and done with. Now let's all get back to fighting about our normal stupid shit!*

We. Were. Wrong.

Chris's parents were kind enough to let us stay in their lake cabin so we could have some privacy, and also because it felt too risky staying with them. The CDC recommended quarantining only with your immediate household and no one else, so that's what we did. On the occasion his parents popped by to say hello, or bring us a Crock-Pot to make chili, we spoke to each other outside, masks on, and from an eight-foot distance. Because we just didn't know. No one did.

Any other time Chris's parents' cabin is an absolutely idyllic place, a beautiful cabin made of redwood from the Pacific Northwest that was delivered on a semitruck, put together by his grandfather in 1960. It was a spot we absolutely loved to visit in the summer, but as we hid out there in the spring of 2020, glued to the news every evening and the rising Covid death count, it felt isolating and dark.

There was also no heat in the cabin, so we slept in layers of clothing with space heaters surrounding us. When I'd open the toasty bedroom door to walk the three steps to the bathroom approximately five times a night, a gust of cold air from the rest of the cabin would blow in like it was from the Arctic. The bedroom was small, and the bed was even smaller. It was Har's dream situation, the three of us sleeping in such tight quarters, kind of like when we went camping and he shared a sleeping bag with me. The freezing cold and the small bed gave the three of us an excuse to cuddle up extra close.

After explaining my partial molar miscarriage to a receptionist and a couple of nurses, I was able to get an appointment for an ultrasound much sooner than my previous pregnancy. A miscarriage and a cancer scare were all it took to get a "pregnancy confirmation" from a doctor before twelve weeks. Who knew?! On the drive to the appointment, I tried to remain optimistic: I listened to my favorite good luck songs, repeated my mantras, made my wishes—all the crazy routines a person does when they're on the edge and grasping. My knuckles turned white on our steering wheel as I prayed there was a heartbeat and that it wasn't cancer spiking my HCG. Even though I'd been cleared by a doctor to start trying, even though my HCG had hit zero several times before we started trying, I still worried. The cancerous tissue can be removed, but not the worry surrounding it.

I waited in our car in the parking lot of the Methodist Women's Hospital in Omaha, Nebraska, as I was instructed to do. When I got the call it was my turn to come inside, I put on my N95 mask but wasn't sure about my plastic gloves. Did I need those only for grocery shopping, or doctor's visits too? My temperature was taken at the entrance and then once again a few minutes later after I'd followed the windy path of back hallways opened by Covid, and I landed in an ultrasound room. I hadn't been in a hospital since the pandemic started, and I was terrified to touch anything. I definitely regretted leaving my grocery gloves in the car. Only a month ago, all these precautions would have felt unreal, and at times they still did, but I was also surprised at how quickly it became our new normal.

The ultrasound tech came in and introduced herself, and we made small pandemic chitchat. I mentioned I'd just moved from Chicago but quickly added that I'd never been exposed and that we'd been quarantining for nearly a month. People were leery of outsiders, especially from densely populated cities like Chicago, so it was best to get that out of the way up front. As the tech got her equipment ready, I tried to take a deep breath to steady myself. But because of the mask or the heat in the room (I'd forgotten what warmth felt like) or simply the overall anxiety surging through me, I couldn't find my breath. I could feel myself starting to hyperventilate, so I began taking short quick breaths.

"Are you okay?" the tech asked.

"I think I'm just having a little meltdown is all. Can I take this mask off for a second? I'm just suddenly feeling very hot."

"No," she said firmly (but kindly).

"Okay, no problem," I said weakly (but also kindly).

I don't really think it was the mask or the heated room causing the shortness of breath; it was just me. *Get it together,* I yelled at myself in my head, or at least I hope it was in my head. I couldn't spend the rest of my life being terrified of ultrasound rooms. Moths? Yes. Ultrasound rooms? No.

Please be okay, little baby, I prayed as the tech began to move her wand across my stomach. *I really want to meet you someday. Please, please be okay.*

"Oh yes, there's definitely something there," the tech said with an optimistic tone that I clung to.

"So everything looks good? Like, like, it's still there? The baby is still growing?" The desperation gushed from me.

"It does." The tech nodded and tinkered away on her computer, connecting dots on her dark screen like she was making her own uterus constellations. "This little dark area right here is the head, and this is the body. It's still very early, so we can't get a read on the heartbeat yet—"

"Is that normal? To not get a read yet?" My own heart started to beat even faster, as if it could make up for the one we couldn't yet hear.

"It's very normal," she said with reassurance. "Based on the size I'm seeing here, I'm going to go ahead and tentatively mark your due date as . . ."—she looked from her screen back to my chart—"probably right around November eleventh. Does that sound right?"

November 11. 11/11. I wiped the lone tear that had found its way to the corner of my eye. "That does sound right."

I had hoped I wouldn't be as sick with my second pregnancy, thinking the endless nausea I felt the first time around was from the partial molar and high HCG levels. And I wasn't, at first. There was even a brief time when I thought, *I'm going to make the best of this pregnancy no matter what!* I was going to focus on being happy and healthy and my magical little due date of 11/11. Bring on the prenatal yoga, maternity dresses, and elaborate dinner recipes full of vegetables and leafy greens. I knew how easy a pregnancy could be taken away, so I was determined to make my gratitude outweigh everything else. *Ha ha.*

Unfortunately, my gratitude and "magical due date" couldn't outweigh migraines, nausea, or the crushing anxiety brought on from a world in a pandemic and a pregnancy following a miscarriage. But I sure tried! I even ordered a floral maternity dress and a new yoga mat. But by the time they arrived, I was done trying. I'd never wear the dress because we didn't leave the cabin, and I wouldn't use the yoga mat because I could barely get out of bed. I knew stress and worry weren't good for a pregnancy, which in turn only made me more stressed and worried.

When I've slipped into can't-get-out-of-bed moments before, I've turned to comedy as my crutch. I've created some of my best characters at moments when I'm feeling really down. When I don't know how to deal with what I'm going through (or simply don't want to), I like to put on a wig and let one of my characters handle it. Unfortunately, all my wigs had been sent away on the moving truck, a decision I deeply regretted, so I had no other choice but to order a new one. I added some fake cigarettes and a cat mask (as one does) to my cart as well because like I said, I was feeling down! And then I just prayed Chris's dad didn't open the package by mistake since all our mail was routed to his office first, because that would have been a tough one to explain.

But not as tough to explain as when a few days later his mom actually saw me hiding in the brush outside of the cabin wearing a cat mask and long blond wig. Any other time Chris's parents had stopped by, I was sleeping in the bedroom, too miserable to get out of bed, but now I was dressed like a cat hiding in the weeds smoking a fake cigarette. I didn't know if I should wave my fake cigarette in the air and say, "Busy day at the office." Or, "The CDC recommends . . ." Or just tuck my tail between my legs and crawl back to bed.

I tucked my tail and knew I couldn't attempt another video until we had our own place.

"When do you think that will be?" Har asked as I shoved the cat mask into the suitcase of sweats I'd been living out of.

"Who knows? Maybe never," I grumbled.

Har loved the cabin; he always had. I never saw what Chris was like at his cabin as a little boy, but I imagined it was something like Har—too excited to stay inside, always finding new paths to explore, different sticks to carry around, and sometimes he was even late for dinner because he was having too much fun just enjoying the outdoors.

"I just haven't felt well, Har. Not like myself."

"A walk will help."

"Not today. I'm too tired." I shut my eyes and turned away and waited to hear Har nudge the bedroom door open, but instead, he stayed with me. However, I could tell from his heavy sighs and groans of boredom, he did so begrudgingly. "Har, just go outside and play."

"Are you sure? I'll stay with you if you want. There's just this one squirrel and—"

"Har, go ahead." And then he bolted out of the bedroom door before I could change my mind.

The longer we stayed in Nebraska, the more Chris and I argued about when we'd finally get to Denver. Neither of us wanted to make Nebraska a permanent thing, so I'm not quite sure what we were arguing about, but we always found something. Sometimes Chris and I do really well about remembering we're a team—that we signed on to a lifelong partnership to love and support each other (remember when he offered to punch a baby for me?)—but other times we forget. And in such a case, we have the capacity to turn into two *very* petty people who gripe at each other for exhaling wrong or not using the correct tone of voice when asking, "Where are the car keys?" Unfortunately, we were entering (or had entered) a phase of the latter. Any word or breath was a battle word.

We'd put our house hunt on pause since we were simply doing our best to get through our day-to-day at the moment. Searching for a home in a new city during a pandemic felt far too daunting. Chris wasn't even four months into his new job—the job that was the reason we left our friends, our home, and what felt like our life in general back in Chicago—and we woke up every morning wondering if he'd be the next one to get furloughed. *Was today the day?* We learned in 2020 that the fear of being furloughed can force you into a complete standstill, scared to make a move or any decision, because if it actually happened, *then what?* It was a harrowing thought I didn't like to allow in, so my way around it was by sometimes not getting up at all. If I never got out of bed, I'd never have to join the world I didn't want to be in at the moment. I furloughed myself from life for a bit. I pretended first trimester sickness was fully to blame for the days I couldn't leave the cabin bedroom, but a good amount of depression and anxiety were always in bed with us as well.

"Do you need anything?" Chris would ask when he could sneak away from the small antique desk where he worked ten to twelve hours a day doing his best to prove he was an employee worth keeping around.

"No," I'd mumble. "I just don't feel well," and I'd turn to face the wall, the wood paneling an inch from my face.

I'd close my eyes and pretend I was back in our Chicago bedroom— the one that was big enough to fit *two* nightstands, had a connected bathroom, and access right to our private rooftop. Our rooftop had an incredible view of the skyline, and I loved to impress out-of-towners with it.

"What? You don't get views like this back home?" I'd joke, my big-city smugness just seeping from my pores.

Luckily, it was usually just my parents or my sister and her three small children who had to hear me gloat in such a way. And I'm pretty sure Jade's kids never gave a damn about the incredible view, which really pissed me off. But whatever.

I missed that view. And I missed running in circles at Pulaski Park with Har. And the trendy coffee shop on Division where I loved to write but was too intimidated to order a coffee because their menu board confused me, so I'd always get a stale scone instead. And the Target where Har threw tantrums if I didn't take him in. I missed all of it. And even though Chicago was on lockdown like everywhere else, in my mind, it wasn't. In my mind, we should have stayed.

One afternoon, as I lay in the small bedroom, blankets pulled up to my chin because it was an especially cold day, Har crept in and put his wet nose near my face.

"You need to come out here," he said softly. "You gotta see this."

"I don't want to, Har. I don't feel good." I turned to face the other wall, but he persisted.

"Just look. Please." He nudged me toward the window. "It's snowing!"

Heavy white snowflakes dropped from the sky, coating the budding trees that surrounded the cabin with their defiance to fall so late in the season. Even from the small bedroom window I could see it was one of those snows where you couldn't tell where the ground ended and the sky began; everything just blended into a cloud of white.

"When did this start?" I asked.

"All morning. I was just waiting for you to come see," Har said.

A late spring snow usually felt soul crushing, but for some reason, this one felt different. I'm not sure if it's because my soul was already crushed from everything the world was going through or simply because I was delirious from staying in the one small bedroom for hours on end, but it felt like my sign to rejoin the world.

"Wanna go on a walk?" I asked, and Har spun with excitement.

"I thought you'd never ask."

Without a car, or even another person in sight, we trudged down the middle of the road as snow built around us and stuck to both of our coats. Well, I guess only I trudged. Har actually ran circles around me, burying his face in drifts and springing from one snow pile to the next. He'd crouch low to the ground, paws outstretched in front of him, then go into zoomy mode as fast as he could.

"I am the fastest in the world, and you'll never catch me," Har shouted with a huge derpy smile on his face.

Gosh, he was happy.

When we reached the trees, their limbs drooped low to the ground from bearing the weight of such a heavy and unexpected storm. But the further Har and I got into them, the less I wanted to turn back. Tired old cottonwoods that had either fallen on their own or been cut down lay across our path, giving Har an opportunity to leap over them or army crawl under. Sometimes both. And sometimes he'd just hop on top so he could run back and forth and feel the thrill of the ground beneath him.

When we got to a clearing in the middle, I sat down and looked upward as the snow fell around me. I took a big breath of cold air and then lay down to feel lost in the whiteness like everything that surrounded me. Just like I knew he would, Har immediately came to my side to join in whatever it was that I was doing.

"I'm glad you're back," Har said.

"Me too."

We stayed like that for a while, lying in the quiet stillness that only a snow day can bring, staring at the silvery sky and the trees that hovered above us trying to meet it. Once the snow started to lighten and my hat and gloves had grown heavy, I thought we should probably head back to the cabin.

"What do you think, Har?" I brushed the damp snow off his back. "Is it time we get moving?" I mentioned that Har hated the rain, but snow? Snow was completely fine with him.

"I've just been waiting on you." He stood and shook.

"Why didn't you say something sooner?"

"Because I knew you weren't ready."

Two days later, we packed up our suitcases and left Nebraska headed west toward Colorado. I found a furnished rental in the neighborhood where we hoped to buy and decided we'd figure out the rest once we got there. A snowstorm didn't make our worries go away, but neither did hiding in a cabin. We needed to keep moving forward and stop waiting for reassurance that might not ever arrive. We blamed Covid for all the uncertainty unfolding around us, but I think if we looked hard enough, it had probably always been lurking there. Covid just happened to pull back the curtain and remind us all of it.

As we drove down the same wooded road that was a winter wonderland only two days ago, I noticed the trees that once bore the weight of the snow on their limbs had returned to normal. It wasn't their first storm and certainly wouldn't be their last, but they'd survived it and were once again standing tall.

a cervix of steel

You don't really know true love until you've had a child.

I was stewing on that line, and I don't know why. I had more important things to think about as I bounced around the small hospital room on a medicine ball, my attempt to stall the Foley bulb insertion, rather than focusing on all the stupid shit people said to me the moment my belly started to pop. More like, you don't really know what it's like to have a balloon inserted into your vagina until you've had a child. There I go again, getting into fictional fights in my mind with people I don't know. One of my favorite pastimes.

"Did you say something?" Chris asked.

Did I? Had I said those words out loud? I was feeling a bit delirious, as we'd been in the hospital waiting for me to go into labor for ten days now. Okay, technically only forty-eight hours, but when you have a team of people constantly checking your cervix the only way you can check a cervix (hint: it's through the vagina), well, time tends to stretch. *Vagina pun not intended, because I would never!*

"Um, I don't think so," I responded.

I was thinking about Har. When we dropped him off at his dog sitter's before heading to the hospital, I thought we'd be away from him for only a day or two (bless my sweet, naive heart).

"I'll be right back, Har," I said as I always did, but I really didn't know we'd be away this long. At the pace I was going, I might not go into labor for another week! Or possibly more?

The most important thing was that our baby's heart rate was strong. The second most important thing was that Chris had stopped narrating my contractions like a sports announcer whenever he saw one spike on the screen.

"Here comes a big one!" he'd declare with wide eyes and a fist to his mouth as if he were the one feeling his uterus contract and not me.

"Thank you, Chris. I'm aware."

"Yikes, that was one of the biggest yet." A line of sweat graced his brow, and I hoped it wasn't too rough on him.

After several days of heavy contractions (and being more than a week past my due date) my cervix had been served a buffet of items to try to soften it up. One nurse noted that I had "a cervix of steel," and before she even left the room, I had updated my résumé to reflect such a compliment:

> Taylor Wolfe @thedailytay
> Writer * Comedian * Influencer
> "A cervix of steel."

I'm kidding! I don't have a résumé. And several cervix checks later, I'd realize it wasn't exactly a good thing.

"Any dilation yet?" I asked hesitantly as a new nurse approached the position, making the same face they all did when given such a task. They'd scrunch their mouths together, squint their eyes, and look toward their forehead as if they were deciding what my cervix needed more of—salt or pepper?

"Not yet," the nurse said.

"Really?" I asked, completely deflated. "How can that be? Cervidil didn't do anything?"

Cervidil, the drug I was given the night before, contained some hormone that was meant to "relax my cervix." But apparently my uptight cervix didn't get the memo. And here I had slept so poorly because I was scared to move, fearful I would accidentally loosen up the string I was warned "could be pulled from my vagina." And then what would happen? Would my arms and legs suddenly shoot out to the side? Would an old circus tune start playing? I didn't know, and I didn't want to risk it. But I guess it didn't matter anyway. My cervix was apparently still clutching its pearls at the thought of what it was being asked to do. That bitch.

"I know it's disappointing, but you shouldn't worry," the nurse said reassuringly. "This is very common."

"But it feels like the baby is literally about to drop out of me," I whimpered. "It's felt like this for weeks." My cervix might have been unwilling to negotiate, but it seemed my vagina was ready to throw in the towel. It was done. I didn't have the heart to tell it that the hard part hadn't even begun.

The nurse patted my arm and spoke with me kindly and compassionately, as did every nurse and doctor I had the pleasure of meeting during my lengthy hospital stay, and she went on to tell me that it was "a new experience for my body, and it simply wasn't sure what to do yet." I appreciated her reassurance, but I also kept thinking, *Well, it figured out how to grow a baby.* Did my body forget to think through step two? Like what would need to happen after growing said baby? If so, typical. Very typical.

"Chris," I said with the heaviest of sighs, "I think it's time."

"For the Foley bulb?" he asked.

"Yes," I gulped. "It's time to bring in the balloon artist." I took one last dramatic bounce on the medicine ball and then returned it to its corner. *That'll do, pig. That'll do.*

I'd only just heard of the Foley bulb, but I was already terrified of it. From what I'd gathered, it was a catheter-like device that was inserted into your cervix, deflated at first, but once inside your womb, the balloon part was inflated with a saline solution and that was supposed to put pressure on your cervix and encourage dilation. I didn't know what any of that meant, but it scared the absolute shit out of me.

Here's the thing—I like balloons. I like them at a children's birthday party or in a balloon arch at a fancy baby shower. Or maybe it's February 1995 and you're at Walmart in Nebraska and the floral section is full of those huge clear balloons with teddy bears and chocolates inside of them. Man, those things really blew my mind. Putting a teddy bear in a balloon? Amazing! Putting a balloon in my womb? Not amazing. My personal motto has always been no balloons in my womb.

But I was about to break that motto because I was ready to meet our baby girl. I was ready to hold her in my arms and feel her skin next to mine. I wanted to gaze into her eyes and finally see the face I'd been dreaming about. I was ready for that piece of my heart to meet the other important piece—Harlow.

..

"I'm going to make the transition as easy on you as possible, Har," I promised him on our final walk before we left for the hospital. It was just the two of us. "It's going to be a big change at first, but the baby will fit right into our pack. I promise."

"Hmm, okay." Har eyed me suspiciously. "I'm less worried about the baby and more about what's going on here. Like, street or curb? Make a choice where you want to walk."

"I'm doing it on purpose. It's called curb walking." I was told it helped induce labor—one foot on the street, the other on the curb. (It didn't help.)

An older woman passed by and gave me a knowing glance. "When are you due?" she asked with a sympathetic head tilt.

"A week ago," I grumbled.

"The last days are so rough, but it will all be worth it," she said with a glimmer in her eye. "And a dog is a great trainer-baby, but you don't really know true love until you've had a child," she added.

I nodded robotically and offered up the best half-ass smile I could muster, and then Har and I continued on our way before I responded something I might regret. Later that night as I lay in bed, unable to sleep, thinking about all that was to come, my body and mind both equally throbbing in anticipation and fear, I stroked Har's velvet ears and gently reminded him that what that woman said was absolute bullshit.

"You know that. Right, bud?"

"Uh huh," he said sleepily.

"You've never been a 'trainer-baby' for us. Not ever. You're our Harlow. That's what you are."

He moaned his Harlow moan and inched a little closer to me, something not as easy to do lately with my bulging nine-month belly. "I know," he said.

It could have been the sight of our suitcases set out ready for the hospital, or maybe it was just my raging hormones and emotions, but Har seemed sad to me our last night together, and it tore me apart. Tears rolled down my hot swollen cheeks as I thought about all the changes on the horizon, and even though I was so excited to be a mom, I was scared to no longer only be Har's mom.

we become mountain folk

DENVER, COLORADO. APRIL 2O2O.

I will forever be convinced that the Colorado mountain water healed me. It healed me from my morning sickness, my pandemic depression, my migraines, even my road rage went away. Okay, the last part isn't true, but only because Denver has some of the most chaotic drivers I've ever witnessed in my life. But everything else? Gone! Were my previous pregnancy symptoms ultimately replaced by new ones because I'd quickly learn that each trimester brings with it a new bag of tricks? Yes, of course. But we'll get to that later.

With masks, gloves, and the fear of stopping absolutely anywhere but to get gas, we made the road trip from Fremont, Nebraska, to Denver, Colorado, all but wearing hazmat suits. But if we could have found some online, we probably would have ordered them. Before our drive, Chris's dad gave us large containers of sanitizer he'd purchased on the sanitizer black market, and my dad gave us a large bundle of toilet paper "just in case Denver didn't have any."

Moving during the height of a pandemic was about as close to living in a post-apocalyptic movie as I'd ever like to get, and I would not recommend it, unless of course you enjoy spraying your shoes and clothes with Lysol after pumping gas.

We were anxious to get to Denver for several reasons, but the most important was that I wanted to find an OB-GYN I felt comfortable with and who I'd see throughout my pregnancy.

We also needed to find a home, get to know Chris's new work territory, and figure out how to start this new chapter in our life. Most of our belongings were still in storage in Chicago, but luckily the furnished rental that I found online a day before we left Nebraska was actually better in person.

"Are you sure this isn't going to be like the yellow Chicago Victorian you found on Craigslist?" Chris joked as we pulled onto Lipan Street in Denver. "The one covered in mold and centipedes but you insisted was a 'great find' for Lincoln Park?"

"That was a decade ago, and it got us out of Topeka, so it wasn't all bad!" I responded, while also hoping and praying I could redeem myself ten years later. "And it *was* a good find! We were close to both Wrightwood Tap and Burwood Tap."

"And don't forget the smells," Har added. "I still have dreams about those rocks where I used to pee."

We drove up to a small navy blue home with white trim and a red front door that looked unlike anywhere we'd lived in Chicago. It had its own yard, its own tree, and even its own garbage bins. It was nearly seventy degrees when we finally stepped out of our car, and the sun hung high in the sky, which was also very unlike Chicago. There wasn't a gust of wind or hint of grayness in the air, only sunshine. The three of us stood in the front yard staring at the house, shielding our eyes from the pleasant weather as if we weren't sure what to make of it.

"The sun's intense out here," Chris noted.

"I feel like I'm already getting sunburnt," I responded. "But seriously, am I red?"

After we commented on the sunshine for longer than I'd like to admit, we walked inside and toured our new temporary home. Har ran straight toward the back door to check out his first backyard. It wasn't big—barely the size of our old living room, but it was a yard, and it was his own. And it even had its own squirrels, albeit we quickly learned Denver squirrels are an entirely different category of evil that make Chicago rats look like kittens, but I promised myself I wouldn't use this book as a revenge memoir against squirrels. (We'll save that for the next one.)

The first evening we spent sitting outside on our new patio under the glowing string lights, watching Har excessively roll around in grass that was his very own, we knew we'd made the right choice by getting to Denver.

"If you like this backyard, just wait until we take you on a hike in the mountains," Chris told Har.

"When do you think that will be?" I asked.

I wasn't quite sure if I was a hiker yet. I'd only been on a few short trails on vacations and spent the majority of the time clapping two sticks together to keep the bears away and complaining that my feet hurt. But if hiking made Har happy, I knew it would make me happy.

"I've heard the mountain towns don't like Denver people coming to them right now, especially Denver people who just moved from Chicago," Chris added. "So, I guess I don't know."

We didn't know because we still weren't sure what the official rules were in this new world we were living in. Were we allowed to go on hikes in the mountains? Or even just go on a walk in our new neighborhood? This was a time when all the public playgrounds were roped off with "closed due to outbreak" yellow tape, and businesses had signs in their windows that read, "If you've been out of the state, please don't come in." The Denver skate park, one of the most popular skate parks in the country, was covered in gravel to keep skaters away. If it seems weird that we weren't sure if we were allowed to hike or not, it's because we were living in a very weird time.

As the newbies in town, we wanted to be on our best behavior, so we decided to keep to our backyard for a while longer. Our small space of greenery became our office, grocery wipe-down area, favorite restaurant, outdoor gym (I'd do five minutes of prenatal yoga and call it a day), and even Chris's barbershop, until, God forbid, I almost "messed up" his beautiful dark hair. That might have been the lowest part of the pandemic for Chris, for us as a couple.

But even with the haircut fiasco and all the uncertainty about what we could and couldn't do, our first weeks spent in Denver were as good as I'd felt in a long time. I started getting up early again and even showering regularly. I blow-dried my hair for the first time since we left Chicago and ordered new makeup since my cosmetic bag had been mistakenly packed away with our furniture. The sweatpants I'd been wearing for six weeks were tucked away in exchange for loose-fitting jeans.

"Look at you all fancy," Chris remarked when I walked into the kitchen wearing both jeans *and* eyeliner.

"Who me?" I said coyly.

Little by little, I started to feel like a new (old) version of myself again.

The first time I decided it was safe to go on a Starbucks run (drive-through only, obviously) was a rush I'll never forget. Turning into a parking lot to be greeted by a line of other cars waiting to pay for overpriced coffee felt like freedom. I get a jolt just thinking about the joy I felt placing my latte order that day, choking over my words because it had been so long since I'd spoken with a menu board. It was the best latte and Puppuccino Har and I had ever tasted. He licked his whipped-cream-covered snout all the way home, both of us giggling like two manic children.

"That was such a delight!" Har declared.

"It really was!" I agreed. "I used to pretend Starbucks was too mainstream for me, but oh my God the way the foam crept out of the top of the lid before it even hit my mouth? What a thrill!"

"Same," Har agreed. "Literally same!"

We continued to go back to the Starbucks drive-through every Wednesday and sometimes Friday too if we were feeling crazy. It became the highlight of our week. The coffee trips emboldened me, and soon we started ordering takeout again. We had to wait outside with masks, at least six feet apart from the next customer until we were called inside to pick up our order, but it was still takeout. *We were living again! Kinda.*

"I think we should take Har on a hike this weekend," I suggested to Chris.

"You think it's time?" he asked, both hopeful and anxious at such a wild idea.

"I do. I saw on the news that the trails are open."

"Well then, let's do it!"

We set out the following Saturday on our first hike as Coloradans, or at least we hoped we looked that way with our brand-new REI hiking socks and boots, Patagonia trucker hats, and our backpacks stuffed with anything labeled "trail snacks" we'd just purchased at Whole Foods. As the city disappeared behind us and the mountains surrounded us on both sides, the three of us were giddy with excitement. We rolled down the windows so Har could let his tongue blow in the breeze and take in the fresh mountain air. Chris cranked Canned Heat's "Going Up the Country," simply because it was the song that was on, but it would quickly become our weekend anthem, the song that instantly brought all of us joy because we knew it meant adventure lay ahead. As three Midwestern kids, we'd only been able to experience the mountains on vacation and the occasional ski trip, but as the steep, winding roads begged us to go farther and farther, it started to feel like they were actually within our reach. Like it was finally real that we got to live here.

When we arrived at the trailhead and there wasn't a parking spot to be found, it felt even more real.

"So maybe we should leave earlier next time," Chris declared as the three of us hiked toward our hike.

"Uh yeah, I think I'm going to be exhausted before we even get to the start," I huffed.

"This is the most amazing park I've ever seen!" Har shouted as he pulled on his leash. "We actually get to go on a walk here?"

I nodded and reminded myself to stop complaining. "Hopefully a lot of walks, Har. But in the mountains, they're called hikes. You're a hiker now."

"I'm a hiker," he repeated with a proud new prance in his step.

Once we actually got on the trail and made our ascent up the mountain, aspen and pine trees gathered around us, and the road disappeared behind us with each step we took. The chatter of traffic, phones, and anxious thoughts were shut off in exchange for the chatter of birds, insects, and rushing water. Both Chris and I noted that the air smelled like a candle, because a candle was as close as we'd ever gotten to the scent of fresh pine and flowing mountain streams. Har pulled even harder on his harness, urging us to move faster. I'm not sure what he was looking for, but he knew it was something worth pulling toward.

"Any chance you can pick up the pace just a little bit?" Har whined when I wasn't walking up to his standards. We were always fast walkers in the city, but this wasn't the city.

"I'm sorry, Har. I'm just a little winded at the moment."

"Let's stop up here," Chris offered. "I could use a break too."

We thought we'd gotten used to the elevation since we'd been living in Denver for a few weeks, but our first hike told us we were wrong. After a five-minute incline, our faces looked like we'd just hiked a fourteener. Being pregnant and always out of breath anyway certainly didn't help. As a former child obstacle-course star, I was shocked at how out of shape I felt. I used to do one-handed push-ups for fun and shimmy up a rope that burned my hands just so I could tap the tambourine at the top. Now I could barely walk a few steps up a mountain without wheezing. All my Presidential Physical Fitness certificates might as well have been stripped from me.

"I can go a little farther," I panted.

"Are you sure?" Chris asked.

"No," I responded.

But Har persisted, making us walk a little longer until we found a good clearing where we could take our packs off and catch our breath. But before we could pull out our hiking snacks, Har found the one small patch of snow that hadn't melted, and he nose-dived across it, skidding as far as he could with his face buried in it until he decided to get up and go back the other way. But this time, he rolled over to give his back a good snow scratch.

"What the heck is he doing?" Chris asked with a chuckle as he filled Har's water bowl.

I watched and laughed. "I think he's having fun." Back and forth Har went. Sometimes his legs were in the air, sometimes only his backside. I had to grab my phone and record him because his joy was so palpable, I wanted to keep it forever. "You having a good time, buddy?" I said as my phone shook from laughter.

"The best time ever!" he shouted as he slid across the snow once more for good measure.

After the patch of snow had turned to complete slush thanks to Har, we rested in a dry spot and broke out our hiking snacks. I hadn't eaten trail mix since YMCA summer camp in the nineties, but I quickly learned anything tasted good on a hike. Peanuts mixed with raisins, M&Ms, more mysterious dry fruit, and a little dirt? Absolutely! Another handful, please.

"This mix is hitting the spot," Chris said as he jumped on a boulder that overlooked the stream below.

"I was literally thinking the same thing," I mumbled as I dropped another sweaty M&M into my mouth.

I watched as Chris stood on the boulder and slowly nodded his head. "Man, I would have loved this as a kid," he said with a youthful flicker in his eye.

Har leapt to his side and looked back at me and smiled. "I think we found it," he whispered.

Found what? I wondered as I looked around. I saw enormous boulders sprawled at the base of trees like nature's ottomans and fallen logs that had become bridges for crossing creeks that led to waterfalls. The trees canopied above us like a giant bedsheet draped across dining room chairs, and I remembered the feeling I had as a child when I built forts in our kitchen and pretended it was a magic forest, or when I sat on the curved tree that hung over the drainage gulch behind our house and imagined it was a mountain stream below me. I saw Chris as a young boy playing in the woods by his cabin, and I realized it felt like we'd found the place we'd always been searching for as children, and I guess as adults too.

"How'd you know this is what we were looking for, Har?" I asked.

He jumped from the boulder and came back to my side. "How did you not?"

Chris and Harlow became obsessed with hiking after they got a taste of that freedom. A weekend not spent in the mountains frolicking in stream water, sharing granola on a boulder, and discovering a new alpine lake nestled among peaks was a weekend wasted, in their eyes. As long as I was promised a hearty lunch after at a nearby mountain grill, I was all in too. I loved nothing more than to see the look on Har's face when we said, "Ready to go on an adventure, Har?" He'd spin in circles and bark with excitement as we grabbed his leash and packed treats in his green hiking vest.

"Let's go, let's go, let's go!" he'd shout, begging to get into the car long before it was time to leave.

The early arthritis the vet detected in Chicago seemed to have all but gone away. I wanted to confirm it with a new vet in Denver, but because of Covid, I couldn't find a single veterinarian that was taking new patients. The first appointment I was able to book wasn't until late November, which was nearly six months away. It made me uneasy to wait that long. Back in Chicago, I took Har to the vet nearly every other month—no lump or limp was too small or insignificant. Harlow was getting older, but he was in the best shape of his life, thanks to our new Denver lifestyle. In the end, Chris and I decided to wait until November. Har seemed so healthy.

just a small bump

"When did you say Har's vet appointment is?" Chris asked as I boiled pasta in the mountain home we'd rented for the weekend with friends as a last-minute "babymoon."

There was a time when I dreamed of myself on a babymoon on a white-sand beach, my belly popping out of a cute polka-dot bikini, fruity drink in hand. Strangers would comment, "Oh, those two must be on a babymoon," and I'd smile coyly and nod, then Chris and I would continue our romantic walk on the beach, hand in hand, soaking up our last alone time before baby arrived. In this dream, I was a very happy and relaxed pregnant woman, with luscious hair and glowing skin, and I said things like, "This pregnancy has flown by" and "I think I'm going to miss my bump." *Ha ha.* I love the person I pretend to be in my head. I also love that she and pretend-Chris hold hands in public. I bet they never fight about who ate the last of the cheddar Ruffles either.

Covid canceled any plans we had for a potential island babymoon, which I feared it might, but I still held out hope until the end. Mostly because we all held out hope until the end, until we realized there probably wasn't going to be one.

"His appointment is next month. Why?" I glanced at Har, who was sound asleep on the couch, feet in the air and snoring loudly, exhausted from a ten-mile hike that I bowed out of around mile four thanks to being thirty-five weeks pregnant.

"He's got a weird bump above his eye that I just noticed."

"Oh?" Anytime Chris "noticed" something on Harlow, my heart beat a little faster. *I* was the one who noticed every new freckle, skin tag, or bump. Chris was the one who talked me back from the ledge and reminded me it was usually only a freckle, skin tag, or bump.

"Do you think he ran into something on the hike today?" There was no way I would have missed a new bump on him; I was always on alert. "Like maybe when he was fishing in the creek? He might have bumped his face on a rock or something."

Since moving to Colorado, Har had taken up several new hobbies, and fishing was one of them. He loved to wade in mountain creeks and lakes and use his pointing skills to seek out any movement under the surface. The moment he saw something, he dove for it face-first. I like to think Har imagined himself as an expert hunter or perhaps a ferocious grizzly bear going after its prey. In reality, he looked more like a toddler bobbing for apples and had caught absolutely nothing, but God love him, he tried.

"Yeah, it kinda looks like he hit it on something." Chris examined Har's face closer. "I don't think it's anything to be too concerned about right now. We just need to make sure the vet looks at it next month if it's still around."

"Okay," I muttered and tried to go back to caring about the pasta.

I checked all Har's bumps. This had to be something minor. Well, I checked all his stomach bumps, and the ones on his chest, and his legs, and hips. *Gosh, he'd gotten so lumpy in his senior years.* But had I checked his head? He'd never had one there before.

I walked over toward Har and put my face in his as I did a million times a day, every day. "Did you hit your head today, bud?"

Just like Chris said, there was a small bump above Har's left eye near what I called his "eyebrow bone." Or was the bump his eyebrow bone? It was so minor that I couldn't tell.

Har looked at me with his post-hike drowsy eyes. "I'm sleeping," he said with a groan and turned away.

"Okay, but I'm making pasta. It's your favorite red sauce."

"I'm up." He sprang from the couch and ran toward the kitchen. Har loved pasta. And any sauce was his favorite sauce.

He was fine. It was just a small bump.

Our friends who traveled with us to Steamboat had a dog—a pointer named Archie—for Har to be competitive with on hikes and a baby around six months for me to learn how to be around a baby. We'll call my friend Kim, and we'll call her baby Roy, because those are their names. I had a notebook full of questions I needed to ask Kim before I had a baby in a month because I knew if anyone would give it to me straight, it would be her.

What is a butt spatula? What is a birth plan? Do I need a birth plan? Didn't someone already establish how this birth thing goes a long time ago? What goes in the top drawer of a changing table? A butt spatula? What does a newborn sleep in? Where does a newborn sleep? How bad did the epidural hurt? Does everyone poop while giving birth? Does anyone care? What's it like having a team of people stare into your vagina? Is the ring of fire real?

"And are you still happy you did it?" I asked with all sincerity.

"Did what?" Kim responded while adjusting the breast pump on her nipples that I tried not to stare at because I hadn't even gotten to my breastfeeding questions yet.

"Had a baby, I mean. Like, you still recommend it?"

Kim scrunched her face to one side and tapped her lip, as she always did when she was trying to decide if I was being sarcastic or not.

"Do I recommend being a mom?" she asked, and I nodded.

The night before, Chris and I listened from the comfort of our quiet bedroom as Roy screamed after a long day of travel. We could hear Kim and her husband walking back and forth trying to soothe him—filling up bottles, playing lullabies, doing whatever it is a parent does to get their child to fall asleep in a new place. It felt like the screaming went on forever, but it was probably only a couple of minutes before I got up and shut our door and turned our sound machine up even louder.

"Is this terrible of us?" I whispered to Chris.

"No," he responded, "our time is coming." And we both fell into a deep blissful sleep, as one does when they know they're about to get eight to nine hours of uninterrupted rest and rise at their leisure.

After Kim's long road trip with Roy, followed by a sleepless night, I wanted to know. "I guess I'm just wondering if motherhood is everything you hoped it would be."

"Tay," she said as she released the sucking tubes from her nipples and wiped dribble from Roy's face all in one motion, "it's even better."

We'd been with Kim's family for almost two days, and I'd hesitantly held Roy only twice. The second time, I thrust him into Chris's arms pretending I wanted to see Chris with a baby, but the truth was, I was still nervous to see myself with a baby.

"That's good to hear, because all of that doesn't look easy." I gestured to the small black bag that contained all her pumping parts. "You carry a booby briefcase with you everywhere now." She used to carry a beer bong.

"Is it easy? God, no. But it's absolutely worth it. There's not a better sound in the world than when you hear your baby laugh. I'd do literally anything to make Roy giggle."

I thought about all the times Har and I had played hide-and-seek, when I'd crouch behind the bathroom door, and the moment I'd hear his nails clicking down the hallway, I'd jump out and scream, "Boo! You found me, Har, you found me," and then we'd laugh and laugh and immediately do it again. I bet a baby would like our hide-

and-seek game. Maybe not at first, obviously, but I'm sure once she got a little older and learned better places to hide, she'd have a lot of fun with us.

After we finished our pasta and the nonpregnant adults in the room poured a few cocktails, I excused myself to go lie with Har and rub some wax on his paw pads to relieve any pain from his hike.

"How are your paws, bud?" I asked as I massaged the wax into the areas I knew tended to crack.

Har looked at me and stretched. "Today was a good day," he replied with pasta sauce still lining his lips, which I quickly wiped before he spread it all over the bed like he did on every white rug at home. "We climbed over rocks and saw waterfalls, and Archie tried to go faster than me, but he couldn't because I'm the fastest."

"You are the fastest." I curled in next to him and pressed my face to his forehead and held it there for a second longer. No matter where we were, Har always smelled like home to me. "I'm sorry I had to stop the hike early. My back was killing me, and Kim had to get Roy home for a nap. What do you think of Roy, by the way?"

"The guy with the beard? Super nice."

"No, that's Roy's dad, Har. I mean the baby—the little human who's been hanging around all weekend."

"Oh, that thing." Har sighed. "Little too noisy for my liking."

"Uh huh," I mumbled, not adding how ironic it was for him to comment on Roy's noise considering whenever too much attention was paid to Roy and not Har, Har basically put on his tap shoes, grabbed his cane, and started singing show tunes to make sure we knew where to direct our focus.

"We're going to have a baby with us all the time soon," I said softly as I stroked his warm ears.

"Uh huh," he said.

"She'll be noisy like Roy. And I'm going to have to hold her a lot and be with her a lot, but you'll be with us too. We'll still do everything together. Baby girl will just be along as well."

Har had either fallen asleep or was pretending to sleep. Sometimes he'd snore with his eyes open, and I'd have to remind him that's not how snoring works, but this time, his eyes were shut and his breathing was steady. I studied the small bump above his eye and decided I'd call the vet on Monday and see if I could get him in earlier.

We had celebrated Har's tenth birthday the month before, and I made him promise me we'd get at least ten more years together. He'd be the lumpiest, whitest-faced vizsla ever, but I wouldn't care. He was my boy.

"Happy birthday to you! Happy birthday to you! Happy birthday to Harlow Har Carl Wolfe Hillis. Happy birthday to you!" we sang as we took Har on a pontoon boat ride around Grand Lake.

"Promise me ten more birthdays," I whispered. "I need my best friend around forever, okay?"

Har stood next to me with his ears flapping in the wind before he lay down and rested his head on my belly. "Forever and ever," he agreed.

My Birth Plan

Have baby.

white butterflies and slithering snakes

After being Denver residents for only a couple of weeks, Chris and I drove to my first appointment at Rocky Mountain OB-GYN. I tried not to think about the dream I'd had the night before about snakes slithering out of the cabinets in our new rental house. I didn't know the meaning of snakes in a dream, but I was certain it couldn't be good. So certain in fact, I refused to Google it, too fearful what I might find. There was a time I wasn't so crazy about dreams and signs and stray feathers I found on walks, but thanks to my miscarriage, that time had long since passed. Everything was a sign to me now, and usually a bad one because those are the games my mind likes to play on me when I'm feeling vulnerable. (Remember earlier when I said you can't just look for bad signs? Yeah, I don't always follow my own advice. But you definitely should!)

Right after I found out about my partial molar and the possibility of cancer in my uterus, a white butterfly followed Harlow and me home for three blocks, and I was sure it was the baby I'd lost. I took to the internet to find out the meaning of such a rare encounter (*a generic butterfly sighting during summer? what are the chances?!*), and even though every site I found said butterflies are a sign of transformation, *renewal and rebirth*, and all that positive fluffy stuff one wants to read when Googling "what is the meaning of . . . ," I happened to find one more site fifty pages down the Google list where no one looks, probably created by an angry teenager hoping to scare an unhinged woman like myself, that said white butterflies are a sign of "bad things to come." And that was all it took. I spiraled. I spent the rest of the night in an anxiety hole, wrapped in a blanket on our rooftop, wondering how soon it was until I died from cancer in my uterus.

When Chris got home and asked what was wrong, I dryly responded, "A white butterfly followed me and Har on our walk, and at first I thought it was our baby, but now I think it was a warning sign that cancer is growing in my uterus and I'm a goner."

"Okay," he said calmly, "do you want some wine?"

"Probably."

"Are you sure it wasn't a moth?"

I knew how insane I sounded, but I also knew how hard it was to rationalize with my crazy thoughts once they got their foot in the door and could sense I was teetering near the edge. Sometimes it felt easier to just let them push me off and see where I fell, rather than grabbing the hand of the one sane thought meekly trying to pull me back.

But not today. I'd worked so hard to step away from the ledge the past few weeks, and I didn't want to go back to keeping my head down, too fearful to look around in case I saw another white butterfly.

"I'm really scared for this appointment," I blurted. Sometimes it was annoying being married to someone so damn logical, but sometimes Chris's reasoning was exactly what I needed. "This is as far as we got last time, and it's all I can think about. What if I've already miscarried and I don't know it and we're going to have to hear those awful words spoken out loud again? I don't want to do that all over again. I can't. I won't." I tried not to cry, but I failed.

"I know, but this isn't last time," Chris said. "It's going to be okay."

"How do you know?"

"I just do, Tay. Everything will be okay."

As we exited onto Colorado Boulevard, I chose to believe Chris because I figured if I could believe a creepy stalker butterfly I didn't know, I could believe my husband.

We rode the elevator in silence with masks on our faces and sanitizer coating our hands. The receptionist instructed us to sit in the chairs covered with protective paper and offered us more sanitizer, which we gladly took because even though things were improving with the pandemic, spotting sanitizer in public was still akin to spotting a Princess Di Beanie Baby in the late '90s. We'd barely sat down on the crunchy paper before my name was called.

"Ready?" Chris asked as he stood.

"Yeah." I sighed and followed the nurse down the hallway.

As she recorded my weight and height, I remembered the person I was nearly a year ago at this time. I remembered the jokes I made about "the baby already costing us" when we paid for garage parking at our genetics appointment in downtown Chicago, the way I complained about stupid baby product names, and the heartbeat I heard—the one I didn't know to appreciate. But I mostly remembered the one I didn't hear. And for the first time that I could recall, I no longer despised that person I was. I had sympathy for her. She simply had no idea.

I took one last hopeful breath and stepped into the ultrasound room.

As the nurse rolled her wand over my uterus, I told myself that just like last time, the heartbeat might not be there. And just like last time, I would have to stand up and walk out there and figure out what to do next. And as I blinked away tears and prepared myself for the worst when it felt like an eternity of time had passed without hearing the sound I so desperately needed to hear, the nurse suddenly said, "There it is!"

Ba bump ba bump ba bump. It was fast and it was strong and it was there.

"Do you hear it? It sounds great," she said.

Chris grabbed my hand, and we both smiled and looked at each other in the way a couple does when the nods come easier than the words, because you've been in the room when you don't hear the *ba bump ba bump ba bump*, and the gratitude you feel for getting to be on the other side of it this time quite literally takes your breath away.

The nurse held it there for a while longer, allowing us to listen for as long as we wanted.

"You were right," I whispered to Chris, but I don't think he heard me because when I looked up, I saw him staring at the screen, mesmerized by the heartbeat he finally got to hear.

A few days later, the Rocky Mountain OB-GYN number appeared on my phone to give us test results, and I had to remind myself it was okay to answer; this time was different. The woman on the other end told us that all our tests came back normal, and then she asked if I wanted to find out the sex of our child. Neither Chris nor I cared what we were having as long as it had a healthy heartbeat, so he'd given me the green light to find out and then pass the news on to him.

"Um yes, I'd love to know," I stammered.

"Well, congratulations," she said in the most joyful voice I've ever heard. "You're having a little girl."

All I prayed for was a healthy baby. But every night when I spoke to that healthy baby I prayed for, I called her my baby Birdie because I just knew she was a girl. I ran inside to tell Chris, and when I reached the back door, a white butterfly fluttered across it. It stopped me in my tracks until I looked around and realized there were several flying in and out of the bushes near our fence line. I decided right then and there those white butterflies were a good sign, because I was the one who got to decide what signs meant in my life. And I wanted good signs flying all over, not bad ones.

On our evening walk, we passed a house two blocks from our rental that was listed for sale. It had been put on the market and taken back off more than a few times now. We knew because we walked by it daily since all we did during Covid was go on walks.

"Maybe we should just put in a low offer on this one and see what happens," Chris casually suggested as we paused in front of it.

The house was nothing like what I originally envisioned buying. It was tall and modern and painted in colors I didn't love. It wasn't the quaint brick Denver bungalow I once had in my mind. But we'd been living out of suitcases since we left Chicago, and my only "must-haves" as of now were a roof and walls.

"Please don't mess with me," I begged. "You know how bad I want to get settled."

"I just don't know if it's a great time to buy yet," Chris said as he pulled a flyer from the for-sale sign in the yard.

"Then let's commit to renting long-term because I can't wait much longer. Once that nesting urge officially kicks in, it won't be good for anyone if we're somewhere I can't start decorating. I could turn into a real nightmare, you know."

"You? Never."

Other than daydreaming about decorating a nursery, I also longed for all the little rituals that make a homebody like myself feel complete. I missed planting myself in the sunken part of our couch with Har on my legs every morning, our favorite furry T.J.Maxx blanket draped over us, my chipped floral coffee mug in hand. I missed the overpriced Anthropologie candles I burned *only* for special occasions and my vases that I filled with Trader Joe's flowers that I inevitably always cut too short or too long or screwed up somehow. I knew these were all things I could do in our week-to-week rental, but it wasn't the same. I wanted to start settling into a place I knew we'd stay for a while. I wanted the feeling of permanence, the feeling of a home.

With gloves on our hands, protective booties on our feet, and masks on our faces, we toured the tall modern house the following day. We were just grateful we could step inside since in-person showings had been put on hold for the past three weeks. The interior matched the exterior with a modern layout, bland fixtures, and more weird paint.

"I love it!" I exclaimed. It was a house, and it was available.

"Are you sure?" Chris asked. "It's not really what we wanted."

"We can make it what we want. Trust me on this."

That evening, we put in an offer below the asking price, and the seller accepted it. *Holy shit! They accepted it!* Never in a million years did we expect to land a house in the Denver market for under the asking price. Chris and I celebrated and then immediately panicked, as one does when buying a home. *Holy shit. They accepted it.*

We were able to expedite the moving and closing process rather quickly and were handed the keys to our new front door only a few weeks later. Chris, Har, and I gathered on our rooftop to film an impromptu reveal party for our friends and family to let them know we were having a girl. I purchased cupcakes from Super Saver and injected them with pink frosting, and like any craft or baking activity I attempted, they looked terrible.

"What happened to those cupcakes?" Chris-the-perfectionist asked. "Did you mean to destroy them like that?"

"Yes, Chris, I did."

"Well, I think they look great!" Har objected.

Thank you, Har.

Anyway, they were not destroyed, *Chris.* The cupcakes were just a little lopsided and sloppy from where I tried to shoot frosting into them using a generic squeeze bottle that I'd also just purchased at Super Saver.

"Whatever. They'll get the job done." My famous last words.

My intent was for Har to take a bite of a cupcake, show the frosting color on the inside, and *boom*, the reveal was done. No exploding golf balls or fireworks or forest fires. Just a good old-fashioned bite-into-a-cupcake reveal.

"Okay, Har, are you ready?" I smiled into the camera as Chris filmed. "Take a bite and show everyone what we're having."

"I'm ready!" Har shouted, and in one swift motion, he swallowed the entire cupcake.

Harlow ate our reveal. And then he ate the second one we attempted as well.

the full moon

For all the lumps and bumps on Har that I obsessively worried about, I chose not to worry too much about the one above his eye. It didn't seem to bother him or grow in size, so when we got back from our babymoon in Steamboat and I wasn't able to move up his appointment, I didn't try to look for another. What was four more weeks of waiting? *Really, though, what was it? I still often wonder.*

We had a baby coming soon, and I was certain she'd be early.

"You know she probably won't be early," my mom told me. "Our bodies just don't go into labor easily. You were a week late, and I had to be induced."

Like most of the phone conversations I had with my mom, I chose to listen to what I wanted to hear and ignore what I didn't. I'd read that a full moon can send women into labor, and we had one approaching—on Halloween, no less! My water was going to break on October 31. I just knew it.

Our nursery furniture was delivered the week before, the wallpaper I had attempted to hang was taken down and rehung by a professional, and the bookshelf was filling up with nursery stories and precious wooden toys I knew probably weren't that fun to play with (*but were so pretty to look at!*). So, whatever. I could worry about the fun part in a year. Or six months? When did babies start playing? I'd look it up later. Everything was coming together just perfectly! To keep my mind off the fact that my water would be breaking soon, I did my first load of baby laundry.

I read each new clothing tag ever so carefully. Heaven forbid I put something in the washing machine that was labeled "hand wash only." *Heaven forbid? When did I start saying phrases like my Midwestern Baptist grandmother? The baby warsh was really getting to me.* I held each onesie, blanket, and footie pajama in front of me to examine its preciousness before I dropped it in our washer. Doing laundry had never been so adorable! *Why do so many moms complain about it?* I wondered as I completed my first-ever wash of tiny clothes and immediately hung them to dry on the drying rack that had never been used before. *Baby laundry was fun and cute and oh so novel.* I'd make sure I never tired of it.

Somewhere in between hanging onesies on beautiful pink felt baby hangers and making more adorable false promises I'd never be able to keep, I felt a sharp pain in my vagina that stopped me in my pretentious little tracks. I looked to my feet expecting to see water but also hoping I had time to move to our wood floor because I really didn't want to ruin the new nursery rug.

But there wasn't a drop of body water anywhere on the rug, obviously. For starters, I had pants on, and that's just not how pants work. Surely I would have felt some wetness before just seeing a puddle at my feet. I shook my head and laughed a little. Duh, what was I thinking? And then ZAP! I felt the sharp pain again. It stung so intensely goose bumps appeared on my arms and legs, and I knew immediately what it must be. The urban legend was true! For the past nine months, my body had thrown more weird things my way than I would have ever expected—a tailbone that never stopped throbbing, darkened nipples (actually, darkened everything), bleeding gums, mucus that never stopped flowing down my throat, an insatiable appetite, but also feeling sickly full after eating two crackers. The list goes on, but I'll stop here because I don't want to give away all the magic. And now I had a new one to add to the list—lightning crotch! Which coincidentally was also the name printed on the back of my Powder Puff sweatshirt in high school.

"Chris, you'll never guess what's happening." I crept down the stairs with a look of shock on my face *and . . . err . . . vagina.*

"What?" He barely glanced away from the TV and whatever college football team was still playing in October 2020.

"My crotch feels like it's being electrocuted."

"Is that normal?"

I nodded. "I think it's lightning crotch."

He stared.

"So, remember when you were a little kid and you'd put your dog's shock collar on and then your brother would shock you a little just to see how it felt?" I asked Chris, really hoping he could relate.

"No, I never did that." Classic Chris, always subtly reminding me how much classier his childhood was than mine.

"Well, fine. It basically feels like our baby is holding a little remote inside of me, and whenever she feels like it, she presses a button, and shock waves are sent down my vagina."

"That's crazy!"

"I know!"

"You really used to wear your dog's shock collar?"

"I thought you were talking about my lightning crotch, but no, not really. We only did that a couple of times."

"What do you think it means?"

"Probably that I shouldn't have had access to a dog shock collar. See what kids used to do without screen time?"

"I meant about the pain you're feeling. Should you call your doctor?"

I sighed heavily. "Oh that. Probably not."

Of course, I'd already Googled my symptoms, and according to

Dr. Google, lightning crotch is often a sign labor is close but not close enough. I still had a few more laps to go while getting shocked, apparently. *Sonofabitch.*

Later that evening, Har and I curled up on the couch together, and I grimaced and squirmed as the baby not only kicked my ribs, but now also zapped me every so often. I resolved to the fact I probably wasn't going into labor tonight, maybe not the next day either, and I sighed with defeat.

"What's wrong?" Har asked as he laid his head on my chest and draped his paw across my protruding belly.

"I'm just tired of being so uncomfortable and in pain." I was feeling whiny and frustrated, as one does during the last nine hundred weeks of pregnancy.

"I'm sorry you're hurting." Har snuggled in even closer, burying his head next to my cheek. "Maybe we should take more naps. Those are so nice."

Har loved the pregnancy naps. All I had to say was "Ready to rest?" and we'd scurry up the stairs together and take a delightful afternoon snooze, snuggled together on the same pregnancy pillow. Toward the end of my third trimester, Har's naps started to last even longer than mine. I'd get up and leave him in bed. I assumed all the hiking must be tiring him out.

With Har's face so close to mine and his paw resting delicately on my nine-month belly, I grabbed my phone and snapped a photo of the two of us. I didn't know how much longer it would be just him and me cuddling on the couch. Pretty soon there would be a third body between us.

It's such a sweet photo, I thought.

Things I Tried to Induce Labor

Making the "magic eggplant parmesan" dish shared all over the internet. *It did not work.*

Drinking gallons of raspberry leaf tea. *Also did not work.*

Eating pounds of dates and prunes. One of the two is supposed to soften your cervix, but I couldn't remember which one, so I doubled down and ate both. *Neither worked.*

Curb walking. *Nope.*

Binge eating pineapple. *Again, no.*

Taking lots of hot baths. *(I couldn't fit in our tub, and my belly got cold.)*

Eating spicy food. *Only more farts, which were already in abundance, so this only did more harm than good.*

Lunges. *Stupid.*

Squats. *Also stupid.*

Sitting in the butterfly pose. *The most stupid.*

Crying. *Helped a little.*

Crying and complaining. *Helped a lot!*

full-blown scary mode

DENVER, COLORADO. NOVEMBER 2020.

I hated that I couldn't take Har to his vet appointment. When I set it up nearly six months earlier, I had no idea that Birdie would only be about ten days old when it arrived. I had no idea what life would be like planning every single errand, task, bathroom break, and breath around a newborn.

"He's going to freak out," I warned Chris. "He hates the vet."

"I know—"

"You don't know!" I interrupted, my postpartum emotions mixed with exhaustion and fear, leaving me in full-blown scary mode. "You haven't taken him in a while, and he's gotten so much worse. He trembles and pants and it's just heartbreaking and it's going to be extra bad right now since he's already on edge with Birdie home. He's going to think we're leaving him there forever." I knew I was overreacting, but I also knew I couldn't control it.

Har was terrified of the vet's office, and he needed me to be with him, but I couldn't. I couldn't because Birdie needed me now too.

She still wasn't back to her birth weight, and her pediatrician was "starting to get concerned." It wasn't until three days previous at her one-week appointment, when Chris and I sat in a doctor's office as very new parents and were told there were health concerns about our new baby girl, that I realized everything I'd thought I'd known about fear was wrong. I knew parts of fear, but I didn't know its ugliest face and what it could do to my insides in only a matter of seconds and with just a few words, until it had to do with our child.

"You think something might be wrong? I don't understand. What am I doing wrong?" How was I already failing at being a mom only one week in?

The physician's assistant told us that if Birdie was nursing as much as I said she was, as well as soiling diapers and sleeping fairly well, then she should be gaining more weight. So why wasn't she?

"I don't know. I guess I thought she was. I nurse her whenever she cries or wakes up, and I don't stop until she pulls away and has that little milk-drunk smile on her face. I even took a photo of it the other day. I can show you!" I dug through my diaper bag, frantic to find my phone to show the photo, frantic to prove I fed Birdie until she was full, frantic to prove I wasn't a bad mom.

"Would switching to bottles help so we could know exactly how much she's drinking?" Chris asked while I tore my bag apart.

"My phone's not in here. I must have left it at home," I said to no one. "But I feed her all the time," I whispered, "or at least that's what it feels like." My throat was hoarse from not sleeping, and my nipples were raw from nursing a baby who apparently wasn't taking in what I thought I was giving.

The physician's assistant told us that we could try a bottle, but that could lead to nipple confusion and there's a chance Birdie wouldn't go back to breastfeeding. If breastfeeding was important to us, she advised we give it a try for another day or two before we offered the bottle.

"I really don't care how she's fed. I just want her fed," I said meekly, feeling as low as one can at the thought I was unknowingly starving my own baby.

In nearly the same breath that the PA told us to wait a day or two before switching to bottles, she also said she was making us an appointment at Children's Hospital to run some tests on Birdie's heart. She "didn't want to alarm us," but they were taking Birdie's weight "very seriously." *Too fucking late. We were alarmed.* Chris and I just sat there frozen in fear, nodding our heads like we thought we were supposed to do, too fearful to question the bottle option any further.

I was also instructed to wake Birdie at least every two hours in the night to make sure she was constantly eating. She had started to sleep for longer stretches, sometimes three to four hours. One night it was even seven hours, and let me tell you, there's not a more confusing/terrifying/gratifying feeling than waking up as new parents and seeing sunlight when you expect to see moonlight. The first time it happened, Chris and I both shot up in bed like the parents on *Home Alone* and ran to Birdie's bassinet to make sure she was still breathing. When we saw she was fine (and even still sound asleep), we danced like we'd just won the sleep lottery. But there would be no more dancing for a while—now I *had* to wake her.

We drove home in silence. I leaned my head against the cold car window and longed to disappear completely into the blackness that had become the day. My anxiety hole was calling my name, and I wanted so badly to drop in it for a day or two, just until I found the courage and energy to face what I had to face. But I knew I couldn't because I had to breastfeed every two hours.

"I thought she was eating, Chris," I said quietly. "I didn't know."

"Neither of us did," he responded, "but now we do, and we're going to do something about it. Are you okay trying bottles *and* breastfeeding?"

"Of course I am." I felt relief at simply the mention of it.

"Then let's double down and do both. The more I think about it, I don't know why we'd wait to try a bottle when we know Birdie isn't getting enough food right now."

"I agree," I said as I sunk lower into my seat knowing *I* was the reason she wasn't getting enough.

"We just need to know how much she's really drinking, and bottles will tell us that." Chris shook his head and scowled, like he was having a divisive argument in his head but wouldn't voice it because that wouldn't be a Chris thing to do. "Fuck what that PA said."

I was wrong. He voiced it.

"Yes! Fuck her!" I shouted. "Why would she advise us to wait but also send us to Children's for a heart scan? It makes no sense!"

"None at all."

We decided to take control of the situation and do what we knew was best for our daughter. We decided to act like parents.

I fed Birdie with the bottle every two hours with breastmilk I'd collected from my "letdown," i.e., the constant drip that came out of one nipple while I was feeding Birdie on the other. For some new mothers, their milk never arrives after they give birth; others may get a lower supply of milk; and then there's people like myself whose boobs grow like a Chia Pet in the night a few days after giving birth, and their breasts are overflowing with milk. I had so much milk our freezer was packed with bags of it, which made Birdie's weight issue all the more confusing. *And dare I say shameful*. I had enough milk to feed a litter, and yet I couldn't feed my one and only.

After I gave Birdie a bottle, I'd breastfeed her as well to try and avoid nipple confusion. Then I'd open up my breastfeeding app on my phone, record how much she ate, how long she ate, and on which nipple she ate. Afterward, I recorded her soiled diapers. It was exhausting doing all this, both mentally and physically, but it was the only thing I could do to help ease the fear until we had her Children's Hospital appointment and knew for sure what was going on, which happened to be scheduled only a couple of days after Har's appointment.

"Har is going to be fine, Tay. I'll make sure of it," Chris promised.

"I just really hate that I can't take him," I said as I washed bottles and pump pieces. "He gets so scared once he realizes where he is."

"I'll get him as calm as I can before I let them know we're there. They said I have to call and then a tech will come out. I can't even walk him in because of their new Covid rules."

"I know." But that certainly didn't make it any better.

"Har, let's go!" Chris called into his office, the spot where Har had been choosing to nap since we brought Birdie home, rather than on the couch in the living room like he always did. I coaxed him out as often as I could, but I also knew Har preferred quiet and calm over Birdie crying, so sometimes I had to let him be. At the sound of Chris's voice, he came barreling into the living room.

"Wanna go?" Chris asked with a leash in hand, and Har jumped up and down.

"Yes, please!" he responded.

"I'll see you in a bit, Har. You'll be right back!" I hugged him and willed the separation I feared had built up between us in the last week to go away. "I love you, buddy."

Once they left, it was the first time I'd been alone with Birdie, which was also terrifying. My mom was at our house when we got home from the hospital, and after she left, Chris's family came to help, so up until now, it had never been only Birdie and me at our house together. Was I allowed to be alone with a baby? *Yes, I'm the mom!* I had to remind myself. But then again, I'd already screwed up the most basic need of simply making sure Birdie was fed. What else could I get wrong?

When I saw her little arms stretch into the air and her eyes start to slowly open, I picked her up and swayed back and forth. "It's just you and me for a few hours, Birdie girl," I said softly.

"I'm so sorry I've failed you already. I can't stand the thought that I haven't been giving you enough." She looked at me with big curious eyes like she was really listening, or maybe like she was really wanting my apology, so I continued. "I'll do better. I promise. I'm just still learning how to do this mom thing, and I know that's not an excuse. I should know, but I don't. And I'm just so sorry."

Birdie gazed up at me and made all the sounds a newborn makes, the little grunts and moans that are adorable and also somewhat similar to the sounds of an aging Yorkie, and then she smiled. I know some people say the early smiles are only gas, but she smiled so big and so sincerely, I knew she understood. And maybe even forgave me. Then Birdie's entire body rumbled with an earthquake of a fart. It was something you'd expect to hear come from an eighty-five-year-old man sleeping in a stained recliner after a second helping of Thanksgiving dinner rather than a precious little newborn, but I knew it was simply a coincidence. The smile and the rumble were not related in any such way.

As I rocked and fed Birdie her bottle, I gently chanted, "Chug, chug, chug," as Chris and I had been doing since we'd started doubling down on both the bottle and breast. I was skeptical how much she was actually taking in while breastfeeding, but at least I knew exactly how much she was drinking when I offered the bottle—around three ounces per feeding, right on par with what we were told she should be drinking. Knowing this, if Birdie still hadn't gained any weight by her visit to Children's Hospital . . . well, then the issue was something that I wasn't ready to think about. *Gain some weight, little Bird. Please, please, please gain some weight.*

Birdie was back asleep by the time Chris and Har returned, which was quicker than expected. When I saw Har sprint toward the sliding-glass back door, no bandages or wound marks, my heart leapt. It had to be a good sign. The vet probably took one look and saw it was only a bruise, a bump from fishing like I'd originally thought, nothing to be too concerned about. Har and I would still get ten more years together, just as planned. And then I saw Chris walking slowly behind him, his shoulders slumped inward and his expression unreadable.

"Hi, Har!" I slid the door open, and he jumped into my arms.

"Please don't make me go back there. I'll be good. I swear." Har leaned into me harder than usual, his energy more anxious than usual. "Just please don't take me back there ever again. I want to stay here with you. I won't even yell when the box man comes. I promise. Just no more visits to that place." His big brown eyes were both desperate for me to protect him and full of relief that he was back home.

"It's okay, Har. You're back. You're home now," I said as I led him inside and patted the couch for him to lie down.

Chris was slower to come in, his face glued to something on his phone. I could tell by the expression on his face he was in research mode.

"How'd it go?" I asked nervously when he still didn't look up.

Chris put his phone on the counter and sighed heavily. "We have to go back."

"Oh no. Why? Was Har a mess?"

"He didn't do well." Chris glanced at Har, who was lying on the couch, giving us his nervous joker smile. It was a grin we saw around the Fourth of July when the fireworks started booming or whenever the Instant Pot came out. "We have to go see a specialist, but luckily this vet was able to call it in and got us an appointment for tomorrow already."

"Okay." I swallowed hard. "Why?"

"He said the bump doesn't look good, Tay." Chris started to cry before he could say much more, and I started to cry before I could hear any more.

My brain felt like it was rolled into a ball and sitting at the very back of my head, throbbing and getting heavier with each tear that fell down my dry red face. I'd cried so much lately, I was surprised I still had enough hydration to produce any.

We both took a seat on the couch with Har between us. He wiggled and nestled near our faces, anxious to make whatever was making us upset go away.

"Guys, stop. Let's play. Wanna play?" He ran to his toy box and tossed Sloth in my lap. "Sloth helps, right?"

"Thank you, buddy," I said as the lump in my throat felt big enough it might choke me. "Sloth always helps."

"He's going to need a biopsy since it's not soft tissue growth," Chris said.

"If they need to remove it, they can though, right? Whatever it is."

"I think that's what we'll find out tomorrow."

"What did the vet think it might be?" I asked hesitantly, but I already knew. Chris could only nod as more tears streaked his cheeks, and I knew it was the thing I always prayed it never would be. "Did they say what kind?"

Har rested his head on Chris's shoulder just like he did the day we brought him home to our small apartment in Kansas so many years ago, and Chris pulled him in even closer. "The bad kind, Tay."

lawless

"Hey, Har? Do you think you could act like a dog just one time in your life and stay in the back of the car?"

It was June 2020, and we were considering staying in our first hotel since Covid. Technically, I think it was considered a roadside motel. But just the idea of doing something so exotic felt exhilarating and lawless. Like how I imagined people felt drinking during Prohibition, or how women felt not wearing pantyhose at a job that "strongly urged" women to wear pantyhose. We hadn't intended to stay the night at the Nordic Lodge in Steamboat, but after our hike full of sunshine suddenly dropped a rainstorm on us that turned into a hailstorm with a grand finale of snowflakes and sleet, we decided we could be a little crazy and stay the night in Steamboat. But first, we had to make sure Har was within the weight limit for their dog policy—or at the very least make sure he wasn't seen upon checking in.

"I will do no such thing!" Har sassed back as he crawled over the rear row of seats and planted his large front paws on the middle console between Chris and me.

Riding in the back was new for Har, as he usually preferred the passenger seat or my lap, but for obvious safety reasons (and with a baby on the way), we knew we had to break him of this habit, and he was rather insulted by it.

"Perhaps if you would have dried me off correctly, I may have considered it," Har griped as he wiped his face up and down my sleeve.

"Oh, Har, calm down. It wasn't even that bad," I responded and struggled to push him toward the back.

It was a good lesson for us as hiking rookies, getting caught in the storm on the mountain without proper rain gear. Luckily, we weren't too far from the bottom when it rolled in, so Chris and I didn't mind getting a little damp as we hustled down. It felt a little wild and thrilling, *like staying at the Nordic Lodge during Covid*, but Har, however, was not pleased one bit. At first, we'd taken cover under a tree, but once we saw it wasn't going to pass over the mountains as quickly as we thought, we decided we'd better make a run for it.

"I'm sorry, *what's* the plan?" Har shrieked when he realized we were getting ready to move again.

"It's only rain, Har. And we're not too far from our car. Just put your head down and run," I tried to reason with him.

"But we'll get wet! From the rain!"

Har wasn't happy about it, but we all made it down safely. Once we had cell service again, we learned there was more traffic than usual on our route back to Denver, and that's when the seed was planted—what if we just stayed in Steamboat for the night? We were wet and cold, and my tailbone throbbed at merely the idea of sitting in the car for an extra couple of hours. Plus, we hadn't done anything so spontaneous since 2019. Wouldn't it be kind of fun to live like we did in the pre-pandemic world (with masks, sanitizer, and social distancing, of course)? A lot of people were starting to travel and stay in hotels again (and actually admit they did so). Perhaps we could too.

"I just can't decide. Do you think it's safe?" I asked Chris because it was my turn to be the Covid-cautious one for the week.

"I think it's probably okay," he said as he pulled into the Nordic Lodge parking lot.

"How exciting!" Har declared as he thrust his paws onto my lap and tried to look out the front window. "We haven't stayed in a hotel in ages! Let me just get one more wipe in so I'm not a total wreck walking in!"

"Carl!" I shouted. "Back!"

"I thought you said you dried him off with your coat when we got in the car," Chris said in a tone I didn't appreciate.

"I did! He's just being a princess. Wonder where he gets it," I mumbled under my breath.

I hated when Chris and Har ganged up on me. They were both so annoyingly fickle about their precious hair. If *anyone* looked like a wet dog in the car, it was me. But you didn't hear me complaining. Okay, technically you did, but only about my tailbone and back throbbing from growing a child inside of me.

"I'll ask the front desk how they're sanitizing the rooms, and we can also wipe everything down on our own. But if it feels weird, we don't have to stay." Chris parked the car, and I agreed it sounded okay.

Two hours later, we walked Har near the Yampa River and showed him where Chris and I toasted with Bloody Marys to celebrate picking up our marriage certificate from the Routt County Courthouse several years previous. We wanted Har to be in our wedding, obviously, but the venue we chose for the reception didn't allow dogs, nor did the resort where we stayed with all of our wedding guests. For nearly three long weeks, we left him behind at summer camp (Chris's parents' cabin) while we got married near a lake in Steamboat and then traveled around the British Virgin Islands for our honeymoon. I swore I'd never leave Har for that length of time ever again, and we never did.

On our walk back, we purchased all the toiletries we needed for our impromptu trip and already had extra clothes because we always hiked with extras. After we'd sanitized the motel room one more time and sprayed all the bedding with disinfectant to make sure it was clean enough for Har to jump from one twin bed to the other, we felt pleased with our decision to stay the night.

"This is what I love about Colorado," Chris said as he tinkered on his phone planning our hike for the following day. "It's like we get to go on a little vacation every weekend."

"Uh huh," I agreed as I struggled to keep my eyes open. "Like a tiring, sweaty vacation that involves a lot of walking."

Which was actually a lot like the vacations of my childhood to Worlds of Fun in Kansas City or the Tan-Tar-A resort in the Ozarks. My family was a big fan of Missouri, the *Show-Me State*, as in show me how many times you can vacation here. Wolfe family: challenge accepted!

"I feel like you don't like it here as much as I do," Chris remarked, and it lingered somewhere in between a question and a statement.

"I was joking, kinda. I do love Colorado. What's not to love—I mean, other than the terrible drivers on 70 and the fact cottage cheese explodes all over my face whenever I open a new container."

"Tay, you just have to poke a hole in the top to release some of the pressure. We've been over this."

"I know, I know. I just forget . . . But I really do like it here, it's just frustrating how hard the hikes are getting for me. I don't think I can really make a fair assessment of our new hiking life in the state I am in."

During my second trimester, I lost my breath walking from our bedroom to the bathroom, or even just while having a conversation that lasted for more than a minute. My belly had started to grow, along with a lot of other things I didn't know grew during pregnancy (arms, ass, legs, moles, armpit hair, etc.), and hiking up a mountain every weekend became increasingly difficult for me. At every OB appointment, I asked if it was safe for me to continue.

"Because if it's not, if there's any risk at all, I will stop."

And I was always met with a cheery response somewhere along the lines of, "As long as you're monitoring your heart rate and you feel okay, hiking is actually a great workout for pregnancy! Keep on hitting the trails. Have you made it to St. Mary's Glacier?"

Ugh, such a Colorado response, am I right? I enjoyed hiking, but would I have also enjoyed lying on the couch cradling a box of Cinnamon Toast Crunch with my feet up watching trash TV? Yes, yes I would have.

"We can skip a hike and drive straight home tomorrow. I really don't mind," Chris offered as I saw him continue to bookmark trails in the area I knew he was dying to get on.

"No, we gotta hike. Har would be devasted if we didn't. Just look at him."

Har was fast asleep with the happiest, derpiest open-mouth expression on his face as he snored away. His legs twitched every few seconds as he caught the fish in his dreams that always got away in real life. I hadn't seen him this excited to be in a hotel since our road trip to Yellowstone when we stayed in Wyoming and our suite "had a view" of the hotel's banquet room. Har could have watched that Casper Class of '99 reunion all night; I think he may have.

"We can let him run near Rabbit Ears Pass, or we can try another hike. I'll leave it up to you in the morning," Chris said.

I thought about the exhaustion I'd feel during the hike (and after). My joints had started to ache in a way I'd never felt before. Perhaps even worse, parts on my body had started to sweat in ways I'd never felt before either. Any time I had to pee, which was approximately every ten minutes, pulling my hiking pants down my sweaty belly and back up again was a workout in itself.

"We're going," I said once and for all, because I also knew the feeling of being sweaty and achy was so short-lived compared to the feeling of seeing Har so damn happy. "Seeing the way the mountains set his soul on fire—and yours too—makes it worth it. But just know I'll want a very greasy lunch after."

"Sets my soul on fire? What?" Chris laughed and rolled his eyes just like I knew he would, but he knew exactly what I was talking about. He just hadn't read the hippie-dippie spiritual books like I had to know the correct phrases to describe it. "Well then, what sets your soul on fire, other than a greasy lunch?"

"Just knowing that I've found a way to live life as I want with the people I want," I said in all earnest. "Luckily, I can do that from anywhere—the mountains or Chicago."

"You just hate being told what to do."

"That's absolutely true," I admitted as I pulled Har closer. "But even more than that, I hate the idea of wasting time, like when I was stuck in those jobs I hated in Chicago and knew deep in my bones that every hour I spent miserable in a cubicle was another hour I had wasted when I should be doing something more meaningful with what little time we have here." I glanced once more at Har. "Especially with time we already know is extra fleeting."

"You're going to talk about that video again, aren't you—"

"I once saw a video about a guy who gave their dog the best day ever before they knew they had to put him down. They spent all day together cuddling, going on walks, playing at the dog beach."

"That's how you and Har spend every day," Chris said.

"I know. It's because I watched that video and thought, Wait, I don't want to give Har just one really good day; I want to give him all the really good days. How could I not, when a dog's time with us is so short anyway?" I trailed off, not wanting to think about a time when Har may not be here anymore. "But we both know he's going to live forever, so it doesn't matter."

"He definitely will," Chris agreed, as he always did when we talked about Har's mortality. "But in the case he doesn't, you've given him a lot of good days."

"But he's given me even more."

the little red wagons

When Har went back for his second vet appointment the following day, he was hesitant to jump into the car. Har had *never* been hesitant for a car ride.

"C'mon, Har. Up," Chris commanded as he held the back door open.

"I don't want to." He looked at me as I stood in the garage in my slippers and postpartum uniform—velour drawstring pants from Target and a gross milk-soaked sleep shirt also from Target, with a baby monitor in one hand and burp cloth in the other. "Please let me come back inside and just stay with you," he begged, and I could see his body was already trembling.

What was I supposed to do? Lie to Har and say he wasn't going to the vet? He would find out, and then I would have sent him away without me *and* lied to him. I couldn't do it. Instead, I did the only thing I could do, which was wrap my arms around his neck and tell him that I loved him and that he'd be right back.

"It will be okay, Har," I promised. "Just get in the car with Chris, and I'll be right here when you get home. Please, buddy."

"Okay," he said with his tail tucked tightly between his legs as he slowly climbed inside.

As I watched them drive away, my phone pinged with a text message from the Colorado Children's Hospital reminding us about our pediatric cardiology appointment the next day. The message told us where to park and how to follow the updated Covid rules and *Jesus Christ, couldn't I just get one second to catch my breath?* Was it too much to ask for a couple of minutes to focus on one ordeal before I got a reminder about the other? My anxiety had anxiety.

As I sat on the couch trying to get Birdie to double fist a bottle and my boob, I wondered what it must be like to be one of those moms I'd seen on social media who declared the first weeks home with their new baby were "the absolute best weeks of their life!"

Getting in all the newborn snuggles! The brand-new baby stage is truly my favorite. Time, slow down—this has been the best month of my life! I am so happy my heart could literally burst all over my phone screen!

They were all lying, right? Or was I just being cheated? Being cheated of a time I was led to believe was supposed to be the most blissful time of my life, one I shouldn't take for granted and should make sure to "soak up every last second of it" to ensure I never forgot a moment of it, even when all I wanted to do was forget it. For someone who has documented every last second of their life in Lisa Frank journals, Limited Too diaries, and BlogSpot blogs, I have very few photos from Birdie's first weeks because I remember thinking to myself, *I don't want to hold on to this feeling.* I didn't want to remember the worry that overcame me with Birdie's feeding struggles or the bump growing above Har's eye, the all-encompassing fear that felt like it was drowning me with its heaviness, the thought that something might not just be wrong with one baby, but both. Birdie and Harlow.

It took a visit to Children's Hospital, where I saw parents pulling wagons full of toys and diapers, alongside large suitcases with zippers bursting. Overflowing bags with even more items sat on top, and the faces that lugged it all wore the same look of weariness and strength as they held the hand of a small child in pajamas and a hospital bracelet. And I realized I had not been cheated of anything. The three of us—Chris, Birdie, and I—got to leave the hospital after our appointment was over while I knew so many others had to stay.

What I was experiencing, what we all are, is something called life. And as a man named Earl once said, "We don't get to only sign up for the good parts; we sign up for all of it." I don't know why we got to leave the hospital after only a visit, with just our diaper bag full of items, while others were in for the long haul with suitcases that appeared much too heavy for one person or one family to handle. But I won't ever forget those families, and I also know there's no sense in trying to compare what we carry, because the only weight we ever really know is the one we're pulling.

Chris arrived back home without Harlow, as I knew he would since his appointment was going to be a longer procedure.

"How did he do?" I asked, and he just shook his head. "That bad?"

"Yeah," he said quietly.

I tried not to think of the fear Har must have felt as another stranger in vet scrubs led him away from our car and into a place that smelled and sounded like sheer terror to him. But it's all I could think about. "I hope he doesn't have to go back for a while. Did they give you any idea when he'd be done?"

"Later tonight." Chris leaned against the island in our kitchen and folded his arms across his chest. "And I spoke with the doctor after she gave Har an initial checkup before they began surgery."

"Oh?"

"She said that it didn't look very promising. That the bump was in a position on his head that, um . . ." Chris choked on whatever was coming next. He rubbed his hands over his eyes and only nodded as more tears fell. "She said it's really just not looking good, Tay."

"Well, she could be wrong though, right? She won't know until they actually test it. Did she say that?"

"They could be wrong."

"They're going to be wrong."

I needed Har. He couldn't get sick on me now. We were just getting started. I needed him as I figured out this mom stuff, and Birdie needed him. We were going to play hide-and-seek and go back to playing on jungle gyms at the park—and hiking! We still had so much to explore in Colorado. We'd only had one summer of the mountains; Har deserved at least ten more. A hundred more. Whatever this was, we would fight it.

A few hours later, Chris got the call that Har was out of surgery and we could go pick him up. Birdie wouldn't need to be fed for another hour, so we strapped her in the car seat and took her along so we could all go together and pick up our boy. We waited in the parking lot for Har to be released. Both Chris and I stood outside of our car so Har would see us immediately, so he'd know we were there to take him home. He burst through the front door, pulling hard at the leash held by the unfortunate employee who got tasked with bringing him outside. Once he saw us, he pulled even harder. I smiled despite myself because would a sick dog be able to pull like a Clydesdale? Certainly not. I crouched to his level as he ran into my arms.

"Hi, buddy. How are you?" His head was partially shaved, and his eyes were glassy, but he leaned into me hard and wiggled with joy anyway.

"Can we go home?" Har whispered. "I just really want to go home."

"That's why we're here, Har. To take you home."

We were told we'd get his results in a couple of days, but I'd learned, thanks to Covid, that could actually mean two weeks or two months. One never knew anymore.

I was worried I wouldn't be able to sleep the night before Birdie's cardiology appointment, but as I lay down in our bed, I could feel that sleep would be a welcome relief. (For two-hour increments, at which point I'd have to wake and feed Birdie.) Har rested his head on my chest, and I held him close as he fell into a hard, snore-heavy snooze. Since we'd brought Birdie home, he'd taken to sleeping at the foot of the bed, either to protest me constantly getting up to feed her or because of her crying or I'm not sure why. But tonight, he was back up in my arms, and I cherished it. I couldn't imagine a night, or a life, where Har wasn't by my side.

When my feeding alarm went off, I was as hazy and confused as I'd been since we'd first come home from the hospital. I immediately pushed snooze, having no idea why my phone was insisting I wake up at such an ungodly hour. Luckily my boobs quickly reminded me, as they began to leak and tingle until I got the hint. I didn't know how pushy and controlling boobs could be until I had Birdie. They're all fun and games until they get a little taste of power (breast milk), and then they blow up and get irrationally upset if you don't follow their every demand. But as I lifted Birdie from her bassinet, I had one second of cloudy bliss where I'd forgotten about Har's appointment the previous day as well as our upcoming visit to Children's Hospital in only a few hours. For just a moment, amid the darkness of the night, my only concern was feeding my baby. As I brought Birdie into our bed, Har nestled back into me, and where his head normally felt so soft and warm, it was cold and shaved, a reminder of what he'd been through and what still lay ahead. My phone pinged with an alert from my breastfeeding app that it was time to record every sip, burp, and fart, and everything I'd forgotten about was right back in my arms.

The next morning as we prepared to leave for Birdie's appointment, Har didn't ask to come along like he usually did. Maybe he feared another car ride would mean another vet appointment, or maybe he understood that some rides only involved Birdie and not him now. Either way, it killed me to see his solemn face pressed against our back glass door as he watched us go.

Chris and I rode most of the way in silence, neither of us sure how to handle the new level of fear that seemed to smother us as first-time parents. *What if Birdie still hasn't gained weight? What if it's more than a feeding issue? What if it actually is her heart? What if...* I think we eventually argued about where to exit or where to park simply for the sake of normalcy. It was inside the parking garage where I first noticed the red wagons. They sat empty next to the elevators, but I was too consumed with our own *what-ifs* to give them much thought.

The Colorado Children's Hospital was enormous on the inside. It felt like a mix between a children's museum and an airport, with colorful decor and cheery lighting, but everyone seemed to be headed somewhere or waiting to head somewhere. Like a children's museum, there was always a helpful employee standing nearby, ready to answer a question, offering a sticker, or cuddling the resident golden retriever therapy dog. It was adorable for a second, but then you remembered where you were and could only hope that you were the next to depart.

The nurse in cardiology who ran Birdie's tests spoke to Chris and me with the perfect amount of patience and kindness that we so badly needed. She was gentle and soothing with Birdie and made sure to keep her covered and warm, until the moment when the blanket had to come off to attach more wires to her tiny body, and Birdie screamed in a way I'll never forget. It wasn't her tired or her hungry cry. It was a new one. It was a scared cry. I knew because I felt like I'd been keeping a similar one tucked deep inside myself. With each wail that Birdie released that I couldn't stop, I could feel myself getting smaller and smaller, like something was gnawing at me from the inside out, hoping to make me disappear completely. I could continue to tell Birdie that we were "almost done" and she was "doing so good"—all that I wanted—but the monster inside of me shouted right back, *She has no idea what's going on. She only knows that you're not stopping it.* And it gutted me. With my head as close to Birdie's as the nurse allowed and every muscle in my body tightly clenched, I reminded myself that giving in to my own fear wouldn't take away Birdie's. As badly as I wanted to fall into the hollow pit of anxiety taking over my insides and curl myself into a ball in the corner of the room, I knew I couldn't. I had to remain standing next to Birdie, reminding her how good she was doing.

I prayed that this would be our last visit to Children's, that we'd find out that it was *just a feeding issue*, and that everything was okay with Birdie's heart. I prayed that the only problem here was me.

After the tests were complete, we shuffled from one room to another while we waited for the cardiologist to review the scans.

"That was terrible," I said quietly to Chris as I began to feed Birdie.

He nodded and paced near the door. "I was trying to read the nurse's face to see if she saw something good or bad, but I couldn't tell."

"You know what's crazy to me?" I said to Chris feeling both completely numb and also like I'd just run a marathon.

"What's that?"

"Before having Birdie, I was mostly worried about the constant crying just because I thought it would be exhausting. I had no idea how physically painful it could be as a mother to hear your child cry and not be able to stop it."

Chris sat beside me and offered to feed Birdie, but I didn't want to let her go. We heard a knock on the door and braced ourselves for what awaited us on the other side. The doctor appeared with a clipboard held to his chest, and I don't remember his name or even if he introduced himself because the first thing I recall him saying is "This looks like a perfectly healthy baby to me." And I nearly fainted with relief.

"Thank God!" I said as I let his words wash over me. "So the only issue is me and my breastfeeding."

I wasn't looking for sympathy or even trying to make a joke; it was just my relief speaking the truth. I was also humiliated and full of guilt, but this appointment had no space for my feelings or ego. This was about Birdie's health, and that was it. But then the doctor gently patted my shoulder and told me that it wasn't my fault—that I was a "good mom," and I crumbled. The faux wall of strength I had tried to build instantly shattered, and it was all I could do to just nod my head and swallow my tears.

The doctor told us that Birdie had gained weight and that we should keep doing whatever we were doing to bulk her up because it was working. I had to continue to wake her in the night every few hours to feed, but once Birdie hit a certain weight goal, I could start to let her sleep for longer stretches.

"That's not a problem," I said eagerly, replaying the doctor's words in my head. *I'm a good mom. I'm a good mom.*

I knew I was (*am*) a good mom, but sometimes the chatter of all the worry, fear, and doubt that goes along with being a good mom gets so loud, I can't hear anything else but the nagging voice telling me otherwise. I don't know why I needed a stranger to remind me of something I already knew, but I did. *I'm a good mom.*

As we left Children's Hospital, I saw the red wagons again. But this time, they weren't sitting empty. They were full of snacks and toys, pillows and blankets, and pulled by moms and dads like Chris and me. One wagon carried a soft pink blanket with silk trim just like the one I had for Birdie in my diaper bag. But as we headed toward the exit, the wagon with the pink blanket went the other way, deeper into the hospital onto a floor we wouldn't visit.

Later that night when my alarm went off telling me it was time to begin the night feedings, I picked up Birdie from her bassinet and cradled her in my arms. I unwrapped her from her swaddle and sleepily brought her into our bed, and Har scooted over to make room. As Birdie suckled her bottle, I draped her soft pink blanket across us and stared into the familiar night sky from our bedroom window and thought, *How lucky are we?*

A Reminder from a Stranger

You're a good mom.

the matt foley bulb

After zero dilation and basically no labor progress whatsoever, it was time for the Foley bulb to be inserted into my vagina. Every time the Foley bulb was mentioned, my mind instantly went to Matt Foley, a beloved character played by Chris Farley on *Saturday Night Live* in the mid-nineties. Foley was a motivational speaker who lived in a van down by the river, which seemed fitting considering I was on day three of my hospital visit waiting for a baby that wouldn't arrive. So if I'd ever needed motivation in my life, now was the time. *C'mon, Matt Foley bulb. Work your magic!*

"Is this going to hurt?" I asked the nurse as she prepared the balloon that was to be inserted into my vagina.

"You'll feel some pressure," she said with a look of both tenderness and concern, and I knew what she probably meant was, "For you, yes."

"Great."

In an attempt to ease my fears, I assume, the nurse added, "But at least it's going in your vagina and not urethra like a Foley catheter. You'd be surprised how hard it is to find a urethra."

No ma'am, I would not, I thought, *because I'm pretty sure I've had one my entire life, and I've never found it.* Then again, I hadn't found my vagina in months, either.

"Well, cheers to finding the right hole," I said and immediately regretted.

Here's the thing. I know some women find the birthing process to be a very beautiful and spiritual thing to go through. Some say they even enjoy it. And I love that for them. But I am not that woman. I have no problem admitting that pretty much every part of giving birth made me wildly uncomfortable. Now to anyone reading this who might have a crippling fear of giving birth (hello, that was me), I'd like to add that toward the end of pregnancy, that crippling fear pretty much goes away. It did for me anyway, mostly thanks to the sporadic vagina shocking and constant ache I felt in nearly every bone and muscle in my body from what I can only assume was my body's way of saying it was tired of being taken over by another tiny body. And on a sweeter note, after nine months of housing a little human, you just can't wait to meet that little human. The feelings of *Hey, it's time for you to get the hell out* and also *I just want to see your sweet face and hold you in my arms* can and DO coexist. So that's the good news!

The not-so-good news is that after three days of people poking and prodding around in a place you don't want poked or prodded, some of the fear of giving birth can sneak its way back in. By the time the bulb was ready to be inserted inside of me, I was dry heaving into a brown paper bag, a fun anxious quirk of mine.

"I'm just really nervous about this," I said in between heaves to Chris. "I've read it can be really painful."

"You don't have to do it. We can try another thing," he said, but I think we both knew at this point we'd tried all the things. It was either a Foley bulb or a C-section.

I was never against a C-section. My plan had always been to just get Birdie out in whatever was the safest way for her. But as of now, my doctor was suggesting the Foley bulb as the next step, so I knew it's what I had to do.

"Can I get an epidural for this?" I asked the nurse, jokingly.

I think it was jokingly, anyway. I'd been wanting that thing since I arrived but figured I had to pass some dilation test before I got it.

"It's completely up to you to decide when you'd like to get an epidural," she responded in a way I definitely knew was not joking. "We're just here to make sure you're comfortable."

I tapped my fingertips on my lips and raised my eyebrows toward Chris as if I'd just discovered an evil plan I wanted to take part in. *Well, well, well, this certainly changed things.* But no! I couldn't. Could I? Why had I always heard stories about women who waited until they were at least nine centimeters dilated, or one push away, or was it nineteen centimeters and zero pushes? I didn't know what they were waiting for, but I knew I'd heard the heroic stories of waiting.

"Interesting," I said out loud to no one and also everyone, "but isn't it normal to wait until you're at least like five centimeters dilated or something?"

"Whatever you choose will be normal."

What a gal, that nurse! She went on to explain the pros and cons of receiving an epidural at this point, and to be quite honest, I don't remember any of the cons other than I'd be stuck to my bed and couldn't eat or drink once I got it—two things I already felt I was doing anyway. The pros were that I wouldn't feel a balloon inserted into my vagina, and the pain of my contractions, which were only getting stronger, would float away.

"Will you judge me?" I asked Chris.

"For getting an epidural? No. Why would I? That was always the plan."

"Well, the plan was to get it when I was . . . you know, dilated. Like at least one centimeter. And I'm not even that."

"Who cares?" Chris shrugged. "If that's what you want, then get it. You've been through a lot."

What a guy, that Chris! But I had a feeling he was secretly think-ing, "*We've* been through a lot," because I know the couch in our hospital room was rather uncomfortable for him, the poor guy.

I asked the nurse if she'd judge me, and she laughed and also said no. She'd seen much worse, apparently. The last person I had to ask was myself. Would I judge me? I thought of a piece of unsolicited advice I'd received before going to the hospital: "Don't be a wimp and ask for an epidural when you're not even like five-to-seven cen-timeters dilated. Don't be that person." Was I going to be *that per-son*? Was there some award if I wasn't? Was it already making me less of a mother or a woman if I decided to listen to myself, rather than someone else's unwanted advice, and admit that I was scared and ask for pain management now rather than waiting? Maybe. But like Chris said, who cared? I wasn't trying to be a hero here. And I know, I know—women have been giving birth since literally the beginning of time without any sort of pain medication, and I respect that immensely, but do you know what else I respect? The beauty of modern medicine and the fact we get to choose not only if we want it, but *when* we want it.

"Let's go for it," I said triumphantly.

When the anesthesiologist came in to administer the epidural, he told me I'd feel some pressure and a little poke as he inserted the needle into my back. With Chris in front of me holding my hands, I took a deep breath and thought of every poke from every blood draw I'd felt in 2019—the good ones that hardly hurt, the bad ones that bruised, and the ones I didn't feel at all because I was too busy trying to make myself disappear from an OB room I didn't want to be in. I thought about waiting for my results week after week, terrified I was only a few numbers away from having to start cancer treatments. I thought about the online molar preg-nancy support groups I'd joined just to lurk but never comment. And I thought about hitting zero in Moab with Chris and Har by my side, clutching the results as a large red arch hovered above us and the Utah sun set slowly behind us. When I finally exhaled, it was all over. And I hardly felt a pinch.

As the medicine surged through my body, my contractions eased almost immediately. "Ave Maria" started playing somewhere off in the distance, the sun danced its way in through the bleak hospital blinds, and two little chirping bluebirds suddenly appeared at my bedside and began transforming my matted hospital hair into two perfect blond braids. Me and my anxiety had never felt so good about a decision in our life.

"Is it working?" Chris asked.

"I think so." I smiled and nodded and hoped the bluebirds would reapply the delivery makeup I applied three days ago when I thought I'd be delivering the same day I checked into the hospital. Lol. Silly me.

"And it's in!" the nurse declared, and it took me a second to remember what she was talking about.

Oh yes, the Foley bulb. That old thing! I hoped the vagina balloon did exactly what vagina balloons were supposed to do. No complaints were voiced, so I had to assume all was good. How lovely.

For the first time since I'd arrived at the hospital, and maybe even since I'd taken a pregnancy test nine months ago, I felt relaxed and content and like I could actually get a few hours of sleep. When Chris mentioned that he was going to step out and get his ten minutes of fresh air for the day (Covid rules discouraged any hospital guests from leaving their room more than once), I sleepily nodded and told him to go for it. A warm feeling was engulfing me, and I intended to give in to it.

My epidural-induced nap came to an end when I heard a new nurse enter the room, and I groggily sat up, assuming she was going to give me a quick vital check. I was also excited to get an update on the progress of the Foley bulb balloon. Had it popped? Or dropped? Or turned itself into a wiener dog by now? I knew it was supposed to aid in opening my cervix, but I wasn't sure how I'd know when that had been accomplished. Perhaps I'd just look out the window and see it floating off into the horizon with all the other Foley bulb balloons, a house with a little old man and a chubby Boy Scout attached underneath them all.

As the new nurse began writing on the marker board, we exchanged polite hellos, but before I could ask my questions, she started to release a slow, but increasingly loud, rip of ass into the air. A fart, if you will. I'll admit I was a bit appalled at first, especially given the nature of the aggressive rip and the fact we'd only just met. It wasn't just a minor slip or something you'd hope would go unnoticed, but it was rather more akin to something you'd hear in a men's gas station bathroom in western Nebraska where another bathroom hadn't been seen for at least seventy miles or so. I had to remind myself that nurses are people too, and I didn't know what she was going through or what she'd eaten for lunch. Whatever the case, it was probably an emergency, so I did my best to give her a slight smile and knowing head nod that I hoped said, "No big deal. It happens to the best of us!" The nurse gave me a bit of a hesitant smile in return, which confused me at first, until I started to understand what was happening here.

It was me.

I was the one farting. I realized this as it was still happening, but there was nothing, and I mean nothing, that I could do to stop it. Apparently once you can't feel your legs, you also can't feel your farts. It was as if the moment my mind realized I had the urge to pass some gas, my body was like, *No problemo. I'm one step ahead of you.* And I was mortified! *Say something,* I begged myself, *like I'm sorry or I can't stop it, or is that a moose nearby? Just, for the love of God, say something!* But I was frozen in both shock and embarrassment, so like an elderly man in an elevator, I continued to let it happen while acting as if it wasn't.

I know nurses have seen and heard a lot worse, but this was too much for me. What else couldn't I control? I'd always been worried about pooping on the delivery table, but now I had to worry about my hospital bed too? I needed this Foley bulb to work, or it was starting to feel like my body had really shit the bed on this whole birthing thing. Literally and metaphorically.

My Acceptance Speech for Winning an Award for Earliest Epidural Given

I am truly humbled to be standing before you today accepting such a prestigious award. If you would have told me ten years ago that I would be the recipient of the "Earliest Epidural Given" honor, I would have said, "What does that even mean?" followed by, "Seriously?" and, "Okay yeah, that checks out."

But I didn't get here alone, no, I certainly didn't. I would be amiss if I pretended this wasn't a group effort. Gosh, where do I even start with who to thank? How much time do I have? (Pause for laughter.) First and foremost, I'd like to thank my pelvis. Why? I don't know—I'm not a doctor. But I'm pretty sure my pelvis did absolutely nothing to help with the birthing process. Same with my membranes. Because if they had, well, I might not be standing before you today.

Speaking of doing nothing, this award truly goes to my cervix and its complete refusal to soften or dilate in the least. The Cervidil, the Pitocin, the Foley bulb, my contractions, the medicine ball I bounced on naked (because I misunderstood the assignment)—we as a group tried everything to reason with my cervix, but nevertheless, it did not budge. It had its own vision board, and widening to allow a baby to pass was not on it.

I can hear the music starting to play, so I'll wrap this up by saying I'd also like to thank myself. A lot of people told me to wait until at least five or six centimeters dilated, or "four at the very least" according to Google or whatever, but after days of contractions (and days of listening to my husband narrate said contractions), I chose not to listen to any of them.

At 0.00 centimeters dilated I listened to myself and a quote I rewrote to fit my own needs: "She believed she could, but she didn't because she really wanted that epidural."

the way back

After the visit to Children's Hospital, we decided to rent a house in Steamboat for a few days so Chris could ski and I could breastfeed/pump in a new place. It sounded fun to mix things up a bit and see if Birdie could kick a full Haakaa pump off my nipple, drenching my entire midsection with breast milk in a different setting. Spoiler: she could! More important, we were still waiting on Har's biopsy results and hoped a weekend in our favorite little mountain town might help provide a much-needed distraction. With approval from Birdie's pediatrician (because I was still in the parenting phase where I assumed I had to get approval to do anything), we loaded up our car for our first big road trip with a newborn. As I hauled Birdie's MamaRoo, DockATot, BabyBjörn, and mesh bath seat toward our car for our two-day trip, I remembered a time when I used to carry on my luggage for a seven-day vacation to Mexico. We were a walking cliché of the parents who pack the entire nursery for a weekend trip, but now I understood why they did it. (Why we did it.) Because you're scared out of your goddamn mind with that first child and have no idea what you're doing or going to need from one hour to the next, let alone one day to the next, so you bring it all. Kindly stop judging us (looking at myself from the past here, FYI).

I rode in the back seat next to Birdie (obviously), and Har rode in the back-back with his head resting on my shoulder (obviously).

"Do I really have to ride back here? I can't even hear what you guys are saying all the way up there," he whined.

"Har, you're literally an inch from my face." I rubbed his patchy head where the stitches still remained. "You're not missing anything. I promise."

"I just feel like such an animal back here," he huffed dramatically, especially considering he had the comfiest spot in the car, thanks to the cozy bed Chris set up for him.

"Just relax, bud. It's a short trip," Chris said from the driver's seat, and I knew it killed Har he wasn't sitting in the passenger seat next to him.

Har was safest riding in the back, especially with a baby on board and all the curvy mountain-road driving we did now. But I couldn't help but think of every nine-hour drive from Chicago to Nebraska Har made as my copilot, happily sitting next to me sharing a bag of Combos from the World's Largest Truckstop in Iowa or Arby's French fries from the outlet mall, also in Iowa. We must have done that drive together at least thirty times, just him and me. Sometimes Chris was along, but more often than not, he flew back because of his work schedule or wasn't able to come at all. Especially in the beginning when the trips were so frequent—when I was just a scared, unemployed twenty-five-year-old with no idea what to do with my life, and I'd look for any excuse to get back to Nebraska. To get back somewhere that felt safe and familiar and with an abundance of street parking and free laundry machines.

"We're making the drive so you can have some space to run, Har, just for a few days," I'd tell him, and even if he knew I was lying, that I was actually driving to Nebraska because I was homesick and couldn't stand another day alone in a big city that felt so foreign and daunting to me, Har would never say it. He'd simply wag his tail and wait for me to open the passenger door, excited to see which self-help audiobook I'd chosen for the journey.

As time went on and we settled into our Chicago groove, my urge to drive back became less and less, as did our self-help listening. Instead, our drives were filled with me rambling off new T-shirt ideas and practicing stand-up sets. Soon enough, Har listened as I gushed about my new engagement ring, planned a wedding, bought our first condo, expanded my business, and began thinking about having a baby. He was there for all of it, with his head resting on the console next to me.

Har sighed with annoyed acceptance behind me as he curled into his bed, and I reminded myself he was okay in his new spot, safer even. But as I turned around to give him a scratch under his white chin, I couldn't help but miss all the years he was right by my side.

After about an hour on the road, with the back of my hand held constantly near Birdie's nose to make sure she was still breathing (their heavy infant heads look so scary in car seats), I decided I needed to pump, feed, and change Birdie's diaper. Chris pulled into a parking lot in Silverthorne, and I realized I either had to breastfeed Birdie in the tight quarters of the back seat or take her into the front seat and swallow my modesty and proudly feed my child for all to see!

I squished myself into the back seat.

I so badly wish I had the confidence to do the latter, and I feel like a bad feminist for admitting I don't, but breastfeeding in public makes me blush. The closest I ever got was putting a handheld pump under my shirt on I-70 and also at our family Christmas when I didn't want to miss out on the name game. Once Birdie was fed, I ran her into the rest stop bathroom, which was situated in a hallway between three very busy restaurants, and apparently after everyone ate their Chipotle, they immediately beelined it to the women's restroom. Other than the visit to Children's Hospital, this was the most people I'd seen in public since 2019. A mix of panic and shame flushed my face as I wondered what in the hell I was thinking bringing my newborn into a rest stop to change her! Would we ever survive such a risky endeavor? It felt unlikely as I vigorously wiped down the changing table that folded down from the wall before I laid down the clean changing pad that I brought with me.

My hands trembled as I tried to unsnap Birdie's onesie as quickly as possible. I could feel the eyes of every woman in line watching me. Were they judging me or taking pity? Was there a difference? *I would have changed her in the car, but it's snowing and freezing, and I'd have to open the door to lay her down and, and, and . . .* , I mumbled in my head to no one. My lack of confidence as a new mother shone brightly in my flushed cheeks as I struggled to clean Birdie up, remove the soiled diaper, and reach for a new one. She started to cry as I pulled the new diaper out, the kind of baby goat newborn cry that isn't worrisome at home—rather sweet and kind of adorable—but in public, it felt like a cry for child services.

"I'm sorry, Birdie girl. I'm going as fast as I can," I whispered.

That's when I held up the diaper and couldn't remember which side was the back and which was the front. Why wasn't it printed on the diaper like all the others? Or was it and I had simply forgotten how to read in the past five minutes? I panicked as I fumbled with the small white straps, and then Birdie panicked, her screams growing louder, presumably because she realized what a moron her mother was. I'd changed a diaper before, obviously. But I'll admit I hadn't changed a lot of them because Chris had taken on that duty in the first weeks as I recovered. Now here I was, stuck in a rest stop bathroom surrounded by germ-infested onlookers, and I didn't know how to change a fucking diaper! In my desperation to just finish the job and get out before our throats started to tingle and our sense of taste and smell disappeared, I ripped one of the small white straps completely off. And I didn't have a backup. Because having an extra diaper in a diaper bag would just make too much sense.

As Birdie squirmed and grunted, I calmly took a breath and did the only logical thing I could think of next—which was call Chris and loudly declare, "The diaper didn't work! It only had one strap.

We seriously need to switch brands. Who's ever heard of . . . Huggies . . . or whatever, anyway?"

I don't know if Chris believed me, or if the other women in the bathroom believed me, or most of all, why I cared so much that they believed me. But it felt like my first public changing was a test that I had failed miserably. I'd failed as a mother and as a mother during a pandemic. For those of us who had the audacity to have a baby during the early-Covid era, we not only received the good old-fashioned mom judgment, we got the Covid-mom judgment thrown our way as well. No choice felt like the right one. If we took our babies out, they'd surely get sick. If we kept our babies in, they'd surely fall behind on social milestones and grow up as isolated weirdos.

Chris appeared in the doorway to the women's bathroom as I held a half-dressed Birdie in my arms with a full-distressed look on my face.

"Thank you!" I said as I took the diaper from him. "That other diaper was—"

"It's okay," he said. "You all good?"

I nodded hesitantly and wondered if Chris was thinking about the bassinet incident. I realized now that that must have been a broken diaper too.

We arrived in Steamboat what felt like three days later but, in reality, was probably only a couple of hours. Chris unloaded the nursery from our car while I took Har and Birdie inside to get settled. Just like I hoped, Har went into full-blown vacation mode the second I opened the front door. He sprinted from room to room, up the stairs and back down, and any door that was halfway closed he quickly nosed back open.

"Are you excited to be here, Har?" I asked as I got my Boppy pillow positioned on the couch, ready for breastfeeding mode.

"Let's play! Let's play!" he shouted as he wiggled at my side, too excited to stay still.

"I just have to feed Birdie first, then we can play all you want!"

Any sign of vacation-Har was a good sign. I watched him run zoomies around the kitchen island and barrel up and down the stairs, and I wondered how he could possibly be *that sick*. He was the same old goofy Har, just with a large bump above his eye. For the first time since his surgery, I was starting to believe that maybe the vet had gotten it wrong. She didn't know him like we did. Nothing could set Har back.

"Tay, come look at this view," Chris said as he pulled back the living room curtains.

With Birdie in my arms, we peered over Chris's shoulder at the picturesque town that surrounded us. Har immediately ran over and placed his front paws on the ledge, his tail zipping back and forth between us. The mountain lit up with a warm purple-like haze from all the glowing homes tucked perfectly into their spots in the snow. Holiday lights traced their borders and illuminated the snow that covered their tops and bottoms. And the moonlight that shone above it all made it seem like darkness would never arrive in such an idyllic little mountain town.

The following morning, Chris planned to ski a few runs while I stayed back with Birdie and Har until it was time to meet him for lunch at our favorite mountainside trailer-turned-restaurant, T Bar. I know a lot of people dream about eating cold cuts after giving birth or their favorite sashimi, but my dream had always been a Bloody Mary from T Bar, specifically while sitting slope side on a cold winter's day as snow flurries fell around me. I held tightly to this vision for nine months of pregnancy and couldn't believe my time had finally arrived.

Being the wonderful wife that I am, I agreed to drop Chris off for his fun (child-free) morning of skiing while I had the pleasure of staying back with the kiddos. While Birdie enjoyed a car-seat nap, I chatted away about what we planned to do for the next few hours (breastfeed) and what time I'd meet him for lunch (as soon as possible). As I pulled onto Apres Ski Way, my phone rang. My heart beat faster in my chest when I recognized the number, and flashbacks of fear flooded my body as I remembered being too scared to pick up my OB's call in 2019. But this time it wasn't about me; it was about Har.

"It's the vet," I whispered to Chris.

"Answer it!" he had to remind me, my hands already shaking in anticipation.

I pulled into the closest parking lot and set my phone to speaker.

We were told Har's biopsy results were in and that the doctor wanted to speak with us directly about what they found.

"Would you mind waiting while I transfer you to Dr. Beauchamp?" the person on the other end asked, and I nodded my head but don't know if I actually said anything.

The power that a simple phone call can hold has always fascinated and scared the hell out of me. I'd learned there can be a certain safety, comfort even, in the few moments of unknowing, but once you know, once you ask "What's wrong?" there's no going back. Snow started to fall, and I stared intently at our windshield wipers as if I'd never seen them work before, mesmerized by their rhythmic swoosh and predictable movements. *Back and forth. Back and forth.*

When Dr. Beauchamp finally came on, her tone wasn't like the other vets I'd spoken with over the last ten years of Har's life. The vets who had told me that the bump on his belly was just fatty tissue, or the black mole near his front leg was just a mole or another skin tag. Her tone was different, and as hard as I tried to focus on the swoosh of the wipers instead, I knew it immediately. The tests confirmed that the bump on Har's head was osteosarcoma.

"I'm so sorry, you guys. I know this isn't what you wanted to hear," Dr. Beauchamp said, and she was right. I didn't want to hear it.

I didn't want to hear that they were pretty sure the cancer would spread all over Har's head, if it hadn't already. That the bump we could see was only the tip of it. The tip of the osteosarcoma that was already working its evil way through my best friend's head, apparently. The head that I had pressed my own against every single day for the past decade when I was sad or anxious or even just happy to see my boy. The one that I'd shared a pillow with since I first brought him home as a puppy, agreeing to let him sleep with us for "just one night" back when I was still under the illusion that Har was just a dog and I was just his owner. I know for some it always remains that way, but not for me and Har. We were the lucky ones. In the past ten years, I'd spent more time with Har than literally anyone else in my life. He was there for everything because I wanted him there for everything. And I wanted him now. I slid my phone toward Chris and crawled toward him. Back to the way back.

"Hey, Har," I said as tears ran down my hot face, a mass of pain and stress already throbbing somewhere deep within my head.

"What's happening? Why are you sad?" He tilted his head from side to side, trying so hard to figure out what was wrong. He hated when I cried. "Are you okay?"

"Are you okay, Har?" I held his head next to mine and tried to understand how I'd missed something so big. How had I not known cancer was taking over? "Are you hurting?"

Har continued to tilt his head in confusion as I sobbed into him, and for the first time in as long as I could remember, it felt like we couldn't understand each other. Did he know? Would he tell me if he did?

Dr. Beauchamp told us that we probably had one to two months left with Har. It seemed so insane to hear spoken out loud that I might have laughed if I hadn't felt so numb. Har was only ten. He was supposed to live until at least twenty, if not longer.

"I'm so sorry," she said once more. "I know how important he is to you."

All I could think was, *No you don't. No one does.*

canned heat

Eight hours had passed, and the balloon still hadn't performed one single trick inside of me. To say my spirits were a little low would be an understatement. What was wrong with me?

A new nurse came in to check on who knows what, and when she lifted the sheets that covered my frozen little legs, she declared, "Your membranes have ruptured!"

My gut reaction was, *Oh no. Was that medical talk for "you pooped"?* It had to be. *What else is lurking under those scratchy white sheets?* I wondered.

"When did that happen?" the nurse asked, and I wanted to shrug and say, *You think I know? I can't feel shit down there. Like actual shit. So you think I'm going to know when some membranes have ruptured?*

Like I said, I wasn't in a good place. But don't worry, I didn't say such a rude thing because I love nurses dearly (especially labor and delivery nurses) and also because I still wasn't sure what a bunch of ruptured membranes looked like. What kind of mess had I made of this bed?

"Did you notice at all when your water broke?" she asked once more, and then I got it. Duh.

"My water broke? My water broke!"

Chris jumped to his feet. This was finally something we both understood. If *Father of the Bride Part II* taught us anything, it was that this had to be a good sign! Here comes baby!

"This is good, right?" Chris asked, thinking the same as me.

"It certainly can be," the nurse said, but she didn't start running around the room frantically preparing it for delivery like I had hoped. "Let's take a look at your cervix."

Yes, let's!

"Any change?" I asked, one hundred percent certain there had to be some dilation going on this time. There just had to be!

But the nurse only sighed, and I knew.

"There is not," she said.

"Not even a little? I'm not even one percent dilated?"

She shook her head. "No, I'm sorry."

WHAT? NO! HOW? WHY? HOW WHY? NO. NO. NOOOOOOO!

I wondered once more, what was wrong with me and my cervix and my uterus and whatever else was supposed to be on the birth-giving team? What if this were the 1800s? Then what? Would I have just carried on being pregnant for another month or two? Or forever? I wondered a lot about women of the 1800s during my hospital stay, or just women from the past in general, I should say. It's not until you find yourself on the cusp of giving birth (or lack thereof) when you really wonder, *Okay, but how have they (we) been doing this forever?* How did they do it without electricity, running water, modern medical technology, or the special post-delivery brunch my hospital promised that I couldn't stop thinking about? I wasn't usually a crab-benedict type of gal, but the photo in the hospital brochure had been haunting me since I first saw it.

My doctor came in shortly after and suggested we start thinking about a C-section. From the very start, Chris and I said that our only "birth plan" was to get our baby girl in our arms as safely as possible, whatever that may be. We'd already discussed the pros and cons at length with our doctor—I believe we did that on hour forty-eight of our hospital stay—and the main concern for having a C-section for my first birth was that it could possibly make future births more difficult should I choose to have "four or five or more children." As much as I enjoyed playing with Catholic families next door when I was a child, having a basketball team of my own seemed rather unlikely for me.

"If you think it's time for a C-section," I said with a deep breath, "then let's do it."

It was around eight p.m. on November 18 when I made this decision, and our quiet hospital room suddenly took a major shift. The flurry of excited energy I'd been hoping for finally moved in. Nurses fluttered in and out at a speed I hadn't seen before, preparing me for surgery.

One nurse gently squeezed my arm and said, "You'll be meeting your baby within the next forty-five minutes."

Forty-five minutes?! Even though I'd technically waited days (months) to meet our baby, this still caught me off guard. I'd be a mom in less than an hour? I was still barely processing all of this when Chris was advised to gather all our things together so they'd be ready to move into the post-delivery room. The anesthesiologist returned to check my vitals and increase my drugs in preparation for surgery as Chris was hustled out of the room with all our belongings.

I wanted things to move a little faster, but this felt like hyper speed. I could barely catch my breath, like literally. The dry heaves were back.

"You really don't need to worry," the anesthesiologist explained. "You won't feel any pain."

Do I look worried? I wondered as more color left my face with each heave.

"But just know that about five minutes into surgery, you might feel the sensation like you can't breathe, and you'll be gasping for air," she continued, and I really wish she wouldn't have because what the anesthesiologist described was my actual claustrophobic nightmare. "Just remind yourself to calm down and take long, slow breaths. Okay?"

"Okay," I said as I started to vomit.

By the time Chris returned, the brown bag at my side was full.

"Is she okay?" he asked one of the nurses.

"She's just having a bit of reaction to the medicine," someone around me responded as they held back my hair. "It's pretty common for some people to get sick from it."

I read all the hospital pamphlets, clicked on all the links about what to expect from giving birth, and watched several romantic comedies on the subject, and not one of them mentioned vomiting. If I would have had a little forewarning that this could happen, I would have packed an extra headband or two in my hospital bag. And maybe some mints.

As I vaguely listened to Chris and the nurses talk about me and what was going to happen next, I realized I was starting to float away. And it felt nice. Oh so nice. How I loved the float-away feeling before surgery. The lights got brighter, and everything inside of me felt warmer and fuzzier than it had before. My bed started to move toward the doorway, and I wondered if it always had this power. I waved goodbye to Chris, but then much to my delight, he glided right alongside my magic bed. He got to come along. How fun!

It was getting harder and harder to focus, and I wanted nothing more than to just give in to the cozy, numb feeling of floating up into the ceiling tiles, but then a little voice reminded me, *You're about to become a mom.* That's right. I was! Wasn't this supposed to be the best moment of my life according to social media and movies? Or at the very least a moment I should be awake for? *Stay present,* screamed the little voice. *This is kind of a big deal!* "But I'm so sleepy," I wanted to whisper back. "It's been a long week." I bet Chris would fill me in on whatever I missed. Right? Right . . . wrong. *Wake up!* I fought with all my might to stay awake to give birth, which for a sleepy Taurus like myself was extremely difficult. The sacrifice a mother makes, am I right?

Once in the operating room, a nurse told me to keep my arms tucked at my sides because they were about to move me "like a human burrito." Before I could ask for more details on what that meant, I was lifted in my bedsheets and transported from my magic bed onto the operating table. Every doctor and nurse that surrounded me, who I also assume helped with the lifting process, took a turn to introduce themselves. I've never been good at remembering names and didn't think now was a good time to try and start, but I studied their faces. And I'll never forget the feeling of comfort and security that washed over me when I realized they were all women. To be surrounded by such a powerful group of strong women put me so much more at ease. Mentally, I mean. Physically, I was still rather sick and only getting sicker. I couldn't possibly throw up throughout my entire delivery, could I? Turns out that yes, yes, I could.

"This will be over in no time. They're like a NASCAR pit crew," my new friend the anesthesiologist told me as she held the bag near my mouth for me. "They'll have your baby out of the sunroof in less than seven or eight minutes."

I laughed in between vomiting and wondered if she and I could get drinks after all of this was said and done.

"Do you have a playlist you'd like us to put on?" someone asked from behind the blue sheet that separated the pit crew from Chris and me.

I was too weak to respond, and for as much as Chris and I love music, this wasn't something we'd ever discussed. But without a second thought, he put on exactly what he knew I'd want to hear—"Going Up the Country" by Canned Heat.

I closed my eyes and imagined we were following the curvy roads through the canyon into the mountains. Har was in my lap with his head out the window, his tongue blowing freely in the wind with my arm riding the waves of the turns next to him.

By the time the song ended, Chris had been summoned beyond the sheet so he could watch our baby girl make her entrance into the world. Janis Joplin came on next, belting her tune about Bobby Mc-Gee, and the lovely mountain drive I was enjoying took a drastic turn when it started to feel like my body was being violently yanked back and forth, but from within. I threw up harder into the bag held by my face and wondered if I'd have any ribs left after, as I was certain they were all being shattered. Did the pit crew know they were breaking my body?

"She's almost here, Dad!" someone announced, and I tried to imagine what Chris saw, what he felt.

Without being able to control it, I started to cry as I threw up because I was so upset that after nine months of growing this baby, I was going to miss her arrival. It was only a thin blue sheet that separated us, but that thin blue sheet might as well have been a brick wall the way it kept me away from the side I so desperately wanted to be on. This was the moment I'd been waiting for, and now I couldn't be a part of it. Wasn't I supposed to be the first one who saw her open her eyes, watch her take her first breath of air, who felt her bare skin against my own? I'd heard so much about the importance of skin to skin right away, and now I was going to miss it? I wiped away my tears of self-pity but hoped they came off as tears of joy, because what kind of mom cries during birth because she feels sorry for herself? Certainly not a good one.

"Here she comes!"

Was she really here? Was she okay? Was she healthy? Who did she look like? I heard the tiniest little squawk, like a baby bird had some-how made its way into the room, and I knew it was her. Our baby girl was here! And then I immediately passed out.

I think I passed out, anyway. I actually have no idea what happened after I heard that first breath of air enter and escape our daughter's body. It was as if I drifted away to the sleepy place I was longing to be once I knew she was in good hands—her dad's. I've asked Chris several times what she was like in those first moments, and he always says, "She came out mean-mugging with her tiny fists all clenched, ready to put up a fight." I laugh whenever I hear it and think, *That's my girl*.

Chris brought her next to me while I was still on the operating table, but I don't remember it. If not for the photo the anesthesiologist took of the moment, I'd probably question whether or not it really happened. But the first photo ever taken of me as a mom shows me lying down with the thin blue hospital sheet pulled up nearly to my neck, an oxygen tube still in my nose, and a blue scrub cap on my head. My eyes are closed, but I'm smiling, or I'm trying to anyway, as my hand rests on the tiny newborn next to me whose eyes are also closed, held next to me by her dad. And I don't remember any of it.

This photo haunted me for a while, an unwanted reminder of how much I felt I missed of what I thought was supposed to be the "best moment of my life." I didn't cry tears of pure happiness or fall instantly in love or feel like my life was suddenly complete like social media led me to believe I should. I just felt nauseous and like I wanted to sleep.

But over time, a few memories have come back, and there's one in particular that I've clung to. It's the one where I got to feel my baby girl's heartbeat outside of me for the first time. I don't know if I'd been in the recovery room for five minutes or fifty, but I lay there in a fog, waiting for someone to come in, when a nurse finally slid open the door and Chris followed behind her. I sat up as straight as I could, trying to muster every bit of strength and cognition I could find, as the nurse extended our little girl toward me and placed her on my chest. I held her as close as I possibly could, her warm skin against mine, and I felt the beat of her little heart near my own. The same heartbeat I'd been hearing inside of me for the last nine months was now outside of me. So, while I may not remember much of the delivery, I remember the heartbeat. I remember the first time I heard it back in March 2020 when I prayed so desperately that I'd someday get to hear it outside of me and at every doctor's appointment thereafter when I lived to hear that little beat, sometimes making up excuses just to go in so I could get a chance to hear it for a few extra seconds. And on November 18, 2020, I finally got what I'd been praying for—to not only hear the heartbeat outside of me, but feel it in my arms as well.

"What do you think, Mom?" Chris asked as he wiped his weepy eyes and cleaned his foggy-lensed glasses for what I can only assume was the hundredth time in the past ten minutes.

"I think she's our little Birdie."

"Is that her name?"

"Birdie Harlow Hillis."

My Description of Baby Items and What They Should Actually Be Called

BABY BOOGER BONG: a tool where one end of a clear tube goes in baby's nose and the other end in your mouth. Once applied you start to suck and pray to God it has been put together correctly and that nothing lands in your mouth.

BABY BOOGER SUCKER SINGER: the thing you buy after the Booger Bong grosses you out too much, with or without boogers ever actually ending up in your mouth. The Booger Sucker Singer does the sucking for you and it lights up and plays choo choo music.

TITTY CUP: a suction cup that you stick to the nipple that doesn't currently have a baby stuck to it and that is used to catch your letdown. Letdown = milk leaking from nipple. Also a fun toy for baby to kick.

BABY COUCH: a hot dog–like pillow with bumpers that you lay baby in so you can get a break from holding baby when your back and arms start to throb. Most likely recalled at some point or another.

MECHANICAL EGG SWING: a mechanical swing that looks like a cross between an egg and EVE from *WALL-E* that is fun for baby to be mechanically rocked in and fun for Mom to watch dreamily and think, *Wow, I'd sure like a Mechanical Egg Swing to nap in.* Also probably recalled.

GIANT NECK PILLOW: a pillow shaped like a horseshoe (or giant neck pillow) that you place around your waist when breastfeeding or lounging so baby can chill on a horseshoe pillow. Also great for dogs! Again, recalled.

PLASTIC CHAIR THING: a small plastic chair that you stick baby in that they can't get out of because their legs are too chubby for the impossibly small leg slots. Definitely recalled.

and then what?

I crawled my way back toward the front before Chris hung up with Dr. Beauchamp. The snow continued to fall from the hazy mountain sky, and excited skiers stomped by our car with ski boots slung over one shoulder and their skis over the other. It was going to be a fresh-powder morning. How exciting for them.

"Is he in pain?" I asked, doing my best to keep my voice from cracking.

"It's hard to tell with dogs," she explained, "because they often choose to hide it from the people they love most."

I wiped my faucet of a nose and looked back to Har and mumbled, "Goddamnit, Carl." Because goddamnit! "Are there any signs we can look for?" We were always straight with each other; I couldn't stand it if he started lying to me now.

"If he's acting like himself and wanting to play and eat and drink like normal, then he's probably doing okay."

But for how long? I wondered. How long would Har keep acting like Har? And when he stopped, then what?

"I know this is a lot to take in," she continued, "and there's no need to make any decisions now, but I'm always here if you want to talk further about the options we discussed."

The options Dr. Beauchamp referred to included removing part of Har's skull (which would also impact his face) to try to eradicate the cancer or starting chemotherapy treatments. Based on the type of cancer and where it was located, it was unlikely that either option would give him more than six months to a year, but both would certainly involve more frequent trips to the vet.

"What would you do?" I asked quietly, knowing I probably shouldn't. "If this was your dog, I mean?"

"Well, that's hard to say because only you can know what's right for your dog." Dr. Beauchamp paused, and I worried she might not continue. "But what I can tell you is that trying to do a procedure like the one we'd need to do to remove all the cancer would be a lot of stress on an older dog for a fairly uncertain outcome."

She went on to tell us that it wouldn't be a one-and-done surgery either. It would require follow-up visits and maybe even chemo as well, and all I could imagine was a tired and anxious Har shaking near our car, tail between his legs, begging me to just please, please let him stay home.

"My advice to you, whatever you decide," she said with another long breath, "is to make sure and enjoy the time you have with Harlow right now. Do the things he loves. Give him extra treats. Spend extra moments just loving on him."

And then what? I fought the urge to ask, because I couldn't help but feel like that's exactly what I'd been doing for the past ten years in hopes that when I someday got the call like we did today, it might somehow soften the blow. Or make the agony of it all just a little less crushing knowing I'd done everything in my power to spend as much time as I possibly could with Har, giving him not just a few months of really good days but years of them. And you know what? I was wrong. There would never be enough time with my best friend.

I reminded myself once more that this wasn't about me; this was about Har.

"I know where we should go," I said to Chris after we'd hung up with Dr. Beauchamp.

"Where?" he asked, still in his ski clothes.

"The dog park."

I sat in the car while Birdie napped, and I watched Chris and Har run through the snow with the mountains at their backside. Chris ran zigzags, and Har delighted in the opportunity to do his infamous "juke" move, as we called it, where he'd fake left and then go right. He did it all the time as a puppy, outrunning every dog he met at the park and stealing all the toys he knew he shouldn't. All across the field, Chris and Har ran, the same way they ran across all the parks in Chicago we'd played in over the years. Har's juke had gotten a little slower and a little more predictable, but we'd never tell him such a thing. Chris still lunged left when he knew Har was going right just to see Har's face light up, thinking he'd beat the person he looked up to most in the world. I watched them run until I couldn't handle it anymore. I needed to play with my boy too.

"Chris," I called from the car, "swap with me."

I wasn't dressed for a snowy dog park. After all, I thought I was just dropping Chris off to ski, but I figured my sweatpants and sneakers could handle it for a bit like they used to on all our snowy Chicago walks. When Chris walked over, I saw that his eyes were red and puffy, and the thought of him playing Har's favorite games while secretly sobbing only made me cry even harder. I put my sunglasses on so Har wouldn't notice.

"Hi, buddy!" I shouted as I joined him in the park.

"Are we leaving?" he asked as he tilted his head toward me.

"No, I'm coming out to play with you." I watched as Har looked over my shoulder toward our car. "Chris is going to be with Birdie," I said.

"You mean you don't have to be with her?"

I shook my head. "Nope, I'm here to play with just you."

"Really? You actually get to play, like without holding her?"

"I actually get to play! Just you and me."

I tried not to let it tear me apart that what had once been a normal thing for me and Har for nearly a decade now seemed like a special occasion. Birdie was only a month old. Of course there would be an adjustment period, but we'd get back to normal eventually. Or at the very least, we'd find our new normal, wouldn't we? I always just assumed there'd be enough time.

"Chase me, Har!" I shouted as I started to run, the cold air stinging my throat in a way I hadn't felt since our Chicago days. My legs were stiff and heavy, and each step reminded me how badly I needed to get back on my and Har's vigorous walking schedule. But Har kept chasing, so I kept running.

I bounded through the snow in my sweats and sneakers until Har's pace started to slow a bit. He stopped suddenly, and I thought something might be wrong, but as I approached him, he faked left, then went right, and left me standing in the snow. The old Harlow juke.

"You still got it," I said triumphantly as he ran one more circle around me.

"Yes, I sure do," Har said proudly as he finally paused to get a good lean into my legs—the kind of lean that nearly knocked me over.

I scratched his belly as he looked up at me with a big smile on his sweet, sugar-coated face, and I decided right then and there, two months simply wouldn't do. Har was going to beat the odds, and I was going to help him.

it's the most wonderful time of the year—for intrusive thoughts and mental breakdowns!

NORFOLK, NEBRASKA. DECEMBER 2020.

We loaded up our car with our entire house once more to make the drive from Colorado to Nebraska for our first Christmas as new parents. I'd dreamed about this moment throughout my pregnancy. I'd listened to all the classic Christmas tunes starting in August just imagining how special the holidays would be with a new baby. If something said "baby's first Christmas" on it, I bought it. Ornaments, onesies, blankets, more footprint frames—this was surely a holiday to remember! What I didn't expect were all the intrusive thoughts that can go along with baby's first Christmas. *"Baby's First Christmas and Mom's First Christmas Having a Mental Breakdown, Certain Everyone Will Drop Baby."* Wonder why we haven't seen that on an ornament before?

On the nine-hour drive to Norfolk, Nebraska, I poured myself

into researching cancer-fighting diets and holistic treatments for
Har, a welcome distraction from the constant pestering thoughts reminding me that if I didn't have my guard up at all times with Birdie,
something terrible was certain to happen. This could include but was
not limited to:

My grandma dropping Birdie (because she was old).
My niece dropping Birdie (because she was young).
*My aunt dropping Birdie (because she was right in between young
and old).*

Truly, anyone with hands could (and probably would) drop Birdie.
My mind convinced me of it. It wouldn't be on purpose, obviously,
but accidents happen. In hindsight, "an accident" was much more
likely to occur on our nine-hour road trip across the interstate during
holiday traffic, but did that worry me? Not really, because it just made
too much sense, and my mind preferred to dwell on the more unlikely
situations. Like, for example, when I became terrified of walking under our garage door with Birdie (because it could drop on her at any
moment, obviously), just like a relative with slippery hands could
drop her, or even one with sturdy hands. Are you sensing a pattern
here? Because I certainly didn't.

I was aware my thoughts were *slightly* unhinged, at least to the
point where I could hear the grumblings in my head of, *Oh, someone
thinks she's the first person ever to have a baby,* and I rolled my eyes at
myself for once again being the woman I never understood. Was I
really going to hoard my baby and not let anyone else hold her? That
was the last thing I wanted to do. I was so proud of Birdie and wanted
to show her off, but at the same time, I was terrified. The intrusive
thoughts hounding my mind convinced me that it wasn't a matter
of *if* something bad happened but *when* . . . so did I really have any
choice in the matter?

I didn't talk to anyone about these thoughts for a while, not even

Chris, because a part of me thought maybe they were just normal mom worries, but on the drive to Nebraska, they spiraled harder than usual. I was trying so hard to focus on what new diet I should put Har on to keep him alive longer while the other half of my mind was whispering, *What about Birdie? How are you going to keep her alive this weekend?* In normal thinking times, I like to believe I could have smacked myself on the head and said, *Calm the hell down. It's just a family Christmas, not a* Game of Thrones *episode, you psycho.* But unfortunately for me and my mind, at only five weeks postpartum, I wasn't thinking normally. So instead, I gave in to the ominous thoughts and whispered back, *Tell me more . . .* and boy was I led down a dark hole.

When Chris finally asked, "What's wrong?" I just stared at him dumbly and thought, *Where do I start?* What were the chances he was also obsessively worried about a scenario in which a relative might accidentally drop Birdie down a flight of stairs, let her roll off a chair onto a concrete floor, or shatter a glass ornament near her bottle, resulting in Birdie drinking shards of glass?

"Um," I treaded lightly at first, "I'm just a little nervous about Birdie meeting everyone."

"Really? I'm excited!" he said easily, and I hated him for it.

"Me too, but like, what about . . . all the germs going around?" That sounded normal, right? It was 2020, after all. A lot of families weren't even gathering for the holidays. Up until a week ago, we were going to be one of those families but ultimately decided a smaller gathering would probably be fine. But per my request, we'd skip the finger foods and snack trays. My mom wasn't happy about forgoing her famous pickle wraps or fondue fountain, but it was a sacrifice she was willing to make.

"Well, do you want me to make sure everyone wears masks when holding Birdie?"

If that would lessen the number of people who held Birdie, then yes. I was scared of Covid, but I was more scared of someone dropping her, and I had to choose my crazy carefully. "What if we just don't let a lot of people hold her. Would that be okay?"

I could see the letdown on Chris's face, and I knew he wanted to show Birdie off as badly as I did, but he didn't have the scary thoughts to go along with it.

"Tay, everyone has been isolating. I told my mom to make sure of it. No one is going to come if they don't feel well. We said we were okay with this, I thought."

"Well," I said as fear surged through me. I knew I had to tell Chris the truth or risk another Covid fight. I think it was technically his turn to be the pandemic-cautious one for the week, but I couldn't remember since we'd gone back and forth so much. "I need to tell you something, and it's going to sound crazy, and I'm aware it's crazy, but I can't stop thinking about it, okay?"

"Okay . . ."

"I have this really intense fear that someone is going to drop Birdie. Not on purpose, obviously, and I know everyone has held a baby before and this sounds ridiculous, but it's really *really* bothering me. Like to the point where it's kept me up at night imagining all the different ways it could happen, and I don't know what to do, so I just need you to be on my team here and understand I can't really control how scared I am right now."

There have been many times in our relationship where Chris has told me I'm nuts or out of line or, worst of all, when he's responded to me in his condescending Chris voice that I absolutely loathe. But this was not one of those times. I don't know if he could see the fear on my face or hear it in my voice, but he listened to me closely as I confided in him about what I'd been feeling. I just kept telling him, "I know this sounds crazy, but I truly can't control it."

"So what can we control?" he asked, and that's where we started.

We could control where relatives held Birdie (only on soft surfaces) and how (sitting down) and if that's what we needed to do, Chris would help make sure it happened. I was mortified with myself that

I felt the need to treat relatives who were seasoned parents as if they were children who had never held a baby before, but my fear kept reminding me Birdie's safety was more important than my humiliation. And simply devising a plan made me feel so much better.

I'd later learn these thoughts were called "intrusive thoughts," and for some reason, naming them and learning that other people experienced them made me feel a lot less crazy. But once I learned about them, I wondered why there was never any mention of them on the countless postpartum depression surveys I squiggled in bubbles for at every follow-up doctor's appointment—both for Birdie and myself. I was always asked the standard questions: *Did I feel like causing harm to myself or my baby?*—which is an important thing to ask, for good reason. But I felt like my answer was the opposite: *No, absolutely not! But am I terrified of a stranger grabbing her from my arms in Target and dropping her down an escalator? Oh God, yes.* And since this was never asked and there was no space to write it in, I assumed I must be fine.

I know most stats are made up (allegedly), but one stat that I choose to believe is that over 50 percent of new mothers have said they experienced intrusive thoughts at some point in their postpartum journey. Intrusive thoughts are scary, isolating, shameful, and completely exhausting, to name just a few ways to describe how awful they can be. I wish I'd talked to someone about them sooner, because as soon as I did, they started to lessen. They didn't go away overnight, but eventually, I learned to recognize them, and I simply didn't allow them to stick around anymore. For a while, I actually spoke back to them in my head (which might have just been another bag of crazy I opened, but whatever). Responding to them in a very condescending Chris-like tone helped me feel like I took my power back just a little. *Hey, shitty little thoughts, as much as I appreciate you trying to scare the hell out of me, telling me the light on Birdie's wipe warmer might start a*

fire in the night or that a stranger is going to pull her from my baby car-
rier on a hike and heave her off a mountain, I actually don't need your
passive-aggressive assistance here. I got this. So, thanks but no thanks. I
found the snarkier I was, the better. Feel free to use this tip if it helps.

Our first stop in Nebraska was my sister's house where my five-year-
old niece, Vivi, had been waiting near the door to meet her new baby
cousin. My sister Jade (the oldest and nicest sibling, if you recall) also
happens to be the most understanding and the one always willing to
do anything to make someone feel more comfortable. After speaking
with Chris, I knew I just had to come clean with her as well.

"I'll just tell Vivi I have to hold Birdie with her. Is that okay? Or
not at all? You just tell me what you prefer, and we'll make it work,"
Jade responded, with zero judgment, I might add.

Vivi had been telling everyone at school she had a new baby sister
(and then Jade would have to explain she meant a new baby cousin
so the rumors didn't start in Norfolk), but Vivi was so excited to
finally meet her baby Birdie, and the last thing I wanted to do was
ruin that joy.

Instead, we set up the safest, softest spot possible on the couch for
Vivi to hold her while we all hovered close by. Once I saw a five-year-
old was capable of holding Birdie and not dropping her, I was able
to ease my fear (a little) and realize others probably were too. But
it wasn't until Birdie went down for the night when I was actually
able to take a breath, let my shoulders unhunch, and relax knowing I
wouldn't have to fight the good fight again until the next day.

Har, on the other hand, was in total holiday mode. He loved nothing more than being surrounded by a home full of family and food.
Har would run from person to person, backing his butt right up
into them, making sure every person in the room gave him the back
scratch he desired.

"Hey, buddy. Come get your dinner!" I announced when I saw

Har had gotten all the butt scratches he wanted and now he had his eye on the buffet table.

Until we settled on an official cancer-fighting diet for him, we'd been making him steamed vegetables with lean meat sprinkled on top. Har loved his new dinners at home, but he knew we were on vacation time in Nebraska, and thus he expected vacation food.

"Oh great!" he said excitedly. "I've been eyeing those meatballs and that cheese tray."

"I've got something even better for you!" I set the bowl of steaming veggies at his paws.

He sniffed around them and only looked at me. "Great. Where?"

"You've been loving this dish at home, so dig in!" My parents' Doberman, Ruckus, drooled closely nearby. "Ruckus would love to eat your dinner. He knows it looks yummy!"

"How about you pass it on down to Ruckus then? You know I get the good stuff when we're here."

It was true. My parents—my dad especially—often treated Har liked the golden child when he came to their house, and he ate like a king.

"Har, we can't." I sat beside him on the ground and tried to feed him from my hands. "We're trying to keep this bump on your head as small as possible, remember?"

"But it's Christmas!" he whined.

"I know. I'm sorry. Just try for me, please?" I pushed my hand full of food closer to his mouth.

He reluctantly took a few nibbles of the meat on top. "Can I get just a small plate of meatballs if I eat this?"

"Just a small plate, I suppose."

What Har didn't know was that I planned to give him a few meatballs with his pills hidden inside anyway. Per the advice of Dr. Beauchamp, he was on a daily painkiller and a few different vitamins. The painkiller hadn't changed Har's mood or activity, but it gave us a little peace of mind that if he was in pain and choosing to hide it from us, the painkiller would help hide it from him. That was our hope anyway and the reason I spent countless hours tucking pills in food twice a day so Har wouldn't notice them.

"Let's take this plate to the guest room to eat so Ruckus doesn't get jealous," I said to Har as I cut up a meatball and sprinkled just a little parmesan on top.

"But I like to make him jealous."

"I know you do, and that's why you're not going to eat in here."

I led Har to the guest room where Birdie slept and held the plate near his face as he devoured everything on it in less than ten seconds, continually licking his lips and jowls to make sure he got every last bite. Birdie was still at that magical age where she could sleep through anything—a door opening, a holiday party, or a dog loudly licking his lips after a plate of meatballs.

"Was that good, buddy?"

"Absolutely divine. Let's do one more plate. What do you say?" Har looked to the door, ready for me to prepare him another helping.

"Sit with me for a second, will you?" I sat on the bed and patted the spot next to me. Har jumped up and rested his head on my legs.

I loved time spent back in Nebraska surrounded by family I didn't often get to see, but my introverted soul also craved its alone moments—the moments where Har and I would sneak away just to take a breath from the chatter and social buzz that sometimes drained me. Our stolen moments had been recharging me for as long as I could remember.

Birdie stirred in her crib, and both Har and I glanced over at her.

"Is she okay?" he asked, and I nodded.

"I think so."

"I can tell you're nervous about her being here—more than you are at home."

Perhaps I wasn't hiding my anxiety as well as I had hoped. Then again, I could never hide my worry from Har.

"I am," I admitted. "And it's exhausting."

"You're tired a lot now," he said as he stared at Birdie's crib.

"I'm sorry. I know it's been hard, but it will get better. I promise."

Har didn't interact with Birdie much, and I never pressed it because I knew (or I hoped) he'd come around in his own time. I invited him on all the Birdie activities—feeding, bathing, tummy time—and in the beginning, he joined and pretended to have fun for my sake. But other times, he preferred to stay with Chris in his office.

"I'm still deciding about her," Har said as he stood on the bed and placed himself between me and Birdie's crib. "I just can't tell if she's good for us or not."

"I know you are, Har, but she is. Trust me, okay?"

The lights on the guest room Christmas tree flickered—because every room in my parents' house had a Christmas tree—and I pulled Har back toward me, and we both relaxed a little more. As we sat in the soft glow of the lights, with Birdie fast asleep in her crib next to us, James Taylor's voice filled the rest of the house. Har stretched his paws outward, and I stroked the bump on his head that was trying to take him away from me and prayed that it didn't win.

"Merry Christmas, sweet boy," I whispered.

"Merry Christmas," Har said as he turned to look at me. "Know what would make tonight even better?"

"What's that, buddy?"

"Another plate of meatballs."

I shook my head and mumbled, "Goddamnit, Carl," as I both smiled and cried a little.

harlow the unicorn

Two months after we were told Harlow probably only had two months left to live, he was running hot laps at the dog park, refusing to leave. I pushed a three-month-old Birdie in her bassinet stroller across the dirt, begging him to go.

"Fine, Har. I'm leaving. See you later!" I threatened.

"Bye!" he responded as he lay belly to the ground, calling my bluff.

"Good luck getting into our house. I bet you didn't even bring keys." This line had never worked, and yet I continued to use it.

He stared at me amusingly before rolling on his back and kicking his legs in the air, and boy did it piss me off.

Birdie started to fuss, and I knew he'd won. "You'll get a denty stick if you agree to leave right now."

"Two. I want two."

"Fine! Let's go."

Har was still very much Har, which was occasionally annoying but mostly a giant blessing we didn't take for granted. Other than the bump on his head, which continued to grow, his mind and body (and appetite) seemed to be thriving. A "critical care" diet was flown in from California and delivered weekly to ensure Har got all the vitamins and nutrients needed to fight the cancer he was battling. So far it seemed to be working.

"I bet he'll show us all and live ten more years and just end up looking like a unicorn with a huge horn on his head," Chris liked to joke.

It felt good to joke about Har's diagnosis, even if it was only a mask for our heavy worry. We prayed spring would arrive early so we could get outside and give Har another season of hikes. Colorado living had also made Chris obsessed with the idea of buying a camper van, and he researched them religiously.

"Do you know how awesome it would be to take a van all over Colorado and just camp wherever we wanted after a hike? Har would love it!" Chris said with stars in his eyes nearly every single night, dreaming about what life must be like on four wheels.

And I supported this dream, assuming it would never happen.

But one Monday in February, Chris mentioned that he found a great Sprinter van to rent for the weekend, and should we give it a go? In hindsight, renting a camper van in the middle of winter was not the best idea, and we both knew it, but we'd been trying to find a way to re-create our magical Utah/Yellowstone trip we took Har on the previous year, and this felt like a way. We knew it would be a trip Har would love, and more important, we knew our time was ticking.

"Let's do it!" I said without thinking it through, as per usual.

"Okay, we're booked!" Chris responded, also not thinking it through, which was rather unlike him, but like I said, van life was his dream, and sometimes following our dreams clogs our vision a bit.

By the time the weekend arrived, the weather took a major shift, and we were about to experience the coldest spell in Colorado since we'd moved there. The Sprinter Chris rented was fully equipped to be in such elements. Heat could run even while the van was technically not running, but I wasn't sure I was equipped to deal with such elements. I'd grown soft since leaving Chicago. We also had a three-month-old now, and what exactly were we supposed to do all weekend while living in a van in five-degree weather?

"Remind me again why we're doing this?" I asked Chris as I loaded a bag full of bottles and breast-pump pieces.

"Because we want Har to experience van life."

"Right." This was for Har.

And from the moment Chris parked the van in front of our house and started loading it with supplies, Har excitedly joined him, planting his butt on the passenger seat, constantly asking, "Is it time yet? Can we go now? What about now?"

Har was happy, so Chris and I were happy. Birdie, however, was somewhat skeptical as we strapped her in the car seat, and her big eyes took in the space around her that was to be her home for the next couple of days.

"Welcome to van life, Birdie girl!" Chris said as he pulled off our street and toward the interstate leading us to the mountains.

Flurries dusted our windshield as we hit the Eisenhower Tunnel, and as Chris and I sat in the front bucket seats looking down on all the other drivers, we felt like we owned the road, and like this was going to be the best weekend ever.

We. Were. Wrong. Holy shit, were we wrong.

Our naivete was almost endearing, as both new parents and people new to van life, because we had no idea what we'd just gotten ourselves into. Roughly five hours later when we finally reached Aspen, Birdie was screaming because she needed to be fed, my boobs were screaming to feed her, and I was screaming at Chris to just pull over already!

"I don't know where to park this thing," he shouted since all the parking spots he'd researched beforehand were full.

Meanwhile, Har paced from the front to the back because the sounds of the van (and probably all the screaming) made him very uneasy. It felt like all hell had broken loose. And then Chris hit a pothole, and the cabinet holding my pump pieces flung open, and suddenly five different pieces meant to attach to my boobs were rattling around the van as well. But it wasn't until we were driving up and down the main streets looking for a place to temporarily park, surrounded by the ritzy folk of Aspen in their furry Gucci snow boots and their furry Gucci snowsuits, all headed into their ritzy hotels, when it dawned on me that we wouldn't be heading into a hotel—not even a crappy one. I always knew the plan was to sleep in the van, but for whatever reason, it wasn't until we got to our destination and the feeling of "I can't wait to get out of this thing" overcame me that I suddenly remembered, *Oh wait. We're not getting out of this thing. Because we live in this van now!* Okay, it was only for the weekend, but it might as well have been forever as I struggled to get Birdie from her car seat, dig through my bags to find wipes and diapers, find a clear spot to change her in the van, and then begin the process of feeding and pumping. All the while, the unnecessary piles of stuff I'd packed were scattered everywhere. Literally everywhere. It was comical (and very stupid) how much crap we brought. If you're an experienced van-lifer, or even someone with a little common sense, imagine packing an enormous stroller, a BabyBjörn bouncer, and numerous outfit changes for a *van weekend*! And then imagine trying to wash pump pieces four to six times a day (and two to three times at night) in a tiny sink where your husband is constantly reminding you to "not use too much water!" But I'm getting ahead of myself here, especially considering we barely made it to the night.

After Chris found a place to park downtown and we all got some food in our bellies, things improved a little, as things tend to do with pizza and a couple of beers. Once Chris found us an easy and rather picturesque hike right outside of town, things improved even more. There was a place where we could let Har run off-leash through the snow, and he frolicked and ran free in a way I think both Chris and I worried we may never get to see him do again after that call in Steamboat. The van trip wasn't a total disaster, after all!

Until it was time to get back into the van. At which point we tracked in slushy, dirty snow everywhere mixed with some blood. Blood? Why was there bloody, dirty snow all over the floor?

"Har, are you bleeding?" I nervously checked his head and face.

"No," he said as he casually licked his paw, and that's when we realized he'd ripped his paw pad.

"What happened, buddy? Are you okay?"

"I'm fine. Let's go back out and play!"

Chris examined his paw closely and couldn't see any signs of glass or what may have caused the tear, but we knew we had to wrap it and that the last thing Har should do was run on it in the snow anymore.

"Well, shit," I said as I held Birdie in one arm and elevated Har's paw in the other. "What now?"

"Let's head to the place where we're going to park and sleep for the night. It's supposed to be this great spot right near a mountain stream, and I bet it will be super cool based on all the posts van people have written about it. We'll make dinner and just have a cozy little night. How does that sound?"

In my head, it sounded quite idyllic. I envisioned a snowy mountain evening overlooking a beautiful stream that engulfed the snowflakes that fell around us. I saw Chris cooking pasta on the little van stove while I sipped wine and held Birdie, Har fast asleep in his cozy bed, all of us toasty and happy in our little camper van. That wouldn't be so bad, right?

We drove around for two hours searching for that spot. When we finally got there, it was dark outside, but not too dark to realize the "idyllic" spot was literally just a shoulder right off a curvy mountain road next to an ominous-looking winter stream that was just waiting to eat Birdie. (My intrusive thoughts had lessened, but they were definitely still around.) Chris and I argued for the next forty-five minutes about what to do next. Neither of us wanted to stay on the shoulder of death, but we also didn't know where to go next. I aggressively cleaned bottles in the tiny sink using the limited water we had as Chris struggled to get service on his phone to find where we should go next.

The only place Chris found to legally park the van for the night was in a grocery store parking lot about an hour away.

The bottles and pump pieces rattled in the cabinets behind us and eventually came crashing out again, and we both knew I hadn't correctly shut the cabinets. But neither of us said a word or even released a sigh. Instead, we just held our angry breaths tight in our chests, as married couples sometimes do when they know the fight is better had in their heads for the time being.

We made it to the grocery store parking lot, got the van ready for our "idyllic" night, and finally took a breath of air once we poured ourselves a glass of wine. We were so exhausted by the time we took that first sip of Sancerre, our anger had all but disappeared, or at least tucked itself away for a rainy day.

"I almost just drove us back to Denver," Chris admitted as he finished his glass in nearly one large sip.

"I know. And I almost booked us a hotel," I admitted.

"I know. Why didn't you?"

"The cheapest I could find was twelve hundred dollars a night." *Fucking Aspen.*

"Tay, this was such a terrible idea," Chris said as he bounced Birdie in his lap. "I usually think things through better than this."

I chuckled, thinking that finally after all these years, I was maybe starting to rub off on him a bit. "It's not so bad to be a dreamer, right?"

"Uh, we're sleeping in a van in a grocery store parking lot with a baby and dog." He stood up and looked out the window, and rather than seeing a mountain stream, we saw a blue dumpster next to a green dumpster.

"And the baby and dog both seem pretty happy, don't you think?" Of course, I was still a little annoyed with the situation myself, but I hated to see Chris so down. He was finally taking a chance and chasing a dream of his (albeit a bit of an odd dream, some might say), but I didn't want him to only see defeat.

Birdie pulled at his beard and giggled while Har chewed a bully stick in the bed we'd made for him at our feet.

"I just really don't know what I was thinking booking a camper van in the middle of winter."

"Yeah, you do," I said as I glanced at Har. "You were thinking about him."

Because what kind of dream was van life if Har never got to experience it?

the part i don't want to write

DENVER, COLORADO. MAY 2021.

The moment the snow cleared from the mountains, we started hiking every chance we got. Birdie seemed to accept her fate as being born into an outdoorsy family and did surprisingly well on most of the trails, except for the few she didn't, and the times I had to carry her up a mountain because she wouldn't settle in her pack were rather stressful (and also painful). She was a heavy baby! But it also made me feel like Superwoman knowing I could carry another body for several miles at ten thousand feet.

I encouraged the hikes, even on the weekends I didn't want to, because in the back of my mind, I worried any one of them could be Har's last. He was still a wild boy on the trails, but at home, he'd started to seem sleepier than normal.

"You doing okay, Har?" I'd ask when I started to leave the room and he no longer followed. Har always followed me.

"I'm just worn out from the weekend is all," he'd say with a yawn as he slept on the couch. "That was a good hike we did. I can't wait for the next."

"Me neither, Har."

He ran like crazy in the mountains, then recharged all week. That seemed okay, right?

"Right, Dr. Beauchamp? Is it okay if we keep hiking with him? I don't want to push him too hard."

"If he's enjoying it and eating and drinking like normal, it's absolutely okay. Keep doing what you're doing. It's amazing to see how well he's done," she told me at every checkup.

So we continued our hikes. But the bump above Har's eye continued to grow. By May it was nearly the size of a golf ball.

My parents rented a house on the beach in North Carolina for Memorial Day weekend, and after canceling so many trips in 2020, I felt the fragility of family vacations more than I had before and knew I didn't want to miss it. Chris wasn't able to attend because he had to work, but Birdie and I jumped on a plane to meet my parents and siblings in Kure Beach.

Our trip was scheduled for Wednesday to Saturday, so we could get back to Denver and still spend a few days with Chris and Har during the holiday weekend and hopefully get a couple hikes in.

On Thursday night, I called Chris to see how things were going at home, and he made small talk about hating work, asking how Birdie liked the ocean, and how was everyone in my family doing? He sounded off, and I assumed it was because he was strapped to his desk (end-of-quarter sales crap), but when I pressed on, I could tell it was something more.

"What's going on? You sound weird."

"Oh nothing. We can just talk about it when you get back," he said, but I have to assume he knew better.

You can't tell an anxious person like me something like that and assume they'll accept it. "What's wrong? Is it Har? Should we come back tomorrow, because we can."

"No, it's okay. He's just acting different, but it's probably because you're gone. He's always weird when you're gone."

"Weird like how?" Har got sulky whenever Chris or I was away because he preferred us all together, all the time. So maybe it was just that.

"He hasn't eaten much, and he started doing this unusual thing with his head, like he couldn't get it to his bowl. Like he tried to dip his head down, but he couldn't figure it out. I called Dr. Beauchamp, and she's supposed to call me back tomorrow, so we'll get it figured out."

"Okay . . ."

"Just don't worry about it, for real. I wasn't going to say anything because there's nothing you can do from North Carolina. So just enjoy your time at the beach, and we'll see you Saturday."

I worried about it every single second until Birdie and I boarded our plane back to Denver on Saturday. What was supposed to be close to a three-hour flight ended up being nearly six hours due to weather, taxiing extra long, and perhaps just bad travel karma because I was flying United. Both Birdie and I got off the plane looking like two disheveled messes. When I saw Chris waiting for us near the baggage claim, I nearly cried. I expected him to pick us up, but actually parking and coming inside? Well, that was next-level.

"Travel day from hell!" I screeched as I handed Birdie over to him. "My clothes are damp, and I have no idea why. It's either milk, water, or pee. Or all of the above."

I didn't ask about Har yet because I wasn't ready to ask. But when we got out to the car, he was waiting for me in the back, as was a travel mug of wine Chris had brought along for me.

"You went all out," I said as I tried not to read too much into it. "Hi, Har. How are you, buddy? I missed you. I missed you so much."

"I just figured after the travel day you had, you could use some wine is all," Chris said.

"You're back!" Har whimpered. "I worried you weren't coming back."

"Har, I told you I'd be right back, didn't I? And I always come back, you know that." I held his face close to mine and tried to read his mind—what he was thinking, how he was feeling—but lately it was getting harder to know. "Are you doing okay, sweet boy?"

"I'm just happy you're home," he said as he buried his face closer to mine.

When we got to our house, I saw that Chris had steaks mari-nating—the finest cuts from a local Colorado farm. I don't love steak, but Har does. Once we put Birdie to bed, I collapsed on the couch and patted my chest so Har would join me.

"So what's going on with him?" I finally asked Chris after feeling hopeful that Har seemed to be acting normal.

"Just wait. You'll see. I'm grilling steaks because they're his favor-ite, and I just want to make sure he'll eat them."

"He's refusing steak?"

"Not refusing. It's like he can't do it. Dr. Beauchamp said it might be because the cancer has moved into his brain."

"What does that mean?" I pulled Har in closer, praying that he'd eat the stupid steak and prove to me that all was okay.

"I don't know, Tay." Chris wiped his eyes and turned away.

For the first of what would be many times, a deep sense of regret overcame me for leaving Har to go to North Carolina.

The aroma of freshly grilled steaks filled our living room as Chris brought them inside, and I held my breath to see what Har might do. He stepped down from the couch and walked toward the plate of sizzling meat, and my heart leapt a bit. Maybe it was all in Chris's head after all! And then I saw his back foot slip. It wasn't much, just a minor slip like he used to do when we ran laps in the winter at Pu-laski Park and we'd hit a patch of ice. But I pretended not to notice because maybe it was just in my head too.

Chris cut up a few pieces of filet and dropped it into Har's bowl, which he'd moved to an even more elevated spot to make it easier for him. *Eat it, buddy,* I prayed. *Be okay. Please, please just be okay.* Har lowered his head, and he ate the steak! Joyfully, I might add, pausing between each bite to turn back toward Chris and me to smile and lick his lips.

"That's a good sign, right?" I looked to Chris, begging him to con-firm he was wrong.

"I'm glad he's eating it." Chris left the sentence hanging, and we both knew there was a "but" coming that neither of us actually wanted to hear, so I interrupted him before it could arrive.

"Where should we hike tomorrow?"

"The weather's not looking very promising. Lots of rain in the mountains."

"I don't care. We have to at least try, right? We have to go somewhere, if only for a little bit. We have to." There was an urgency in my voice that surprised even myself.

But I needed to see mountain-Har happy and free on a trail doing what he loved. Certainly he would be himself on a hike. I was sure of it.

Ready to go in all the waterproof gear we now owned, we set out the following morning for a rainy Sunday hike.

"Wanna go on an adventure?" Chris asked as he brought Har's green hiking vest inside.

"Always!" Har responded as he waited near the back door, his tail zigzagging back and forth.

I let myself believe for a second that this hike was going to solve everything. The mountains would cure Har, and we could go back to normal, back to joking about him being a diva and griping at him to leave the dog park. All I wanted was our normal. But as Chris loaded our packs and boots into the back of the car, rather than jumping in before the trunk door had even fully opened, Har just put his front paws up and looked over his shoulder for assistance.

"Need some help, buddy?" Chris asked as he lifted Har into the back.

"Just a little," Har said quietly.

We played Canned Heat as we drove to the least rainy area Chris could find. A light mist coated our windshield, and I prayed the rain would subside enough for Har to enjoy the hike rather than get upset about getting wet. When we got to the trailhead, the lot was surprisingly empty, a benefit of the weather, perhaps. Once we got our boots laced and Birdie situated in her pack, the rain had all but stopped, but it made sure to leave a green tint hanging in the air as a reminder it could return at any moment.

Chris opened the door to the back, and instead of jumping out at his first chance like usual, Har once again looked to us for assistance.

"You up for this, Har?" I slowly lowered him to the ground. "Because we can head home if you want."

"Turn down a hike? Never!" he said with a smile as he hustled toward the trail.

Chris and I looked to one another with hesitant yet hopeful smiles. Maybe the past few days were just minor setbacks? And then we saw it. We saw Har's back paws start to drag—not a lot, but enough that we both noticed it. But Har pressed on and didn't want to turn back, so we did the same.

I knew in my soul this was an important hike for Har, but I didn't know it would be his last. Or maybe I just wasn't ready to admit it.

so many good days

DENVER, COLORADO. JUNE 2021.

We rearranged our rugs and cut up all my yoga mats so Har could walk on our main floor without slipping on our hardwoods. Like a children's game of "the floor is lava," as long as Har stayed on the soft spots and patches of mat, the lava couldn't get him.

"Har, do you remember when you chewed a perfect square in the middle of this yoga mat our first summer in Chicago?" I asked as I cut it into even smaller pieces. "I didn't want to buy a new one, so I just continued to bring a mat with a random square chewed out of the middle to class every week."

"I did no such thing," Har said with a smirk. "But I think that was the same week I ate all of the dollar bills you left out on the counter."

"They were twenty-dollar bills, Har."

What made Har's decline extra painful was that his body may have been failing him, but his mind and spirit were still very much Har. Sometimes even Carl. When he barked at the doorbell when the mail carrier stopped by, I nearly cried tears of joy.

"That's right, Har! You protect this house," I shouted.

Given the number of times I'd explicitly told him no more barking at the doorbell (because of Birdie sleeping), he looked at me like I was crazy. "So now this is okay?" he mumbled with a side eye, and I'd never loved a glare from him more.

The rainy hike we did only two days ago, Har wouldn't be able to do today. He could barely make it to the park a few blocks away without dragging his back paws on the pavement. I bought him a wagon because I thought that might help, but he hated it.

"This is humiliating," Har said when I tried to pull him down the alley.

"No, it's not. It's fun!" I said with false enthusiasm.

"Oh yeah? Then how about you ride in it?"

I also bought him gripper socks, gripper shoes, and nail pads, but these were all just Band-Aids. When I saw the vet's office number pop up on my phone, I took a deep breath and stepped outside. I'd been practicing trying to keep it together for this call all morning.

"So, I hear Harlow is starting to have a rough time," Dr. Beauchamp said slowly.

"Yes, he . . ." I couldn't say anything more before I started to weep. "I'm sorry. I thought I could talk without doing this." I hiccupped and choked on my words as my face leaked from everywhere. "It's just really hard."

Dr. Beauchamp saw him only a month ago, and he was doing so good. "Remarkably good," she had said, and I wanted to hold her to those words. *You said that, Dr. Beauchamp. Remember?!*

"It sounds like what's happening now is what we expected to happen back in December or January, but thanks to your incredible care, you've gotten him so much longer. I know you don't feel lucky right now," Dr. Beauchamp explained, "but you are."

I appreciated her sympathy. I really did. But I also couldn't help but shake my head and wish she'd just shup up. I was losing my best friend. What was so lucky about that? *I don't make friends easily, Dr. Beauchamp,* I wanted to shout. *Har is my friend. It's been him and me every single day for the past ten years.* Didn't she understand this?

"How will we know when it's time?" I asked timidly.

"Well, there's a few things we always look out for—"

"His tail still wags," I interrupted, feeling this was crucial information Dr. Beauchamp must know before she continued. "He still wants to be with us. I can tell."

But even as I said it, I knew Har would always want to still be with us, so his tail may never stop wagging.

"That's definitely good, but we also look for things that keep a dog independent. Like can he go to the bathroom on his own? And is he still eating and drinking?"

"He is!" I said with excitement.

We no longer fed him food flown in from California because once Har realized he could have steak or meatballs instead, he wouldn't eat anything else. We raised his bowls even higher since it was becoming increasingly hard for him to lower his head, but Har was still able to do it. Sometimes I fed him with a fork, but that was always because I wanted to.

"Then today isn't the day, and tomorrow might not be either."

"We don't want him to be in pain." I glanced inside where he was fast asleep on the couch. "Or to keep him around just for our sake."

"Then you just need to be aware he could decline quickly."

"I am," I said as I swallowed my guilt for going to North Carolina the previous week.

"He could walk just fine when you left," Chris had tried to remind me. "You couldn't have known things would change so quick."

But I should have known. He's my Har. He needed me, and I left.

Even with the scraps of yoga mats, soon the stairs were no longer manageable for Har either. And that's when I started to carry him. In the mornings, I'd bring Birdie down first and get her situated in her activity center, then I'd run back up and grab Har.

"Hi, buddy. Ready to go out?" I'd ask when I saw him waiting at the top for me, his tail always wagging.

"I'm ready," he'd respond with a sleepy look on his face. The bump above his left eye had grown so big he was no longer able to fully open it.

As I'd bend down, careful to get a good grip on Har's big body, I'd think about all the mornings I'd asked him this over the years. From our small apartment in Kansas to every brownstone rental and condo in Chicago and finally our home in Denver.

"Here we go," I'd say as I lifted and Har leaned into me.

Unlike the wagon, he didn't object or complain. But instead, Har rested his chin on my shoulder as I carried him down, and I felt like it was because he knew this was the first step toward getting our morning started. And oh how we loved our mornings together. We always had. Whatever home we were living in, Har would wait on the closest rug while I prepared his breakfast, his tail swooshing back and forth like a proud puppy who had just learned to sit while he watched my every move. Har no longer looked like a puppy anymore—far from it—and yet I swore I could still see it in the mornings.

Before I put his bowls down, I'd lean over and give him a hug. I know most dogs don't like hugs, but Har was never like most dogs. I'd tell him how much I loved him and that we were going to have a good day, a little ritual I started back in Kansas—my way of telling him he wasn't going to chew up any shoes or remote controls for the day—and it hadn't stopped ten years later.

Har devoured his breakfast, still loving the leftovers we let him feast on. And as long as he continued to eat and drink, we still had more time. I helped him onto the couch and prayed Birdie would take a long morning nap later so I could get some alone time with him. I needed our morning routine. I needed our chats. I needed us.

"Har, are you okay?" I'd ask when I sat with him, hoping he'd tell me or give me a sign if he wasn't.

"I'm okay. Are you okay?" he'd say with his head tilt, studying my face as if he too was looking for a sign.

"Because if you're ready to go, you can tell us," I'd say quietly, not sure if I really wanted him to hear it or not. "I don't want you to be in pain."

"I'm just sleepy is all," he'd respond, never willing to acknowledge any pain or why I might be asking.

And once he rested his head on my legs and closed his eyes, I'd let go of the tears I'd been holding in since the last time he napped.

Before the sun rose the following morning, I woke up to whimpering in our bathroom. I bolted from our bed, confused and upset with myself that I hadn't heard Har get up and been able to help him. I found him standing in the shower with his tail tucked tightly between his legs.

"Har, are you okay? What's going on?"

"I'm sorry," he whined. "I didn't want to wake you, but I couldn't hold it. I'm so, so sorry."

Behind Har, in the corner of the shower, were three very loose piles of stool.

"Oh, buddy. It's not your fault. Please don't feel bad. This really isn't your fault." I carried him from the shower toward the stairs.

"What happened?" Chris asked when he finally woke up (always the late one to the middle-of-the-night wake-up game).

"He pooped in the shower, and he feels awful about it."

Even in my arms, Har hung his head away from Chris and tucked his tail.

"It's okay, Har," Chris said as he cupped his face. "Don't worry about it. No one is mad."

Chris scrubbed the shower while I took Har outside and cleaned him up. I made a bed for us on the couch and decided we'd better sleep downstairs in case he had to go out again.

"I'm really sorry," he said once more as he laid his head on my chest. "Are you upset?"

"Not at all. It wasn't your fault, sweet boy."

"You promise?"

"To be honest, Har, I'm kind of impressed. I know Chris is too.

Pooping in the shower is way more thoughtful than pooping on the rug like you used to do as a puppy."

"I didn't think it was the worst idea," he admitted with a hint of optimism in his brows.

"It truly wasn't. I'd take it over the white rugs you used to choose any day."

"I just wanted us to have a good day today, is all." Har burrowed his head into the crook of my neck.

"We will, Har. We'll have a really good one."

We've had so many good days.

i'll be right back

We spent Har's last day near a mountain stream where he could lie in his bed and feel the sunshine on his face and the early summer breeze blow through his ears. Walking at all was a struggle for him now, so he wore a vest with handles that allowed us to assist him. We would have just carried him to the stream, but Har still wanted to try and walk. He even wanted to chase the squirrels but settled on just watching them from his bed.

Birdie, Chris, and I sat on a blanket next to his bed, and while Birdie ate dirt and clapped rocks together, Chris and I took turns telling our favorite Har stories. Har basked in the attention and continued to request we "tell one more, tell one more," by slapping his paw on our arms if we had the audacity to stop talking about him. When Chris carried Birdie away for a moment to collect some wild succulents that we intended to bring home and plant in Har's honor, I plopped down next to him and pulled him into my lap. I draped his head with a crown of braided grass like I used to do when he was a puppy at the playgrounds in Chicago.

"King Harlow!" I sang as I twirled his ears between my fingers. "The king of all the playgrounds where he's technically not supposed to play, but we always do anyway! Remember when I used to sing that?"

He looked at me with his big brown eyes and nodded and then sighed heavily.

"Are you okay, Har?" There was something different about this look, about his sigh.

"I think I know now," he said softly.

"What do you know?" I held his face close to mine, studying every part of it for what he was trying to tell me.

"That she's good for us."

"Who, Har?"

"Birdie." He looked toward the spot where Chris carried her on his shoulders, and she giggled as he held her small hands in his. "I wasn't sure at first, but now I know. She can make you guys happy."

"Oh, Har," was all I could muster. I'd been trying so hard to not let him see me cry, but I was failing. "You've made us so happy—happier than I could ever tell you."

"And now Birdie will. See, you wanted to make sure I wasn't in pain, but I had to do the same for you, because that's always been my job. And I couldn't leave until I knew. But now I do."

..

I had an in-home euthanasia specialist waiting on standby for when Har told us he was ready to go. As we drove back to Denver from our time spent near the stream, I called and scheduled an appointment for later in the evening. We dropped Birdie by my cousin's house so we could have some last alone time with Har and then rolled down all the windows in the car and played "Going Up the Country" as we drove home.

Chris and I spent the next few hours lying next to Har telling him what a good boy he'd been and how lucky we were that we got to be his. He lay with his head in Chris's lap and his paws outstretched in my lap, gazing at each of us periodically to let us know he was listening. The paws that once looked so comically oversized on Har when he was a puppy now felt so fragile and small as I held them in my hands today.

When the veterinarian arrived, rather than cowering and panicking like Har did at every vet's office, he remained relaxed and content, safe in his own bed. There was some relief, even if it was quite minimal, in knowing we got to say goodbye at home instead of the place Har hated most in the world.

The veterinarian, a soft-spoken man who told us to call him Paulo, explained the process to us as we numbly filled out the necessary paperwork. He told us that the first injection was a sedative to relax Harlow so he wouldn't feel any pain and that the second injection was the one that stopped the brain from functioning, which ultimately stopped the heart from beating. I felt like I'd gone into a robotic-like state—signing my name where I had to and saying yes when asked questions that needed a yes—simply to keep the process moving. But if I really stopped and thought about what the process was, I'd crumble. So, I didn't. I kept moving forward knowing that at this moment, Har needed the full version of me, not the one about to break into a million heartbroken pieces.

Before the first needle was administered, I somehow pulled Har even closer than he already was.

"I want you to know something, Har." I held his sweet white face in my hands, as I was ready to say the words that I had held in my heart for years now but could never quite articulate. "We didn't decide to have Birdie because you weren't enough. I finally knew I wanted to be a mom because you've been so much, Har."

"That was my plan all along," he said softly. "I couldn't leave you with just anyone. God forbid another dog," he mumbled, and I laughed despite myself.

"God forbid," I agreed as I wondered who would ever make me

laugh again the way Har did. "I love you, buddy. I love you so much."
I buried my face into the folds of his neck, hoping to muffle my sobs.

I took in his scent as best as I could, a smell that felt like home and
comfort to me, and the warmth of his soft, floppy ears that were velvet against my skin. I took it all in, never wanting to let go.

"I'm scared, Har," I finally admitted. "I'm so scared." I shouldn't
have said it. This was my time to be there for him, and yet there I was,
still leaning on Har like I always had.

"Don't worry," he whispered as he nudged me with his nose, his
pushy way of saying "listen to me." "You don't have to worry."

"How can I not? You're leaving me."

"But it will be okay. I promise."

"I don't want you to go," I cried. "I can't do this without you. I
really can't."

"Yes, you can." Har put his paw on my arm and stared at me intently, the kind of deep stare that always made people remark what
human-like expressions he had. "Because I'll be right back, okay? I
promise. I'll be right back."

epilogue

A Very Long Epilogue About Missing My Best Friend

After the first needle was injected, Har closed his eyes and never opened them again. I was warned it was the second injection that took him away, but to me, it always felt like it was the first. I never got to see his soft brown eyes gaze at me again after that first dose or feel his warm breath on me after a big yawn. After Paulo administered the second injection, he waited a few seconds before checking for Harlow's heartbeat, but I knew he was gone. I didn't need anyone to confirm it. With a spirit as big as Har's, the world immediately felt a little emptier the moment it left and has ever since.

I woke up in the middle of the night following Har's death, certain I heard Birdie crying, only to realize it was me. I was the one sobbing. Sleep had always given me an escape from a pain I didn't want to feel, but not tonight. There was no escaping the blackness that engulfed me as I woke up in a panic that Har wasn't next to me and never would be again. I ran to the blue velvet chair in our bedroom that he wasn't supposed to sit in, arguably the one thing in our house that was off-limits, which of course meant it was his chair of choice, and I collapsed in it, gasping for a breath I couldn't find.

"Give me a sign, Har. Please!" I begged like a maniac. "Please give me something. I just need to know you're still with me. Send me a sign!"

I prayed to see a vizsla walking by our house at that very moment. That would be my sign, and I was just sure Har would send it. And you know what? There was no vizsla walking outside of our house at three o'clock in the morning, because of course there wasn't. I went back to bed only because it was a better option than sitting in the blue chair, staring into the darkness, waiting for a sign that wouldn't arrive.

Before Har's death, I did my best to prepare for all his lasts. Our last walk to the park together, our last nap on the couch, the last time I felt his scratchy paw stretch into the ball of my foot after he crawled under the blankets next to me. But when I got up the first morning after he was gone, I realized I'd forgotten about all the firsts. I looked at the bare spot in our bed where he always was and said to myself, *Ready to go out, Har?* . . . because I didn't know how to not say it. His leash remained hung near the door and his bowls, empty. Sloth stayed in the toy basket.

In the days following, Birdie was a welcome distraction. If not for her, I don't think I could have gotten out of bed. My friend Tyeler, a busy mom with three small children, dropped everything on her schedule to fly out and help me, an act of kindness I don't think I can ever repay. Never one to hide her opinions, Tye admitted she never quite understood my "weird relationship" with my dog, but she clearly understood my love for him. I'd soon learn a lot of people did—more than I ever knew.

Our house overflowed with flowers from friends and family offering their condolences. Chris said that our kitchen "looked like a funeral home," and he was right. Har would have loved all the attention. When I shared on my Instagram that Har was no longer with us, the messages came flooding in. Over a hundred sat unread within the first hour after I shared. To those who shared they'd also once lost a dog they loved dearly, and their hearts ached for us, I responded, "When does it go away?" I really believed there might be an expiration date on the pain I felt. Was it a month? Two months? How long would it take until I felt normal again?

I've learned the only honest answer to this is that the grief doesn't go away; it simply changes, and in doing so, it changes you. But it's taken me a long (annoyingly long) time to accept and understand this. In the beginning, I searched high and low for a remedy for my heartache. Certainly there was a book I could read or crystal I could rub that would end my grief or, at the very least, lessen it. I simply couldn't live with the pain of missing Har so much, especially when I knew the one thing that always made my ache go away was . . . Har. At one point, I even got the grand idea to call a pet medium "just so I can talk to him one more time," I told Chris, who simply nodded and said, "Whatever you think will help."

Sadly, I quickly learned it wasn't as easy to call my dead dog as I had hoped. When channeling Har, the medium spoke in a thick Jersey accent and talked about how much Har loved the Vegas strip and thought "Denver was so vanilla." *Har's never even been to Vegas* was all I could think as a stranger I'd found online continued to ramble about my dog like he was from the Jersey Shore. She finished the call by telling me Har would come back into our lives right before Birdie's second birthday. I wouldn't have to worry about finding him because he'd find me. *Sure, sure, sure. I'll look for him at the craps table.*

I stopped trying to call Har after that interaction because it only set me back. I had to learn to move forward without him or, at the very least, appear as if I had. Unlike when a human dies, I learned pretty quickly there's an appropriate timeline for mourning "just a pet," and I'd certainly passed mine. Even though everything inside me screamed, "Har was never just a pet," and I wanted to justify my grief somehow, I didn't know how to without seeming crazy or, worse, insensitive to those who'd actually lost humans. There was a hierarchy for grief, and dogs weren't at the top of it.

I did my best to establish new morning routines, new walking patterns around the neighborhood only for Birdie and me. *I can do this,*

I told myself while another voice whispered, *but I don't want to.* There was a constant battle in my head of trying to be an adult and "just move on" and an angry toddler who wanted to slam my fists against the wall and shout, *I just want my best friend back.* In trying to force my grief away, I turned it into anger and frustration instead. I cried myself to sleep at night and then would yell at Har in my head for leaving me behind to deal with all this all alone. *Goddamnit, Carl! How dare you!* And after I yelled at him, I yelled at myself. What was wrong with me? He was just a dog! (I'd try to belittle myself. Certainly that would make me feel better!) But seriously, why *couldn't* I just move the fuck on? I knew I had a deep bond with him, but this grieving was a little much, wasn't it? And then, somewhere in the midst of my tantrums and hating myself, a little voice whispered, *Your grief is a lot because your love was a lot. You don't get one without the other, and grief does not care who or what you loved. It simply knows that you did.*

He was just a dog. But he was a dog who was by my side more than any human. Har loved me unconditionally and without reserve, even in times when I did not love myself. Through layoffs, a miscarriage, meltdowns, and breakdowns, he was always there. I'm not sure exactly what all that means, but I know how it feels. And it feels like there's a gaping hole in my heart that may never fill back in, like the lump in my throat won't get smaller or the homesick feeling in my stomach will never go away, because Har was my home.

Surprisingly, once I was able to accept my sadness and that my grief didn't take away from someone else's, even someone's grief that ranked higher on the invisible hierarchy scale, I felt better. Or, better-ish.

I no longer cry about Har every night, but the cries still come on occasion, and I let them happen. I've stopped my weird rituals of checking coat pockets for old receipts that are time stamped to a date when Har was still with me. And I've long since washed all the clothes that still had little threads of red vizsla hair on them. But do I sometimes still smell his old leather collar? Oh, absolutely. I also talk to the succulents we picked from his last day near the mountain stream that are planted with some of his ashes as well as those little red hairs. But the good news is that I no longer swear at them. I simply glance at the succulents as they bask in the morning sunlight and whisper, *Hi, Har. Hello, sweet boy.*

··

Two months before Birdie's second birthday, I received a random Instagram message in the random Instagram message folder that I never check. But for some reason I'll never really know, I happened to check it on this day. It was from a woman I didn't know, as they all are, but she was reaching out on behalf of her dad, Earl. He was a farmer from Gridley, Kansas, and she was pretty sure he was the man who had given us Harlow so many years ago. They'd just had a litter of vizslas after not having any for several years, but they had one little boy left and wondered if I wanted him. He'd be ready to come home late October, right before Birdie's second birthday.

I'd just found out I was pregnant with our second child, and we'd also recently rescued a senior vizsla a few months previous. The last thing we could handle was a puppy! Can you even imagine the madness? A toddler, a baby, and two vizslas?

There was no way I could say yes to a puppy simply because some weird pet medium told me it was Harlow reincarnated. I'm not *that* crazy. Then again, I've just written an entire book about a talking dog . . . so . . . *Goddamnit, Carl.*

acknowledgments

Thank you to my parents, Jay and Sandy Wolfe, for raising me as a child with a wildly inflated sense of confidence, leading me to believe I could do anything. More importantly, thank you for kindly suggesting I go to college and study writing rather than moving to California to become a surfer simply because I watched *Blue Crush* once.

And a huge thank-you to my mom for all her edits, feedback, and compliments. (She knows I prefer compliments.) I'm not sure when she and I will get to the Oscars, but I know it will happen someday.

Abby Saul, my literary agent, has been incredible every step of the way. I'm forever thankful for her advice, her guidance, and her never telling me to stop panic texting/calling her because she's an agent, not a therapist, as I often seemed to forget.

Sydney Rogers, my editor, helped me bring this story to a new level while also crying with me on several phone calls about how much we love dogs. And thank you to Kate Walker for all her amazing support behind the scenes and helping bring the cover I had hoped for to life. The entire team at HarperOne has literally made my dreams come true with this memoir: Judith Curr, Anna Paustenbach, Maya Alpert, Suzanne Quist, Stephen Brayda, Dwight Been, Yvonne Chan, Aly Mostel, Julia Kent, and Laina Adler.

Thank you to my sister, Jade, for her unwavering support and belief in this book. And to my brother, Jordan, for his same support and response of "yeah, whatever" when I asked if I could share the ear story. Hopefully he'll read it someday!

To my Gump chat—Audrey, Adrienne, Sarah, Taylor, and Jake— thank you for being some of the most talented, kind, funny humans I know.

To Joyce Novacek, thank you for all the phone calls and discussions about writing. Without those calls, I'm not sure I would have had the confidence in myself to finally actually finish a manuscript.

A special thanks to all the amazing teachers in the world who recognize something in their students and take the time to tell them. For me it was Mrs. Morgan in fifth grade and Mrs. Grey in middle school.

Thank you to Chris's parents, Bob and Dian, for raising a guy like Chris. I'm also very thankful for the time they spent walking Gunny and Vinny and watching Birdie while I cried in Pinwheel Coffee Shop finishing this memoir.

Speaking of, thank you to Pinwheel Coffee Shop in Denver.

Finally, so much thanks to baby Goldie for being the chillest newborn in the world, allowing me to put the finishing touches on *Birdie & Harlow* while I hold her in my arms, even knowing her name isn't on the cover. Luckily, she gets the next book.

about the author

Taylor Wolfe lives in the Pacific Northwest with her husband, Chris; daughters, Birdie and Goldie; and two vizslas, Gunny and Vinny. Anything else you probably already know because you just read an entire memoir about her.